Mary Tyler Peabody Mann

Juanita

A romance of real life in Cuba fifty years ago

Mary Tyler Peabody Mann

Juanita

A romance of real life in Cuba fifty years ago

ISBN/EAN: 9783337051082

Printed in Europe, USA, Canada, Australia, Japan

Cover: Foto ©ninafisch / pixelio.de

More available books at **www.hansebooks.com**

JUANITA

*A ROMANCE OF REAL LIFE IN CUBA
FIFTY YEARS AGO*

By MARY MANN

BOSTON
D LOTHROP COMPANY
FRANKLIN AND HAWLEY STREETS

CONTENTS.

CHAPTER		PAGE
I.	AFRICA	7
II.	HAVANA	14
III.	THE SALE	36
IV.	LA CONSOLACION	51
V.	THE DOGS	79
VI.	THE MARCHIONESS	94
VII.	THE DINNER	112
VIII.	THE DRIVE	130
IX.	JUANITA	150
X.	CAMILLA	161
XI.	THE CHICKEN-HOUSE	169
XII.	THE AMERICANS	183
XIII.	FANCHON	196
XIV.	THE NEW YEAR'S BALL	204
XV.	COCK-FIGHTING	218
XVI.	THE CACTUS.—THE SLEEVE OF WIND	222
XVII.	PEDRO AND DOLORES	235
XVIII.	DOÑA JOSEFA	245
XIX.	LA MODESTIA	251
XX.	THE TURTLE-DOVES	266
XXI.	PARTED FAMILIES	288
XXII.	DON ANDRES	311

XXIII.	Tulita .	323
XXIV.	The Flight	351
XXV.	Sewing .	355
XXVI.	Deception . .	369
XXVII.	Consequences .	376
XXVIII.	Repentance . . .	383
XXIX.	Homeward Bound	392
XXX.	Dissipation	402
XXXI.	The Return . .	411
XXXII.	Cuba	423

JUANITA:

A ROMANCE OF REAL LIFE IN CUBA FIFTY YEARS AGO.

CHAPTER I.

AFRICA.

In a beautiful valley on the border of a river, about fifty miles from the western coast of Africa, a party of natives had assembled under the shade of a copse of trees to celebrate a rustic wedding. The valley was nearly closed in by a circle of low hills. From one of these summits a stream dashed down and wound its way like a silver serpent, glistening in the sun's rays, through meadows, and by bosquets of plumed bamboos and heavily laden mango-trees. The feathery, acacia-like foliage of a clump of tamarind-trees shaded the group of figures as they reclined on the bank of the stream, waiting for the decline of the burning tropical sun before they consummated their simple ceremony, which was to be followed by a festive dance, for, like other savage nations, the Africans consecrate all national and social observances by the dance.

War and rapine had never invaded this little valley of peace. It was separated from any other tribe by the hills that surrounded it, and the wants of its unsophisticated inhabitants were amply supplied by the productions of nature around them.

The plantain, the fig banana, the orange, and the bread-fruit tree, the maméas or tree-melons, the yam, and innumerable other fruits and vegetables; the delicate fish of the rushing stream, that shot through the valley with the first impulse from the hills that had given it birth; the light game found in the woods, and the birds that made the air alive with music, furnished them with all the necessaries of life. Two varieties of dwellings stood in the valley: light bamboo structures, interlaced with cocoa-leaves; and more solid structures, formed of mud and pebbles, which the sun soon baked, and which were designed for shelter in the rainy season. In these, abundant stores were laid by for future use.

The Ayetans, for so we will call them, from the name of their river, Ayete, had heard stories of invading white men who stole their dark brethren from their homes and bore them away on the backs of great birds, with snowy wings; and, not a great many years before the time of our story, some young men, more enterprising than the rest, had ventured beyond the hills, and were never heard of again. A narrow opening, which the kidnappers had never espied, wound into the valley between two hills, and the native curiosity of man had led them to explore it. But the Ayetans had by their seclusion escaped the common fate of the tribes of western Africa thus far.

On this day, with the native taste which characterizes the African, they had chosen the prettiest grove in their lovely valley to celebrate the nuptials of their youthful chief with a maiden he had chosen from the tribe. He was a tall and well formed youth, and she was a lithe and bright-eyed maiden. Labor had not stunted their growth; but fishing, hunting, and chasing the antelope, had developed their limbs in graceful proportions, and in their simple way they were as happy as savages could be — gentle specimens of savage nature. The older members of the party were resting in the shade; the younger girls and lads were chasing the innumerable butterflies of all hues and sizes, and pulling off their brilliant wings by way of preparing the more solid parts of these "flying jewels" for what was to be the wedding cake, — a favorite food of the Africans, which was to be made with their bodies and with honey from the wild bees' nests, and cooked over embers that were burning on a little reach of pebbly beach by the river. Groups of little children were paddling in the edges of the stream or rolling upon the green sward.

A distant shout and the noise of fire-arms suddenly startled them all from their repose and amusements, and in a few moments, as they stood huddled together, the dreaded white men, of whom they had heard, followed, alas, by a savage troop of howling negroes, burst into their midst. Then, like frightened deer, they fled. But it was in vain. Their enemies carried the lightning and the thunderbolt in their hands. It was the first sound of fire-arms that had ever assailed the ears of the natives. It proved far more terrific than their imaginations had pictured it. At every flash of that concentrated lightning, and at every peal of that mimic thunder, their companions fell dead to the ground. The rest turned and knelt suppliant to these evil gods; but they were bound hand and foot, and borne away on the backs of these black and white demons—for their own countrymen were there transformed into fiends by the cruelties and bribery of the white men.

Only a few old people and very young children were left in the valley, for such do not survive the horrors of the middle passage.

On this festal day, many of the natives were ornamented with chains and bracelets of the soft gold which was found in the rivers and in the sides of the hills, and which they knew the art of moulding into these decorations. These did not escape the eyes of the kidnappers, who commissioned a few of their number to sack the rude habitations and store-houses of the negroes for more booty of a similar kind. But the natives had hoarded little gold. It was only preferred in their eyes to the flowery chain because more glittering and more permanent. They knew no other value for it. Its discovery, however, doomed the beautiful valley to desolation and still farther carnage, for other parties soon came to inquire for the locality of the gold, pitilessly massacred all the inhabitants that were left, fed upon their stores, and dug into their hill-sides till they had exhausted the supply of the treasure for whose possession they had become the fiends they were.

When the kidnappers were weary of their burdens, and knew their prisoners were too much exhausted by the torment of their bonds to be able to make any resistance, they unbound their limbs, and, tying them together, led them by the thongs a weary march to a barracoon near the coast. There they were thrust into pits, and earth was shovelled in around them till it reached the chin, and thus they were left till they could be safely embarked. Enough food was given them to sustain life, and this they were made to eat whether they wished to do it or not. A guard was stationed over them to prevent any sound from issuing from their mouths, for these were deeds of darkness, that must not be exposed. Some compassionate ear might hear and betray, for English vessels were occasionally nearing the coast for this very purpose. Straw and other rubbish was piled up in the corners of the barracoon, ready to be scattered over the heads of these poor victims if 'any symptoms of approaching danger were scented in the air.

One wretched night and long day passed before the negroes were released from their agonizing positions. They were then huddled, in the dead of night, between the decks of a vessel, where they were laid side by side. There they were left to move about what little they could, but if they endeavored to thrust their heads out of the loopholes for a fresh breath of air, they were beaten back from without, such was the kidnapper's fear of capture. Occasionally, when out at sea, a few at a time were allowed to come upon deck. Every day their dead were drawn out and thrown into the sea, and thus they crossed the ocean to the Spanish islands.

We will not dwell upon the countless sufferings, the impotent ravings of the middle passage. From this earthly hell they were glad to be set on any shore, to breathe again the sweet breath of Heaven, to look at one another by the sun's light, to count over the ranks of kindred and friends to see who were left. All the sins of selfishness that had developed themselves in the hours of suffering were forgotten and forgiven. Hatred was felt now for the oppressor only, and they still had the privilege of uttering their common sentiments to each other without being comprehended by their tyrants. Every natural sign of hostility must be suppressed, but the burning word of their native dialect still remained to them, and this gift of untrammelled speech was the only earthly boon they now possessed. They no longer owned themselves. Who could tell how long their simple souls would be their own?—for it is not probable that they ever consciously realized the possession, or would be likely to retain it, amid the temptations and degradations of bondage.

Hitherto they had worshipped an unknown God as the birds do, by song and dance, and by happiness — but had not their God forsaken them?

CHAPTER II.

HAVANA.

It was a lovely day, of golden sunshine and balmy air, in the Island City.

On the veranda of a spacious court-yard, enclosed on all sides by the mansion of Don Miguel Arbrides, sat some ladies, earnestly engaged in conversation.

The setting sun was shining upon a mass of brilliant clouds that rose to the zenith, and their reflection threw a rosy tint upon the marble walls of the mansion and the shrubbery within the court, while a sparkling fountain threw up its spray from a clear basin in the centre, giving one a sense of coolness that was most refreshing after the heats of a tropical day.

Below the veranda, or piazza, which ran all round the building, were the domestic offices. They were unusually spacious for a city, for Don Miguel was a successful slaver, and, in addition to his household dependents, often had a supply of slaves in preparation for the market. He had just returned from a profitable voyage, and the numerous people seen below were some of the fruits. He owned extensive slave-pens in the country, within fifty miles of the city; and from these depositories small gangs of *bozals*, as the newly arrived negroes were called, were from time to time brought into the city by night, and placed in this domestic slave-pen, where they were attended by a skilful physician, who prescribed for the maladies incurred on the voyage; and when such a gang was pronounced by him in good condition, it was sent to the slave market in the vicinity of the city, and few slaves there sold brought such good prices. Formerly slave-pens were within the city walls, where medical men attended regularly, but since the treaty of 1817 with England, which made all slaves contraband who were brought to the island, it was safer to land them upon some unfrequented part of the coast. Thence, so many as were not disabled were marched, chained together, to such plantations as required recruits and had engaged them beforehand, and even to the villages of the interior where they were sold, for no troublesome English commissioner resided in the country, and the one in the city took no pains to inform himself of disobedience to the treaty, knowing that the Captain General received so much a head from the slaves, and was therefore specially blind and deaf upon that subject, which made his commission practically abortive. The usual form through which he passed when he did confiscate a cargo, was to throw the captain into prison, from which, after a few months, he would be sent into the country by a physician, on a plea of ill health : and, very possibly, a week or two later the commissioner would meet him in the street, just ready to re-embark in the employ of some other slaver, like Don Miguel Arbrides, who was wealthy enough to pay the fine and all collateral expenses. It was not often that a wealthy slaver commanded his own vessel, but Don Miguel, though a pleasant gentleman at home, had practical proclivities, and liked the excitement of the chase ; and even looked forward to taking his own son with him when he should be of suitable age. But of this anon. Less popular or less wealthy men would not have brought such slaves into their own places of residence within the city, for fear of inconvenient consequences ; but who wished to give offence to such a man by saying that those were *emancipados*, and had a right to their freedom ? Not the people who visited his splendid mansion and partook of his lavish hospitalities! In such communities it is not considered good manners to complain of one's neighbors and acquaintances. The enslaving of fellow-men who are defenceless is a trifle in comparison.

As far as practicable, such slaves were sold into the country, for in the city they might in time learn of their rights from the free negroes, of which Havana contains some forty thousand, and every addition adds to the constantly impending fear of insurrection.

In one corner of the court-yard, a knot of people, who, apparently, had no part in the domestic service, were gathered together and earnestly engaged in conversation in a language which no one else could understand. The slaves of the household occasionally mingled with them, but evidently could not communicate with them. A beautiful little boy, son of Don Miguel, might be seen threading his way amongst them, and giving them oranges and little articles of confectionery.

Tulita, the dark-browed Spanish maiden, was the very embodiment of loveliness and goodness. No tenderer heart ever beat than hers for her friends, for her pet dog, her birds, for the poor padre who begged at the door, for the sick negro who was consigned to the domestic hospital of her father; but she had never questioned the propriety of his seeking slaves on the African coast, or selling them at home. Her father was a kind and tender father, though his wealth was acquired by the theft and sale of his fellow-beings. Indeed, it was a jubilee all through the family circle, which was large and well-to-do, when Don Miguel returned from his voyages, for his return was the signal for many a festivity, which he specially enjoyed and liberally promoted; and he was always well furnished with the soft golden chains and trinkets made on the coast, which he distributed among his friends. He did not own any plantations, for his occupation was on the high seas; but there were many on which he was a welcome guest; and when he was at home in winter, the season for visiting, Tulita passed brilliant and joyful days in the country.

Miss Wentworth had gone to visit a friend in Cuba with the northern feeling upon the subject of slavery. At that time, it might be said to be rather a negative feeling. It was before the agitation of the question of human rights had stirred the foundations of society. The controversy between abolitionists and colonizationists had just begun. She knew that she was going to a land of slavery, but she had no expectation of being plunged into the midst of it. In her childhood she had heard a respectable old negress, who lived in the neighborhood of her mother's house, tell the story of the abolition of slavery in Massachusetts, when she had emerged from a mild form of that institution into the enjoyment of perfect freedom and ownership of self, and she told it eloquently but without entering into the details of cruelty and injustice. A respectable community of colored people resided in the town, and Miss Wentworth had seen them, arrayed in their best attire, congregate together on the anniversary of the day of emancipation, which they celebrated with dances, sometimes with revels, which were laughed at but not sympathized with. She had known

excellent persons of color in domestic service.
She had helped to teach their children to read,
and had gathered them in the Sunday-school. She
knew that their mothers were afraid to trust them
out after dark, for fear of the kidnapper; and
this had been her most painful knowledge, for
she knew slavery was not far off, and that that
was a real danger. She knew the colored people
were not allowed to ride in public conveyances, and
had indignantly sympathized with her own nurse,
who was obliged to pay largely for being carried
into the country, in a private conveyance, to
see her old mother. She had shuddered over occasional accounts of the horrors of the middle
passage, but her mother had tenderly guarded her
children from the knowledge of extreme cruelties,
and her impression was that they were exceptional. Indeed, slavery was a name rather than a
reality to her. The pecuniary interest northern
people had in southern plantations — often the
ownership of them — made it invidious to dwell
upon the subject, and sealed the eyes of humanity, down to the time when Garrison boldly
attacked the monster crime. Even long after
that, it was considered not genteel to say
too much about it, — all which condition of
things threw dust in the eyes of society. Colonization had excited some interest in the benevolent, but the general voice condemned any
suggestion of immediate measures of emanci-

pation, or relief for the oppressed. There was no faith in human nature large enough to compass the idea that emancipation from bondage would call forth any but the baser passions of revenge and indiscriminate destruction. It yet remained to be seen that the long enslaved would receive freedom on their bended knees, and with songs of thanksgiving. It was supposed that, like the Anglo-Saxon race which had enslaved them, they would turn and rend their oppressors. That they can feel gratitude and affection for kindness among their oppressors when in bondage, did not suggest the inference that they would be much better, instead of worse, for the boon of liberty.

A few days' residence in a slave-country had rudely waked Miss Wentworth from her comparative insensibility to the fact of slavery. She now saw the degradation and helplessness of a class of men and women whom she had hitherto looked upon practically as almost fabulous. She learned with a shudder that she was residing in a house of a slave-catcher, — a class of men whom she had previously thought of as the embodiment of all that is brutal and demoniac in human nature, but one who was, in fact, respected in society, outwardly like his fellow-men, and possessing many of the qualities of a man and a gentleman. She had accidentally learned that day that the slaves below were about to be sold at auction, and she had inquired, with startling earnestness, whence they came and whither they were to be sent.

Tulita, with all simplicity, had revealed all the arcana, which those more conversant with non-slave-holding communities would have concealed. The wife of Don Miguel had visited American cities before her marriage, and had some glimpses of the state of feeling on the subject; but courtesy to a guest, and that guest a young lady, had prevented her feelings from being hurt, or even roused by it. She was now for the first time, as a mother, made aware of what the feeling might be; for her husband had already intimated that he should take his son with him, when a little older, to initiate him into the business. Her maternal instinct made her sympathize with Miss Wentworth's ill concealed disgust and indignation, but she wisely concealed it, in the fear of her husband's displeasure. Nothing makes a slave-holder so angry as any question of his rights, as he calls them.

"Did your father go for them himself?" asked Miss Wentworth, her blood boiling within her at the thought of the courtesies she had received at his hands.

"Ah, yes, indeed!" said Tulita, "and they will be so much better off now. They were all ill when they came, but they are all well now."

"Poor creatures!" exclaimed Miss Wentworth;

"they were brought forcibly away from their homes, I suppose."

"Yes, but papa says they are taken from the most cruel slavery on the coast and brought here to a Christian land. They were all baptized a few days ago, and now can have Christian burial when they die," and Tulita crossed herself devoutly.

"A Christian land!" exclaimed Miss Wentworth, with an emphasis that brought a surprised look into Tulita's face. "But there would be no slavery on the coast if there were no slave-traders."

"Oh, yes, there would!" said Tulita. "The African tribes make slaves of their enemies, and it is a mercy to them to bring them here! These people whom you see below are much more civilized than usual. They were all baptized with Christian names the other day, and Carlito and I chose the names. They were so pleased, and all spoke their names very well. None of the rest understand their language, so we can't find out much about them. Carlito spent a great deal of time teaching them their names, and he says mamma Francisca thinks those two you see talking together are lovers, and he has been teasing papa to let them be married."

"They will not know what it means, perhaps, but it may keep them from being separated," and with these words Carlito, who had climbed up, threw himself over the balustrade, and climbed down from the gallery like a squirrel.

"Separated!" repeated Miss Wentworth, the truth beginning to dawn upon her. "Are families separated to be sold?" she almost gasped out.

"Oh, yes, to be sure; that is, sometimes," said Tulita, for the first time thinking anything about it. "It does seem cruel, but papa says they don't care."

"Not care!"

"Oh, they are not like us, you know."

"I do not know any such thing!—they must have human affections if they are human beings!"

"I should hardly think so," said Tulita, "for papa says they are in the habit of killing their own children."

"Probably to save them from slavery," said Miss Wentworth. "I like them all the better for it."

"But they do it in Africa—it is an African vice."

"Did you not say they were victims of slavery there, too? Probably the vice does not exist except in connection with slavery. It is too unnatural a one. Animals love their young and defend them frantically when attacked, without taking any precautions for themselves;—it is impossible that human beings should be below the animals in that respect. Nothing could make me believe it. I know the colored people of our own country. They are below the generality of whites in education or position; but many of them are good people, and some of them quite respectable in intellect. I am sure of it, for I have taught some of them to read."

The conversation, to the great relief of Tulita, who was beginning to see what she had never seen before, was here interrupted by the entrance of Padre Jean, a jovial, benevolent-looking Irish individual, in a Franciscan garb, whom Tulita greeted very warmly and introduced to Miss Wentworth.

"And how is the Señorita, your mamma? and how is my boy Carlito?" he inquired.

Tulita told him how he was engaged.

"Foolish boy!" said he, "is papa going to indulge him? Where are his lovers? I suppose they will only quarrel the sooner if they are married, but I will marry them if Don Miguel says so," and the fat priest laughed merrily.

At this moment Carlito came scrambling over the balustrade in great excitement. "Oh, where is papa? I want to see him this minute!"

"Carlito, you have not spoken to Father Jean."

"Oh, how do you do, Father Jean? but where is papa?"

"I think he is at home; but what is the matter?"

Papa evidently heard the demand; for he now entered, asking Carlito what he wanted in such haste.

"My boy is crazy over some negroes we have below, whom no one can understand, so he cannot gratify his curiosity about them."

"Oh, papa! let me tell you. Juacomo has just come back, and he says they came from his country, and he can understand them — and mamma Francisca was right! they are lovers, they were just going to be married when they were carried off. Juacomo says he is Dolores' uncle; he came away a great many years ago, when she was a little girl. He says Pedro is the king; and oh, papa, he did so to him," — making obeisance. "That is the way they do to their kings when they speak to them. I asked him if they would like to be married now, and he said they would. Oh, papa! won't you let Padre Jean marry them? Padre Jean, will you marry them?"

"Oh, yes, if papa says so, I should like to marry them. But Juacomo must tell them what it means, for they will not understand what I say; perhaps Juacomo can tell you how they marry people in the place where he came from."

Carlito was over the balustrade and out of sight in a moment, shouting, "I will ask him."

He soon returned, breathless.

"Juacomo says they jump over a stick, and somebody takes a long shawl or a string, and winds it round them, and then they dance together. Oh, how pretty it will be! papa, you will let them be married, won't you?"

"I think you had better have waited till you found out before you went quite so far, my boy. I suppose they know all about it now, and Juacomo will be greatly disappointed if it is not done, but this is the last time you must ask such a thing, Carl," and Don Miguel looked more grave than was his wont.

Carlito did not wait to discuss the matter, but, securing the permission, he was soon out of sight again, and came up the other way, dragging the two astonished negroes after him, followed by Juacomo and a crowd of men and women, with a stick and a long scarf, which he had obtained from one of the house-servants.

"Ah, these are some of the people I baptized the other day. Lend me your ring, Miss Tulita, and I will soon have them married."

Juacomo laid the stick upon the floor, and held the scarf ready. After Padre Jean's ceremony and the placing of the ring, at a signal from Juacomo, the two took hold of hands and jumped over the stick, and Juacomo wound the scarf around them. At this moment, the negroes present, with one accord, clapped their hands, which was a signal for the dance; but Don Miguel, with one wave of his hand, signified to Juacomo that that could not be allowed, and they descended to the court below, where instantly the whole crowd threw themselves in wild excitement into the most violent contortions, accompanied with measured clapping of hands and wild screaming, and for a few moments it was as if pandemonium was let loose; but this again was of brief duration, for as soon as the order could be communicated it was hushed, and they were all driven to their quarters and locked in. Don Miguel was undoubtedly aware that he could not go too far in his violations of legal provisions; and, although it seemed hardly possible that any amount of noise in that closed court could be heard over the incessant and uninterrupted din of the city, it could not be risked. But the few moments in which nature had resumed its sway over these savages made a fearful impression upon Miss Wentworth. It seemed to her that in those screams she heard the long suppressed agony burst forth, which the new surroundings of these unhappy people had pent up within them. With an excuse she left the company, and Tulita followed her. For the first time the latter had realized that the African slave had sentiments like her own, for marriage is not promoted by the slave-holders, and this was the first time she had ever witnessed such a scene. Doña Lucia mastered her tears, as she had often done before, and Padre Jean was left to take counsel with the elders.

Francisca was summoned to put Carlito to bed, when he gave his father the good-night kiss.

"This will never do," said Don Miguel. "Let us have no more such fooling, Carlito, or I shall never let you go down among the people again."

Carlito had never before heard a word of reproof from his father, and evidently was not acquainted with that face in anger. It was indeed a changed face. This was the slaver, and Doña Lucia shuddered when she saw the expression of which his countenance was capable.

The friar tried to turn the conversation, but it was impossible to guide it into a gay or happy channel, and he soon took his leave. His was not the mission to turn the sinner from his ways, and he regretted that he had called that day.

So great was Doña Lucia's dread of the subject of Carlito's future, that she commanded herself sufficiently to sit down to her piano, which, she knew by experience, could soothe her husband's ruffled feelings; for her playing was of no ordinary merit, and he had a Spaniard's love of music.

Throwing herself into the luxurious boutacle that stood by her window, long and deep was Miss Wentworth's reverie. Her life had been one of many experiences, though she was not advanced in years. She had been a daughter, a sister, a friend, and had felt all these relations to society keenly. She had buried parents, brother and sisters, friends. She had seen the loved go astray, and had labored long to conduct them into the right path again, sometimes without success.

She had loved nobly, and not in vain; but she had seen the object of her affections die an early death, while in the prime of life and usefulness.

All the resources of a cultivated intellect, of high principles, of sanctified affections, had been called into requisition to enable her to bear up under these calamities, which deepen the character they do not discourage, and set the world's shows in their true light. She thought she had sympathized with the oppressed of all climes and of all times; but her home had been in the freest nation of the earth, and in the most advanced portion of that nation. Her forefathers had been prominent in service and suffering for the cause of human rights, and she had been nursed upon the stories of these sacrifices and these sufferings. She now felt as if oppression and slavery had been mere words to her. Within a few hours, the deepest crime against man had been brought forcibly to her notice, and the perpetrators of it had an honored position in society, practised the common social virtues, and would undoubtedly feel insulted if their characters were called in question. Could she stay where all distinction between good and evil seemed to be obliterated? At first she thought not.

"How could Isabella have consigned me to the keeping of such a family, even for a few days?" she asked herself.

But a second thought suggested that she had no right to lose this opportunity of observation, for was there not the same plague-spot festering in the heart of her own country? The noble Follen, the saintly Channing, were her friends, and from this standpoint she comprehended the feeling that had thrown them into the ranks of that small and contemned party which was laboring at home to waken society to a full conception of its duty upon this momentous theme.

Before her feelings had regained any measure of composure, Tulita entered her room to invite her to drive to the public square, to listen to the music of the black band, that played from nine to ten every evening in the square before the Governor's palace. Glad to receive any relief from her present feelings, she accepted the invitation, and stepped into Tulita's beautiful *quitrin*, which accompanied that of her father and mother.

Governor Tacon had been but a short time in office, but among his many improvements in the outer world of Cuban life was the transformation of the city of Havana from the most dangerous to the safest city in the world. Two years before, no man could walk the city after nightfall with safety. A powerful banditti held it in bondage. Murders were of common occurrence, and, the moment there was any disturbance in the streets, every inhabitant who had a shelter rushed under cover, and locked the doors, for the sword that hung over the city was the fear of insurrection. Members of the banditti would call the householders to the door, and demand enormous sums of money, on the penalty of shooting on the spot, or by threats which the victims knew too well would be fulfilled, and that none would dare to complain or to testify against the murderers. The victims of assassination in the streets were not picked up by their friends, because the judiciary was so corrupt that legal action would soon impoverish the richest man. If robberies were committed in the warehouses and shops, the owners would carefully obliterate all vestiges of the deed the next day, for the same reason. It was less costly to lose in the one way than in the other, for litigation might be prolonged for years. If a man was thrown into prison, the chances were that he would linger there all his life, his expenses charged to his estate or those of his friends. Not long before Tacon's administration, a wealthy man was assassinated by mistake, in the street, taken for another man. The family claimed his body of the authorities, and the litigation continued until his widow was obliged to buy up all the papers, at great cost, to save herself wherewith to live. No decent woman dared to set her foot upon the pavement except to step into her volante, and an evening ride must be well escorted to be safe. Foreigners sometimes infringed upon these customs, but only in emergencies, and then at the risk of losing caste unless their infringements were pardoned by Spanish courtesy as sins of ignorance.

But all this was changed. The square before the Governor's house, which was formerly a quagmire whenever it rained, was now laid down in what looked like polished marble, a cement made of the lime of the country and the red soil, and pounded, while still wet, to a fine consistency. This platform, splendidly illuminated, was filled between the hours of nine and ten with crowds of ladies, of all ranks, who owned or could hire a volante. They paraded the stone floors arrayed in their most elegant attire, sparkling with jewels, and unbonneted, as in the ball-room, listening to the divinest strains of Italian and German music, played by the matchless band, whose fame is world-wide. I say listening, for the decorum of Spanish society is to be quiet, instead of talkative, even in their dances, and especially when music is the entertainment.

The banditti was suppressed. Tacon's rules were imperative. No man of any rank was allowed to be in the streets after nine o'clock with a weapon of any kind. The espionage of the Governor bordered upon the miraculous. It extended even to the villages and plantations of the interior, and every one who was ready to keep order breathed freely and enjoyed life.

An ancient tree, which had stood in the square, and had the reputation of being the tree under which Columbus is said to have reposed, and which was very dear to the Habaneros, was ruthlessly removed by Tacon, to make way for his platform; all men stood breathless before his decrees. He had a large standing army at his beck, and exercised his despotic power without regard even to the remonstrances of his nobility, which had hitherto been lawless.

Nothing could be more in consonance with the feelings of Miss Wentworth than the impassioned strains of Bellini's "Pirata," which was at that moment the favorite music of the Habaneros, performed every night at the opera by the Pedrotti, and reproduced on every musical instrument in the island, but chiefly and most marvellously by the black band of the city troops, who had no other occupation in time of peace than to improve their music. This band was composed of colored freemen, many of whom enter the profession of music, and in whose ranks have appeared composers of music which has been played throughout the musical world.

Every noise is hushed in that great city while the four bands of the regiment play in the four respective squares. The muleteer arrests his steps and sits in profound silence upon his willing animal during the hour; the *calesero* * checks his horses to catch the near or distant strain. No bell is struck. The crying child is shut within the house. The barking dog is soothed or muzzled, for Tacon has decreed that it shall be so; and this decree, added to the love of music in the southern heart, hushes every sound, as in former days the matin or vesper-bell arrested all worldly pursuits and turned every thought heavenward.

* Volante-driver.

Such holy pauses in life are of inestimable worth amid the din of cities, where it is so difficult to turn the mind from the world and its pleasures and strifes. But, like all other religious observances, the vesper prayer ceased at the time when the revolutions in Spain produced anarchy and misrule in the colonies. The Sunday morning mass would probably have followed, but the custom of going from that to the cock-fight kept up the observance. A quarter of an hour in the church and the rest of the day at the cock-fight! This is the Havana Sunday, and, indeed, the custom is the same all over the island. Men are apt at times of political revolutions to think liberty means license; and here the undevout, once liberated from the pressure of public opinion, never returned to his idols, and national religion was at an end.

But I wander from the scene I was describing. When the clock struck ten, the music ceased, the company ascended their carriages, and in half an hour or less the square was empty, and the natural sounds of the city life resumed their sway.

Thus far Tacon had made himself respected as a just though a severe ruler. None dared to disobey openly, not even the hitherto privileged class, the orders of Castilian and sugar nobility. The last mentioned class was composed of those sugar-planters who had acquired sufficient wealth to buy titles from the mother-country. The sugar-plantations cannot be confiscated for debt. This bounty upon titles robbed the island of that wealth which should have been expended for its improvement, and up to that day there were not even high-roads upon it.

Of late, the new Governor had given some indications that he was no respecter of persons if any one interfered with his plans; but privileged classes find it difficult to realize that they are amenable even to wholesome laws. So corrupt is society in this respect, whether in despotic Spain or in our own country of boasted freedom, that in both, in spite of the popular cry against rank, the wealthy and the powerful are safer from the earthly consequences of sin than the poor and lowly.

CHAPTER III.

THE SALE.

EARLY on the morning of the day after the wedding, as Carlito called it, the doomed party emerged from their quarters under Don Miguel's proud mansion, neatly but coarsely arrayed, washed, combed, and ready for the sacrifice. Bozals are preferred on many accounts to older residents, particularly on plantations, where they learn less of the rights of slaves than in the cities. These rights, according to Spanish law (violated by custom), are many, and, in some respects, humane. Still less would they be liable in the country to learn that they were in truth free men.

After recovering from the effects of the terrible voyage, they were fresh and unimpaired in strength. The exposures of field labor on the plantations, and of sugar-making in the mills, abridge negro life very much in the Spanish colonies. But both coffee and sugar planters have concluded that it is cheaper to work gangs to death, and then replace them by new purchases, than to take care of their health as they do of that of their cattle.

The Ayetans knew not on this day what was to be their fate. No freemasonry had enabled them to learn it from the slaves of the household, whose grave looks when they parted from the new-comers were only explicable on the common ground of social sympathy. Juacomo had evidently not told them anything. The experiment would have been too dangerous for himself, and of no use to them. The comfortable quarters, the medical treatment, the good food, the kindness of the children — for Tulita, as well as Carlito, had often visited them, laden with sugar-plums and fruit — had restored them not only to health, but to some measure of good spirits. Don Miguel was still an object of terror, for, though he had apparently released them from the barbarous treatment they were subjected to on the African coast, they knew him to be the presiding spirit of the vessel of torture that had borne them across the ocean. Before the family had risen, the whole party, to the number of forty, was marched under escort to a place on the edge of the city, where they were exposed for inspection during the day, to be sold at even-tide, at a public auction. Here sat, or stood, or walked about, men, women, and children of all ages — infants at mothers' breasts, stalwart youths, athletic maidens, old men, boys, middle-aged men. Some were barely covered with a scant garment; others were neatly attired; some were ornamented with trinkets; but all looked sad and apprehensive. Tearful mothers clasped their little ones to their bosoms as if for the last time; husbands and wives exchanged words which might be their last; youthful sons and daughters clung lovingly to the sides of their mothers, from whom they for the first time feared separation. The more attractive were the daughters, the more intense were the fears of the mothers, who scanned with agonizing penetration the countenances of those who came to buy.

Dolores and Pedro had left aged parents in their native valley, and knew nothing of their subsequent fate. They had left brothers and sisters on the coast where they had landed, for when detailed for the city there was no consultation respecting kindred, but thus far they had each other, and while together they were not utterly desolate.

New parties continued to come in in the course of the day, and these remained there without food or means of rest till late in the afternoon. Many of them were evidently bozals, but others might be known by their dress and language to be either creoles or long residents.

Some of these latter were unruly servants, who could no longer be trusted in the city, from the greater facilities it afforded for disorder and even for escape. Others were slaves, who, by their intelligence and thrift, had been hired out by their masters, and, after having completed the tasks assigned them, had earned nearly money enough to purchase their freedom, which can be done in Cuba for five hundred dollars. To prevent this consummation, they had been despoiled of their hard earnings, and were now to be sold into the country, separated from all they loved, to toil in the fields and be again "broken in." No disgrace is more keen to a well trained and accomplished household slave than to be made a field hand. This mode of treatment quells rebellious spirits if any human measures can do it.

The hour at length came, and terror and heart-sick despair took possession of many a bosom that had long been trembling with vague apprehension. Dolores and Pedro saw mothers part with nursing babes, who were given into the rough keeping of banditti-looking men, to be conveyed they knew not where; daughters who were sold to the highest bidder for their comeliness, and sons who were to be sent to distant provinces for their manly independence, which made them dangerous fellow-citizens. Wives were separated from their husbands, the aged from all youthful supporters. The bozals could understand the natural language of grief, terror, and despair, and when Dolores and Pedro were placed upon the stand and examined like fattened beasts in a stall, the blackness of darkness came upon them, too, illumined indeed by one ray of hope, which a few moments' time served to quench in eternal night.

"Dolores and Pedro! husband and wife," said the slave-dealer, "to be sold together — young and strong — healthy bozals — just married — hear!"

"Whom do you belong to?" said a purchaser, rudely seizing Dolores by the chin, and jerking her bent head towards him.

Pedro made one step forward, his eyes flashing fire and defiance, but a cutting lash across the face sent him reeling and bloody to the back of the platform, where he was seized and bound hand and foot. A scream of agony from Dolores as he disappeared from her sight was the parting sound that rang in Pedro's ears long after he was conveyed from her presence. Not even a momentary sympathy was elicited from the crowd. Such demonstrations of human feeling are too common in such scenes to attract any notice, and the by-standers only crowded nearer, to lose nothing of the spectacle, thus blocking up the street.

A volante drew up suddenly, to avoid riding over the people. Dolores caught sight of Carlito's sweet countenance, and stretched out her arms to him with a supplicating cry, which made the slave-dealer turn to look in the direction of her eye. He immediately recognized Don Miguel, to whom he lifted his hat respectfully.

"Oh, papa! there is Dolores all alone! — Where can Pedro be? Do you think he is sold without her?"

"I am afraid so, my boy; but we cannot help it now."

"Oh, papa, perhaps you can, if you ask that man. Do ask him, papa."

"He is doubtless taken away before this. It is of no use."

"But, papa, I think it was Dolores that screamed so just as we drove up — perhaps he was only just carried away."

"Hush, boy. Drive on.— Rascal! why did you come round this way?"

"Oh, papa, Juacomo came this way because the troops blocked up the other street — don't you know? He tried hard to go the other way."

"Yes, I remember, but let us get out of it as quick as possible — turn round, if there is no other way — mamma does not like to be sitting here."

Carlito turned to his mother, whose kind eyes were blinded with tears of compassion. She begged him to be still.

Carlito always obeyed his mother, and sat down. The crowd gave way and they drove on; when Dolores, who had stood in an attitude of intense hope and expectation, saw this last earthly resource fail, she fell senseless to the ground, with another wild scream.

Carlito stopped his ears, and hid his face in his mother's lap. The volante turned a corner, and whirled them into the Paseo. Tulita and Miss Wentworth, who were immediately behind, had with bitter tears witnessed the whole scene, but Tulita had checked the impulsive movement of Miss Wentworth, who started from her seat to add her voice of supplication to Dolores' and Carlito's. Tulita knew too well that it would be of no avail.

The Paseo, which was the object of the drive, is a shaded avenue of several rows of trees, in which the Havana ladies take the air and the fresh at nightfall, beautifully dressed, and their male friends and cavaliers walk by the volantes as they slowly wend their way, enjoying their society. Intercourse is so restricted by forms that there is little free interchange between men and unmarried women, who must meet the opposite sex under the superintendence of their mothers or elderly female friends, if they wish to preserve a fair reputation. These guarded interviews are eagerly sought.

There were no handsomer quitrins on the Paseo than those of Tulita and her mother. The show of dress, which was of the richest quality, the ladies unbonneted, which is the style in Havana, and often covered with jewels, would have been a fair one to Helen at any other time; but she only looked upon it then as we do upon any scene that offers itself to the eye under overmastering emotions — mechanically; and it was even a relief to her to be at last whirled home.

When they emerged from the gay scene, it was

illuminated by one of those gorgeous sunsets so often seen in that latitude; but, by the time they reached home, the sudden twilight, which is an equally striking feature, had succeeded, and all was dark and gloomy as they ascended the long flight of steps, silent and sad.

Don Miguel scarcely joined the evening circle. Miss Wentworth's presence was oppressive to him. As they sat upon the veranda in the cool of the evening, Carlito climbed into his mother's lap, and said : —

"I am never going to sea with papa."

"Why not?" said Don Miguel, who was pacing the veranda, and heard this half whisper.

"I should not like to bring people away from home to be sold."

"Not if they were all the happier for it?"

"How can that be, papa?"

"Because they are always fighting in their own country. They are savages, and make prisoners of each other, and are very cruel to each other. There are no wars here, and Padre Jean has baptized them all with a Christian name, and now they can be good Catholics, and be buried in holy ground when they die."

"But they can't understand what Padre Jean reads to them out of his book."

"They will learn by and by."

"But nobody can tell them what it means, because nobody can speak their language."

"Perhaps they will find some one, just as they found Juacomo."

"Papa, do you know I found Juacomo crying, when he was washing Rosillo? I never saw a man cry before. He was thinking of Dolores," and Carlito burst into a wail of sorrow.

"Let us not talk any more about Dolores. Think how happy Francisca is when she is saying her prayers. By and by some one will teach Dolores, as Tulita teaches Francisca." And Don Miguel paced away, and turned the corner of the house.

Carlito sobbed long and convulsively. It was his bed-time, and, as soon as his mother had soothed him, Francisca was summoned to put him to bed. His mother soon followed them, and, when she sat down on his little canopied tent, he rested his head upon her knee and said: —

"Mamma, I mean to go and live in Miss Wentworth's country; Tulita says there are no slaves there. I won't live in a place where people are sold!" And he burst into another paroxysm.

At last nature triumphed, and the weary, heart-stricken child fell asleep.

Tulita had stolen to the piano, to change the current of talk, if not of thought, and played some sweet strains, for she could not find her voice to sing, till the carriages came to the door for the evening drive to the Governor's square.

The brilliant scene that formed the accompaniment to the music passed before Miss Wentworth's eyes as a pageant. She could only look upon its attractions as bought by blood and tears. Again she listened to the despairing wail of Imogen, which only by the refinement of its agony silenced for the moment the memory of Dolores' wild screams.

The barricaded street again obliged them to make a circuit, but Juacomo made it in a different direction, and gave Miss Wentworth an opportunity of seeing the noble cathedral by moonlight. Its architectural beauty seemed to her the only true worship that was likely to rise from such a desecrated spot of earth. She did not know then that the convent beneath it was filled with the friars and their families, or that the very semblance of celibacy was dispensed with by the colonial priesthood.

As they approached the public stocks, in their circuit, the appalling sound of the lash startled her ear. She almost sprang from the carriage, but Tulita held her firmly, and said, by way of explanation : —

"It is not the slave stocks; it is some punishment given to those who go out armed after nine o'clock. It is a police regulation, which makes everything safe."

As they passed the spot, they saw a carriage drawn up before the stocks, into which the form of a young man was lifted by the calesero and footman.

"It is the volante of the Marquis of Carova! What can it mean?" whispered Tulita. "It looked like José himself, but it cannot be. It frightens me to think of it!"

José was the son of the Marquis of Carova. Tulita had but half an hour before pointed him out as the favorite cavalier of the young ladies, not only of his own rank, but of a still lower one, in which he visited unsanctioned by his father.

The young marquis expectant was a handsome and talented Spaniard, possessed of every grace and accomplishment that makes youth captivating; but his father was poor, though titled, which made it difficult for the son to ally himself to one of equal rank. He had that evening been very attentive to a young citizen on the platform, whose mother had long had her eye upon the young marquis, wishing to purchase his title with the wealth which had been hoarded up for that end so desirable to a Habanero. The young lady's beauty and accomplishments were such as to excite the admiration of all who saw her: and as the young cavalier walked by the side of her volante, he was challenged by a sentinel, who inquired if he was armed. With the presumption of his class, he answered defiantly, not stooping to a falsehood, and the sentinel collared him, not suspecting his rank in such company.

The young nobleman drew from his breast the knife that had betrayed him, but was instantly disarmed and hurried to the stocks, where the thirty lashes were administered, decreed by recent law as the punishment for carrying arms after nine o'clock. In vain he had protested his rank and its immunities. Tacon's orders were not to be questioned; and, though the sentinel might have allowed him to pass unchallenged if he had known his rank, the possession of the knife was inexcusable.

The volante the young man was escorting had driven on to his father's mansion, which was not far distant, and arrived just as the marquis and his lady were alighting at the door. The good woman who carried the intelligence was delighted to have the opportunity of speaking to so great a personage, even under such circumstances; and, as soon as she informed him of the arrest of his son, he remounted his carriage and returned to the spot, where he arrived before the operation of flogging was concluded, and just as the carriage of Don Miguel passed by his servants were lifting his son into the vehicle.

"Ah, mama! was that José?" whispered Tulita to her mother, as they ascended the steps.

"I think so, my child," said Doña Lucia.

"Horrible, mama, is it not?" said Tulita. "What a disgrace! whipped at the public stocks, like any one else! was such a thing ever heard of before? the son of a marquis!"

"There must have been some mistake, my child. The Governor would not have had one of his rank publicly whipped, surely. Do not be alarmed; it will all be made right," and with these words they entered the saloon, where Don Miguel was already pacing the floor.

"Good enough for him! I am glad his plumes are plucked," said he. "His pride will be humbled now, I hope."

"It must be some mistake, I think," said Doña Lucia, timidly. "Surely, the Governor would not sanction such an outrage upon the person of one of the nobility."

"Nobility, indeed, nobility! Tacon has too much sense to let that make any difference! What is this youngster worth beyond Luis Gonzallo, or any other high-mettled youth who has been punished for disobeying orders? You may be sure Tacon is only glad of the chance of showing these proud nobles that they cannot cross his will. The Marquis of Carova has done it several times of late, and this makes the account square. For my part, I am glad it has fallen just where it has. Did you see the fellow dancing attendance upon that pretty girl to-night, Tulita? She has plenty of money to fill his empty pockets. You see, you have lost your cavalier, hey? but, never mind! there are plenty more."

This was more than Tulita could bear, and she was hastening after Miss Wentworth, who had said good-night, but her father called her back.

"What! going to bed without kissing papa? that is something new."

Tulita returned and kissed her father, but not as usual. He drew her upon his knee, and whispered something in her ear which made her start back with an exclamation, "Ay, papa; how can you?" and, bursting into tears, she left the room.

"Now he is disgraced, perhaps his father will let him marry the slaver's daughter, and you may yet be a Marchioness," were the words Don Miguel had whispered into the ear of his daughter.

When Tulita reached her own apartment, the young slave who attended at her toilet stood ready to bathe her feet in the usual manner, and Tulita suddenly dried her eyes and suppressed all evidence of unusual emotion; for she knew that on the morrow this untoward event would be bruited from one end of the city to the other; and Tekla, the pretty lady's-maid, was the queen of gossips, and knew enough of her young mistress' affairs to make it dangerous to admit her to any confidence. Pleading headache, Tulita sank into her boutacle, and threw her handkerchief over her head, while Tekla bathed her feet; but, declining to have her hair combed as usual, she quietly undressed and threw herself upon the bed. When Tekla had retired, her mother stole into the room to give her the accustomed caress and blessing, which were more tender than usual, if possible, but accompanied by few words, and it was not till she left her that Tulita gave way to a passion of tears, such as only the young and hopeful shed when grieved and disappointed. Tulita's heart was yet pure and uncorrupted; but she was destined to be made the tool of the ambitious and the selfish, who were old and wise in the world's ways. Yet such are the fetters of custom that she suffered more when she thought of the disgrace and momentary suffering of a favorite than for the despair of the bondswoman, for whose fate there was no redemption.

CHAPTER IV.

LA CONSOLACION.

THE arrival, from the plantation of La Consolacion, of the housekeeper who was to be her escort into the country, was announced to Miss Wentworth one evening on her return from the music; and, after parting words with her hostess and Tulita, she hastened to her room to make arrangements for starting at daybreak, in order to avoid the noonday heats. Tulita had formed many plans of entertainment for Miss Wentworth, and was much disappointed when she had heard of the arrival of Mrs. Warwick. The housekeeper of the Marchioness of Rodriguez was an American, whom Miss Wentworth had sent to Cuba eighteen years before as nurse to her friend's first-born. The Marchioness had lived too long in America to be willing to give her child into the care of a negro slave.

Mrs. Warwick had retired much fatigued from her ride, and would have been very glad to have lain over for a day's rest, but no such intimation was made, and Miss Wentworth was only too glad to escape the necessity of exchanging any more courtesies with Don Miguel, who was more and more repugnant to her feelings. When her preparations for the morning were made, and she had dismissed the young waiting maid who had been assigned her in Doña Lucia's hospitable arrangements, she threw herself on her bed, but it was not to sleep. So far from that, her whole past life seemed to come up for review, and what astonished her more than all things else in this review was the fact that, with what she did know formerly upon this subject, she had not sought to know more. The intensity of Channing's emotions upon it was now explained to her. In pursuit of health he had sought the climates of slave-lands, and had seen slavery for himself as she now saw it. She saw now how the general atmosphere of opinion influences the mind, if experience has not given it the means of throwing it off and judging subjects by principles. She remembered her mother's enthusiastic ejaculations when speaking of Wilberforce, and referring to the sufferings of the middle passage. The reference was somewhat vague, for she was a child then, to whom her mother would not recount the details of horrors. Her mother had long since passed away, but her daughter remembered the stories of sacrifices and sufferings her family had experienced in leaving their English home for the love of freedom — freedom, whose significance she now for the first time realized. She had never known anything else but freedom, and had compared it with nothing else. It covered far more than worshipping God according to the dictates of conscience, which was the Pilgrims' shibboleth. Follen had sympathized with down-trodden nationalities, and had defended them before European courts at the risk of his life, and when he came to America it was coming, as it were, to ideal liberty. She was familiar with the story of his life, but saw now how little she had appreciated it, enthusiastic as was her feeling at the time. She remembered, too, his pain when the knowledge of slavery first dimmed the fair picture he had drawn of America. She with others had criticised what were then called Garrison's extreme views as they appeared to her through the medium of other minds. She had wondered at the opposition of decided anti-slavery men to the scheme of colonization; but she understood it now. She now saw why the slave-holders favored it — not because of their humanity to the race, but because it would be so convenient to have all the freemen of that race removed from the vicinity of slavery, whose peaceful existence their freedom threatened. She had heard Follen state this strongly, but then thought he went too far in judging ill of his fellow-men, kind and just as he was on all other subjects. Such, again, was the influence of prevailing sentiments. The great upheaval had not yet come; when it did come, it was demonstrated that these lax judgments were founded on self-interest, for the northern portion of her country proved to have been deeply involved in the pecuniary gains of slavery, and therefore blinded to its heinousness. She remembered the intelligent colored boy in her grandfather's village, where she went to school in her childhood after her parents' death. He was the best declaimer in the school, and a manly boy in every sense of the word, who grew to be a respected member of society, intrusted with town interests, and his name another word for honesty and fidelity. How long ago she had forgotten John Gibson! with whom she had studied and recited and played as with any child of her own color. She remembered, too, the bright girls in her own Sunday-school class in the African church at a later period, one of whom became a distinguished proficient in American history, and wrote sensible articles in the anti-slavery papers. More strongly than ever she felt it her duty to stay and learn all she could, that she might help to clear up doubting minds. She hoped she had seen the worst — it must be better, she was sure, in the rural districts.

What were likely to be her farther experiences in this fearful land? This subject had never been a theme of the correspondence she had kept alive with her Cuban friend for the last twenty years. She knew she had married a slave-holder, but she knew him to be a devoted husband and father.

She even knew that he loved his horses with a special affection. Could she doubt that he had feeling for his brother-man? She did not yet fully realize that his brother-man had passions and will of his own, that made him hard to govern — that, in order to keep him in subjection, he must be treated despotically, and that irresponsible power was liable to ruin the best organized natures and silence all the best instincts of the heart. She had often heard that the wildest and most excited horse could be instantly calmed by the touch and voice of the Marquis of Rodriguez, and she found herself imagining this benign influence exerted over human beings, till the tumult of her soul was calmed, and she fell asleep, to be roused — as it seemed to her, immediately — by the summons to start upon her journey.

It had been arranged that, if the good Mrs. Warwick concurred, Carlito should accompany them for a short visit; for the accident that had opened up to the child the horrors of slavery had so affected his happiness that he could not sleep, and both father and mother wished for a change of scene, hoping the impression would fade. Mrs. Warwick consented to take him, although she knew the Marchioness kept her children very much apart from others less guarded in their lives than their own, and he was so overjoyed at the prospect of the visit that he rallied at once and left home and his mother in high spirits. His father promised to bring him home when he should take Tulita to a neighboring plantation, which would now be very soon, as the Christmas holidays were approaching, and at that season the plantations, otherwise dull places to the young, were given up to gayety.

The relief afforded by nature, seen in such a different aspect from anything that had before met her eyes, was inexpressible to Miss Wentworth, and the prattle of Carlito aided its effect.

After leaving the white limestone formation that surrounds the city of Havana, and which is very dazzling and trying to the eyes, they passed into the deep, rich, red soil of the interior, which makes such fine contrast with the luxuriant foliage. No fences mar the beauty of the scenery, but the plantations are bordered with broad lime hedges, impervious, by reason of their spines, to man or beast, and often covered in their turn by a little blue convolvulus, whose delicate vine trails over them and the adjacent earth. No houses are seen from the road, but gates, sometimes of great architectural beauty, and always more or less pretentious, shut in long avenues of trees, at the end of which, within ample squares, stand the low rambling houses, usually built with posts of the lignum-vitæ wood, which is impervious to the attacks of insects, and filled in with cocoa or bamboo stakes, plastered. These houses are floored, within, and on the broad piazzas that surround them, with the same concrete as the platform in the Governor's square, made of lime and the red earth, laid down wet, and then pounded by enormous piles into a consistency which resembles marble and takes a very fine polish. These piazzas are often made with circular openings for plants, which form little gardens, as it were, that the ladies of the house can enjoy, without stepping upon the soil, which a large portion of the year, that of the rainy season, is of the consistency of hasty pudding, to borrow a familiar image, the earth not having a pebble in it of the size of a pin's head.

Heavy rain in the night — very unusual at the season, which was midwinter — had made the roads almost impassable. They were fearful to an inexperienced traveller, and many times the trusty negro who headed the escort had lifted Miss Wentworth and her heavy companion, the housekeeper of her friend, from the volante (Carlito took care of himself), and placed them on a dry spot while the vehicle was pulled from the deep mud-holes in which it occasionally sank. Gullies, fifty feet in depth, had to be descended on one side and ascended on the other, and the driver, who sits on the outside horse, and guides the one that is between the bars at arm's length, did not seem to have any fears of a successful transit unless water stood at the bottom; but the enormous wheels of the volantes, wheels of the size and width of our largest cart-wheels, must not sink too deep, or they cannot be extricated, so the occupants of the vehicle must alight and be carried over on the sides of the declivity, or, perchance, through the mud and mire, in the arms of attendants. Women never travel in the rainy season, and men usually on horseback; but in exceptional cases, like this, unknown perils may be encountered, and it seemed to Helen, sometimes, that all hopes of a safe arrival were futile. The old lady who served her as escort took the perils very quietly, which somewhat reassured her, and when the sun became pretty high, and threatened to be intolerable, they entered an avenue of beautiful trees, at the end of which stood a hospitable mansion, where they were received as if expected. There are no inns by the way in that country, but the hospitality of the people is unmeasured, and always freely invoked.

Miss Wentworth could speak the language, and found that the tidings she brought from the city amply compensated her hosts for the trouble of entertaining her for a few hours, and, after doing her best thus to requite their kindness, she gladly accepted an invitation to rest her wearied limbs in a luxurious hammock, where she was considerately left to sleep until she was roused to continue her journey. The worst roads were passed, and when she entered the circle of San Marcos, not far from the mountains of San Salvador, she found the plantations of the Castilian nobility distinguished for their cultivation and beauty. The one which was the scene of the chief incidents of my story was approached by a long avenue of palms, which seemed to throw their slender columns so high because they worshipped the sun which had drawn them forth from the rich, red earth of that region. Such, at least, was the thought suggested by their columnar beauty to Miss Wentworth as she leaned back in the luxurious volante which was winding its way through their ranks, that seemed interminable. She had long ceased to utter the transports of her enjoyment to her companion, who, less youthful, less enthusiastic than herself, had fallen fast asleep — besides which, she had no words in which she could appropriately express her admiration, for, as she rode on, the enchantment increased. Carlito was beside himself with delight, for this was his first visit to the interior of the island.

The sun was just setting in tropical glory, and as they passed, crossing avenues of these peculiar trees, the vistas were illuminated by a roseate light, which gave them the effect of colonnades of marble pillars. The rich evergreen of the leaves of the coffee-plant formed a fine relief to the snowy whiteness of the palm shafts; as they approached the house, shrubs of various flowers were interspersed with the trees, till in the more immediate vicinity of it they gave place to others as new to her; to the mango, with its pear-like fruit, to the orange-tree, the laurustinus, and the bamboo, which seems to sweep the sky with its plumes, and forms an arch of shade impervious to the sun; the ground being carpeted like our pine forests with the fallen leaves. On emerging from this cool shade, the road opened into an area whose centre was occupied by a spacious marble basin of water, which was immediately surrounded by a hedge of roses in perfection of bloom. The hedge was cut so low as not to intercept the view of the water from the carriage. Within the hedge, on the edge of the basin, was a rich garden border of flowers, among which stood many classic vases where vines had strayed from their bed and found their way to the waters of the pond, festooning the whole edge with the most splendid colors of the floral kingdom. Into this area opened avenues from every direction. The calesero dashed into one of these, and, suddenly quickening his pace, whirled the volante to the piazza of the princely Rodriguez mansion.

Here Miss Wentworth was folded in the arms of her old friend, whom she had not seen since they resided on her grandfather's farm in Berkshire County, Massachusetts, twenty years before. The matronly beauty of the Marchioness was even more attractive than that of her youth had been, and when she greeted Helen with the affection of a sister, amid the perfume of roses and the play of a fountain, which stood like a familiar household spirit in an opening on that *floor of luxury*, as the beautiful Castilian idiom designates the highly polished composition piazzas that surround the houses, it seemed to her that she was in the very gates of Paradise. Voices are more mellow, objects more soft, in that delicious climate, than elsewhere, and the air seemed full of music as well as of perfume.

Miss Wentworth, or Helen, as we will now call her, was in the prime of life. The heyday of youth had not only passed, but she was perhaps prematurely old in the experience of life, and had never again expected to be taken captive by any beauty whose inmost reason for being she had not penetrated, but from the time she had been relieved of her fears of perils by the way, and had breathed that divine air loaded with tropical sweets, her blood had flowed with the vivacity of youth, and, wearied as was her frame, she was completely intoxicated with the scene and the joy of the meeting. When she afterwards remembered how painfully and suddenly she was disenchanted, it seemed like a dream of surpassing beauty for whose ingredients she looked in vain. The next morning, the glory had faded from the skies, the clustered roses, wet with dew, appeared like angels with drooping wings mourning over lost humanity; the palm-trees, which the evening before had seemed to stretch toward the skies in order to worship the sun, now appeared to struggle upward because they loathed their parent earth. Their stiff leaves looked like the fixed gaze of despair; they were but the emblem of desolation, standing apart, with no wish to mingle with humankind, lest the wail of sorrow should pass along their ranks. But I anticipate.

Guests are not allowed to sit late in the damp evening air, which insidiously affects the stranger in that climate, and after the sudden twilight of tropical latitudes had succeeded the brilliant sunset, and they had taken a few turns on the luxurious gallery, Helen was taken in to look at the precious jewels, her friend's children, who had been taken to their little tent beds just before her arrival, tired out with their day's play. Carlito was told that they would have been kept up to welcome him if he had been expected, but the party had not been looked for so early.

The spacious saloon, which constitutes the chief apartment of a country mansion in Cuba, was more simply furnished than that of Don Miguel Arbrides' pretentious abode in the city, for in Cuban country-life all ceremonies and etiquette are relaxed, and comfort rather takes the place of show. Not that it can be called comfort in the New England sense of that term, but in a climate where one only needs shelter from the sun and rain, and no protection from chilling and changing winds, much fewer appliances are requisite to supply the natural wants of man. Deep leather boutacles, lounges covered with the same material, before which stood light sofa-tables, bamboo tabourets of various sizes, whatnots of the same material for books and articles of *virtu;* high massive sideboards, on which stood silver candlesticks, protected by cut-glass *guardabrisas*, or wind-shades, of glass, stood upon the highly polished floors, which were uncarpeted, for insect life in the tropics renders the use of carpets impracticable. The hall was unsealed, the partition walls reaching only within a foot of the rafters, which were handsomely carved, but left naked for the free circulation of air. These spacious apartments have a desolate air to the eye of a stranger accustomed to close and carpeted rooms, sheltered by glass windows and curtains, but art had done something for this one to relieve it of the effect of its extent and barrenness. A wreath of fruits, flowers, and birds was painted all around it on the plastered walls, of a light sky-blue, so gorgeous and luxurious in hue that it riveted the gaze even by candle-light, and illuminated what would otherwise have been the darkness of the apartment. Behind this apartment was another wide piazza, curtained by heavy duck, with a border painted somewhat in the same style; this gallery was used as the dining-hall, where the party partook of light refreshment, and were then conducted to their own apartments. There were large rooms on either side the hall, one of which was the sleeping-room of the Marchioness, around which were smaller apartments for the children's little tented beds, and beyond these Miss Wentworth was ushered into her own spacious apartment, near which was a smaller one, in which Carlito was quite ready to be put to bed by the kind Mrs. Warwick.

A nice little ebony lass stood ready to bathe Miss Wentworth's feet and to help her undress, but these were offices she had always performed for herself, and, with a painful remembrance of her late Havana life, she gently declined the aid of the young girl, who stood in silent wonder to see the lady wait upon herself.

"Solidad is much disappointed," said the Marchioness, who had followed Miss Wentworth to her room. "She was much delighted at being appointed lady's-maid to the long-expected friend; but you will soon learn the luxury of being waited upon, in this climate."

"She shall be my little maid, if she wishes it," said Miss Wentworth, "but not my little slave. It does not seem to me, now, that I can ever let any one wash my feet, in that capacity."

"I shall leave it to Solidad to persuade you," said the Marchioness. "When you have met her half a dozen times a day, at your chamber door, with a tub of warm water upon her head, you will capitulate, and make her happy by allowing her to wash your feet; and then she will hold out her hand for a *medio*, for the slave does not like to serve you for nothing, and if you wish for their good services you must buy them."

"She shall have the medio this time, for her good-will," said Miss Wentworth. "Is it the fear of losing it that makes her look so grave?"

Solidad's face brightened again with a smile when Miss Wentworth dropped the medio into her hand, and then despatched her to her quarters.

As she glanced round the room, after her friend's parting kiss, before she threw herself upon the mosquito-netted cot, which was two-thirds hammock, she was aware that her walls were adorned with what she supposed landscape papers, and her attention was for a moment riveted upon a scene that she remembered to have been sketched by the Marchioness in her girlhood — for the Marchioness was an artist, and this must have been her work. But she was too weary to examine it, and the only light in the room was afforded by carved gourds containing brilliant *curculios*, a beetle which is of the nature of a gigantic fire-fly; and it was but a few moments after Isabella left her before she had sunk into a slumber such as can be enjoyed only in that atmosphere, which seems created for sleep, so soothingly does it bathe the limbs and faculties in repose.

Her last thought, as she fell asleep, was the comforting reflection that here she should be spared the pain of witnessing any distressing features of the institution to which she had had so appalling an introduction. But her little bark of sleep seemed to her scarcely launched on the sea of night before she was roused from her refreshing slumber by the most piercing and heart-rending shrieks, from many voices, accompanied by the terrific sound of the lash.

She sprang from her bed, and grasped the handle of a door that led upon the gallery. Voices reassured her as she rushed from the room. How can I describe the scene to those who are yet novices in such horrors? A man who looked more like a demon than a human being was applying his instrument of torture to the old negro who had been Miss Wentworth's kind and attentive escort. His blood was pouring from the wounds inflicted by the lash. The groans of the victim, the shrieks of his wife and children, were maddening to her ear. The friend of her youth, whom she knew to be the milk of human kindness, stood motionless, though pale and weeping. The Marquis, who had appeared to her, the evening before, to be the embodiment of all her fancy had pictured as the noble knight and the "preux chevalier," paced the gallery with a hurried step, but did not interfere.

Miss Wentworth looked at them a moment in unspeakable amazement, and then, as if impelled by energies that had never before been roused, darted from the piazza, and seized the arm of the wretch who was inflicting the punishment. At the same moment, a youth of twenty, whom she had not seen the night before, but whom she knew must be the oldest son of her friend, ran from the house, exclaiming, "My God! I will shoot the wretch"; and held up a pistol as if ready to discharge it. His father struck back his arm, and sternly commanded him to go back into the house, where he followed him, and probably forbade his reappearance, for he was seen no more.

Miss Wentworth's impulsive movement had arrested, not only the attention, but the arm of the overseer: but his wrath was not expended, and, seeing that she was not seconded, he continued his flagellations — with more passion than before, if possible.

The deep slumbers of the children were not disturbed by the noise, thanks to the construction of the mansion. The rooms in which the family lived were approached by a flight of twenty or thirty steps, but Manuel had been roused by his brother, so the circumstances could not be wholly concealed from him.

The Marquis called the overseer to his apartment, and the wife and children of the slave removed the poor old man from the blood-stained ground.

The Marchioness called Miss Wentworth from her room, and, throwing herself into a boutacle in the saloon, burst into tears. After a few moments of convulsive weeping, she commanded herself sufficiently to say: —

"Poor Carlo! he was never whipped before, nor did my children ever before witness or listen to such a scene; Ludovico is old enough to know all the penalties of slavery, but we have kept everything we could, even from Manuel, that would distress them. This wretch is a temporary overseer, and has brought badly trained bloodhounds, who frighten the people, and then he punishes them for defending themselves. I assure you, my dear Helen, this is the first time I have seen such a spectacle since my marriage."

"I am glad it is not common," said Helen, unable to suppress her indignation; "it is bad enough that it is possible, Isabella."

"Ah, it is not so uncommon," said Isabella, "but all the whipping is done at the other plantation, for my sake and for the sake of the children. When I returned from the States, my good father indulged me by discontinuing the custom of having the punishments inflicted before the house, and my husband has done the same here."

"Then it is a favorite spectacle with slave-holders!" said Helen, more indignant than ever.

"Oh! no, Helen, but it is done in the presence of the master, that he may control its severity. The slaves look to him for protection against the overseer, whose power, while in office, is absolute, and necessarily so, or he could preserve no discipline."

"Protection! discipline!" were all the words Helen could utter.

"You will surely agree that there must be discipline of such savage creatures."

"It is not the discipline for human beings, and you are satisfied when you spare your own feelings by not witnessing it!" exclaimed Helen.

Isabella burst into fresh tears. "Indeed, Helen, you are cruel. We women cannot help this thing. Would you deny us the small boon of having it out of our sight?"

"My dear Isabel, you must forgive me if I am unjust; but the horror of my mind is such that I hardly know what I say. Tell me why you did not interfere if you were displeased with this. Has a master no power over his overseer? Of whom are you afraid?"

"It is for the sake of the poor people that we must be cautious, for the overseer must not be exasperated. I assure you we shall not keep such a man longer than we can help; but it is difficult to find a good one, for the occupation brutalizes all ordinary natures. We have had an excellent one,—a Frenchman,—but he was called to France a week or two since, to inherit some property, and could not wait for my husband to supply his place, as he would have wished to do. Poor Carlo is my husband's foster-brother, and devoted to him. He was never punished before. All his family are my house-servants. Carlo was fleeing to his master for protection when this wretch caught him. He called the negro driver who is under him to whip Carlo, but Carlo is Jacobo's godfather, and he refused to do it; so he did it himself, all the more angrily."

"What had Carlo done?" asked Helen.

"Simply threatened the dog that bit him, they say; but Don Ermite has been much irritated about his dogs, which have given us a great deal of trouble the last two weeks. I have been afraid to let my children step off the piazza, though well trained dogs never snap at a white skin."

"Everything you say in extenuation only increases my horror. The faultless, faithful servants are punished as if they were the worst; the discipline, as you call it, would be a cruel one for beasts — are no sentiments ever addressed in these people but fear?"

"Slight punishments do not subdue them; they only exasperate them. It is necessary to break their wills, and some of these people have very stubborn wills, and will even fight till they are subdued."

"I see more and more horrors —"

"All would be anarchy and confusion on the plantations if they were not subdued; but on well managed plantations, as this has been, definite rules are established, and they can escape punishment if they obey them."

"If the overseer happens to be a decent man, you mean."

"Yes, there is that chance, and it is a fearful one. But they must feel there is an inexorable power over them, or they would kill us all. The most faithful are not to be trusted in extremity. How can we expect them to be faithful if they see a chance of liberty for themselves? They might not take into account the retribution that would come upon them. Oh, my dear Helen, I felt just as you do when I first came home, but I have resigned myself to necessity. What else can women do? All I can do is to be as good a mistress as I know how, make no unreasonable requisitions, and bear all the evils that I see. My house-servants are never punished when we have a good overseer. Carlo is a house-servant, and all his family are in the house. They do horrible things sometimes, but we have to bear them; and I never let them have much to do with the children. They are beside themselves to-night. I am afraid that wicked overseer will punish them all for interfering with him. They undoubtedly thought my husband would interfere."

"Can it not be prevented?" exclaimed Helen, shuddering at the thought.

"I do not know what my husband can do with that creature," said Isabella, "but, at any rate, I am afraid our good Jacobo must suffer."

"Who is he?"

"He is the negro driver who refused to whip Carlo to-night. He is a good fellow, and must have known the danger to himself, though perhaps he thought his master would interfere for

Carlo. Carlo is his godfather, and he is very affectionate."

"He must be a hero, indeed, if he can risk such a danger," answered Helen; "but cannot he be saved? Let us go and see if we cannot intercede for him. Has your husband no authority whatever over his household? Pardon me for asking —"

"It will do no good," said Isabella, sadly. "What you have done to-night, my dear Helen, will only make the matter worse for somebody. Planters and overseers will not be interfered with. Wait for me one moment; do not go to bed till I come back," and the Marchioness suddenly left the room.

The request was unnecessary. Sleep was never farther from Helen's eyelids. Every fibre within her trembled with the excess of her indignation. It was as if the lake of fire which some theologians describe as the retribution for sin was suddenly opened before her. The lurid light that shines from evil deeds sent a searching glance into realms of hitherto unimagined suffering. The faithful, trusted, beloved servant was thus a victim to the uncontrolled passions of man, without the power of an appeal to any earthly friend or tribunal, and God meddles not between man and man. The ocean that rolled between her and her bleak northern home looked to her like an interminable waste of waters, but one which must soon separate her from such scenes.

But, as on a former occasion, the next thought was, Is this right? Should not these things be known? Perhaps I may be a humble instrument for enlightening society upon this fearful topic.

How differently did the hooted and persecuted friends of freedom appear to her now! She respected them before as well as she knew how, but how little she had known! They were, perhaps, not perfectly wise in all their methods, but earnest, humane, self-sacrificing. She had dared to criticise them. A new aspect of human duty had presented itself to her. She determined to hush every selfish feeling, and look with a keen eye — a calm one, if possible — into this monster iniquity. But she must possess herself, and still the tumult within her. She could not believe that her friends were willing to be cruel, and she felt that she might trust herself to do them justice. She believed their personal benevolence would make them kind masters up to the limit of their possibilities, but had any one a right to remain in such circumstances? And then again came the thought that if there were no humane masters, what a pandemonium earth would be! She could not yet realize how the prejudices of education, the weight of custom, and the workings of self-interest, blinded them to the full sense of the iniquity of such a position. She hoped with trembling that she might help them to see their farther duty.

When Isabella returned, she saw by her countenance that her mission, if it was one, had been unavailing. The exasperated overseer threatened to leave the plantation the next morning if interfered with any farther. Carlo had been bitten by one of his untrained dogs as he was crossing the lawn on his way to his cabin, and had uttered a threat of revenge against it, which the overseer overheard. He immediately ordered the driver, whose office it was to execute his behests, to give Carlo thirty lashes. But Carlo was the master's personal servant and his foster-brother, petted, loved by all, respected by the other slaves, the godfather of all the younger portion of them, among whom was the negro driver himself, and he refused. The passionate overseer seized the lash, and, swearing vengeance against Jacobo for disobedience, inflicted the punishment himself. Nothing would now satisfy him but to wreak his anger upon Jacobo. The wretched victims of slavery are not even allowed the sad privilege of weeping for their suffering brethren, except in secret. The shrieking wife and frightened children, who had felt hitherto that the old husband and father was safe from punishment, now shared his tortures by personal suffering as well as by sympathy. Can an outsider believe that this had to be submitted to? Isabella had pleaded for the negro children, and saved them, but the old wife was punished with her husband. Isabella, however, did not tell Helen of this, but had to confess that the intercession she had made for Jacobo proved ineffectual. The Marquis had given his wife a solemn promise that not a day should pass without his seeking a substitute for this tyrant. This, however, was not to be intimated, for if it were not done cautiously there was little doubt that his life would be the sacrifice, and, in the slave-holder's code of honor (I might perhaps say his code of self-interest), his overseer's life must be protected, how many lives of negroes soever might be sacrificed to it.

"And what," said Helen, "will be the effect upon the family of household slaves? Will it not destroy the very germs of that faithful devotedness which you say has actuated them, to find that you are powerless to protect them?"

"I fear so, indeed," said the Marchioness, "but they have not an unkindness to remember from me. Yet I may not be allowed to enlighten them upon the reasons why we could not interfere to prevent this injustice. They must not be let into our counsels, for they could not keep the secret. Half these slaves are raw Africans, hardly yet broken into their traces: and we stand on a volcano if they are not thoroughly intimidated; for many belong to tribes that it is very difficult to reduce to slavery. Carlo is a Congo, one of the easiest tribes to govern."

"I cannot believe this is the only way of making human beings docile," said Helen.

"They can hardly be called human beings," said Isabella.

"And why should they be?" said Helen, indignantly. "Have they not been robbed of themselves, and treated like demons?"

"True; we should expect nothing of them, and we do expect nothing. They cannot be trusted. We are few against many, and must convince them of our superior power."

"And yet you are willing to live on under such a system and bequeath it to your children," replied Helen, with rising excitement, for she again began to take command of herself.

"Oh, be just, Helen! Am I not powerless? But I am wholly unnerved as well as you. Let us talk no more of it to-night. I have nothing to say in defence of this wrong — only of myself. I will not leave you alone, but lie down by your side. Let us try to sleep and be strengthened for the morrow. I have given orders not to be disturbed."

Helen acceded, and said no more; and Isabella soon fell asleep, but not so Helen. It seemed to her that sleep would never more visit her tortured brain; and, when she saw the soft light of dawn through the crevices of her shutters (for the Cuban country-houses rarely know the luxury of glass windows), she quietly opened the door and stepped out upon the cool piazza. All traces of the fearful scene had been carefully removed. She descended the steps, but she could not walk on that side of the house, and turned the corner. Here, on the other side of the path, were the raised platforms, of masonry, which served for drying the coffee. Mounting these, Helen walked to cool her burning head in the soft dews of the morning, which weighed down every leaf. Beyond these coffee-driers stood the cabins of the slaves — light structures of bamboo stakes, inwoven with the long leaves of the cocoa-plant, now stiff with age. As she descended from these driers, and passed the nearest dwelling, stifled sobs struck her ear, and, trembling with her suspicions, but irresistibly impelled by sympathy, she pushed open the door, which stood ajar. Stretched on the bare earth, with but a small blanket under each, lay the victims of the last night's brutality; with the exception of the poor old man, who had been taken to the hospital, which is prepared for the reception of such victims, who often do not emerge from it for many weeks. A tall negress, with a countenance expressive of much dignity as well as of the deepest sorrow, was tenderly bathing the wounds of the sufferers. At first Helen's knees trembled under her, and her senses reeled again with horror; but the next moment she was on her knees, joining in the humane service, and assisting the solitary attendant in her charitable work. The poor wife of Carlo fixed her wondering eyes upon Miss Wentworth's face, but their grateful expression changed instantly to one of terror when Helen inquired for Carlo. "In the hospital, and my husband too," said the negress in attendance, who was the wife of the negro driver, "but you must not stay here, lady," she said to her, in the same language as that in which Helen had addressed her. Her fast-falling tears called forth those of the poor woman, who threw herself upon the ground, wailing piteously. Carlo's wife motioned to Helen to go, and, startled by the expression of her face, Helen instantly obeyed, and darted from the cabin, regaining the driers as quickly as possible; and, hoping no one had seen her, she entered her room softly, and took her place by the side of Isabella, who still slept.

CHAPTER V.

THE DOGS.

ISABELLA was still sleeping, but not quietly. Helen lay down by her side, and resolved to keep her own counsel, if possible. Exhausted by weariness, strong emotion, and want of sleep, she soon lost herself, and when she awoke the sun was riding high in the heavens, and she was alone.

As she stood at her dressing-table, Helen again caught the outline of the Berkshire hills on the wall. It riveted her gaze. Two years spent in France with her father, before returning to the island, had given the Marchioness the opportunity of becoming conversant with other works of art than her own, and her native genius had developed wonderfully, so that Helen, who had given her her first childish lessons in painting, felt herself wholly distanced in skill; and she was now breathless with admiration. The beloved hills! the land of liberty! She could have knelt to them.

A plate of fresh oranges, nicely peeled, stood on the table at her side, and, refreshed by their cooling juices, she dressed and went out to seek her friends.

What a contrast was this day to the scene of the preceding evening! Isabella and her husband were pacing the piazza, and the former greeted her with the affection of a sister, but she fancied she perceived some constraint in the salutation of the Marquis, who had received her so cordially the night before. One fine boy of six was standing by the door, with eyes swollen with weeping; two beautiful little girls were playing with a little dog, and they looked at Helen with wondering eyes, but when their mother told them this was Aunt Helen, whom she had been so long expecting, they began to smile upon her, and when Helen told them she had seen them before, a sweet little four-year-old thing held out her arms to be taken up, and asked her if she would talk English with her, — Mrs. Warwick and Ludovico had taught her to say some things in English. Helen made many promises, and was soon intimate with these little ones, who were not strangers to her, and many of whose childish sayings had been the theme of their mother's letters.

The children of the Marchioness of Rodriguez had not been trained, as most of the children of slave-countries are, by negro nurses, but, with good Mrs. Warwick's help, their mother had trained them herself, and presided even over their baths and their meals, — for Isabella had brought with her, from her old New England life, impressions and principles regarding the education of children that her Cuban life had never corrupted. Helen's good aunt had always presided over her morning toilet and her retiring hour for the night, not trusting hirelings in those trying scenes and precious hours of children's days.

It is usual for each child in a well-to-do family in Cuba to have its special nurse, and much of its character is determined by its "mumma," as the negro nurse is called; but no such function existed here. Mrs. Warwick was the other mother, and she was a stanch New England woman, of the best type. But Manuel had always had his morning ride on old Carlo's head, when the latter went to feed his pig, — that cherished object of a negro's affections, because the only thing, except his chickens, that he really owns. He did not own his wife or his children; but he did own his pig and his chickens, and had the disposal of the money for which he could sell them. That money went into the little fund that a thoughtful slave always hoards, secretly, towards the making up of the five hundred dollars that can legally buy his freedom. The fact that everything that can be done to prevent its accumulation is done, does not discourage the slave from the attempt to gather it; nor the fact of the few cases in which they are successful. But this is a digression. It was not the selfish loss of a pleasure, merely, that wrung Manuel's heart this morning, but the cruel wrong that had been done to Carlo, whom he really loved, and about which he knew enough to demand the relation of the whole, which his mother had reluctantly given. The little girls had been more easily put aside, and he was charged not to tell them what he knew. It was Manuel's first unselfish sorrow, and the little girls had in vain endeavored to comfort him, or to ascertain the cause of his trouble other than the disappointment about his morning pastime. He had consoled himself as far as possible by feeding Carlo's pig with corn and oranges, reserving a huge orange, which he carried under his arm, for Carlo, and was waiting with what patience he could till his mother was ready to prepare Carlo's portion, in which she had promised that it should be an ingredient. She always attended personally to the rations for the hospital, and, in ordinary cases of illness, Manuel always accompanied her in her visitations to the hospital; but she could not take him in cases of punishment, without revealing too much of the fearful arcana of slavery.

"Do you know what is the matter with Manuel?" whispered Pepita to Helen; "he will not tell me." "I think he is cross," said Louise. "Oh, no! he says he is unhappy, and that people don't like to be talked to when they are unhappy," and Pepita's little eyes filled with tears. Helen could not restrain her own, as she pressed the little darling in her arms, whose musical voice in broken English sympathized so deeply with the unknown sorrow.

"I wish everybody would not cry!" burst from Pepita, as she broke into a passionate fit of weeping.

"Mama cried, too, when she dressed me," said Louise, who, though of more sturdy mood, was not proof against the general depression. Manuel's tears began to flow afresh.

"Let us all try to make each other happy," said Helen, making a strong effort over herself; "if every one would do that, no one in the whole world would be unhappy. What is your little dog's name? He does not like to see people look sad. Dogs always know when people are unhappy. Let us have a little frolic with him." Helen caught an orange from the buffet, and rolled it across the floor. The little girls, whose sympathy with the afflicted was indefinite though real, were soon absorbed in the frolic. But Manuel walked away; he could not bear it. Relieved from his depressing presence, the children soon recovered their spirits, and played horses on their long Guinea-grasses without him.

The Marquis had retired to his own apartment, and Isabella silently seated herself at her worktable, grateful to Helen for the relief her care of the children afforded her.

At this moment an old negress, with preternaturally active motions, bustled into the hall, and began to dust the furniture, lifting up the heavy chairs, and setting them down again with a great noise.

"Ah, Camilla," said the Marchioness, a little impatiently, "I thought you had done dusting."

"Ave, Maria! oh, no, la Marquisa, not yet; poor Jacobo! — poor Carlo! — poor Maria! — Ave, Maria! good morning, miss" (in English), courtesying to Helen — "good lady" (in Spanish), "ah, the dogs! — the dogs, lady! — French ladies walk! — poor Carlo! — poor Jacobo!" — and Camilla continued to go round and round the room, venting her excitement upon the chairs and tables and every article upon the large buffet, which she dusted over and over again.

"Take care, Camilla! you will break the guardabrisas," said the Marchioness, "and those delicate little vases! do not touch them again! — you have moved them all once — do you hear me, Camilla? let the things alone!" for as her lady remonstrated the clatter increased rather than diminished. "Ah, yes! pupil of my eyes! much dust, much dust! — poor Carlo! — poor Jacobo! — the Marquis, the Marquis walks — the Marquis walks too fast — the Marquis walks in the night — the Marquis does not sleep — the Marquis should sleep — my lady slept a little — the young lady had better not walk — the dogs — the dogs — the young lady must not walk alone — good lady — good lady — the dogs, my lady, the dogs!"

"What does she mean, Helen?" said Isabella, in English. "I went out upon the driers last night, while you were sleeping, to cool my head," said Helen, aware that she had been seen.

As she spoke, Camilla stopped short, and listened intently, pretending to be attending to something out-of-doors.

"You must not do that, dear! — those dogs might attack you!"

Camilla shook her head. "The dogs — the dogs, my lady — the French ladies walk, oh, yes!"

"Which way did you walk?" said Isabella. Camilla crossed her bony fingers over her breast, and listened intently again.

"You have dusted enough, Camilla," said her mistress; "you can go now."

Camilla reluctantly walked away, but soon returned to pick up her duster, which she had, probably, dropped designedly. Helen waited before replying, and, after adjusting one or two chairs again, the old crone went away, and, seizing a bunch of brush, began sweeping the path before the steps, evidently wishing to hear more.

"Camilla pretends not to understand English," said Isabella, "but we are sure that she does. Wait till she is fairly out of sight before you answer my question."

This was what Helen was doing, and, after

raising the dust before the house pretty effectually with her broom, Camilla finally disappeared.

"I walked a little way down one of the avenues," said Helen, as calmly as she could.

"Did you see any one?"

"I did not see Camilla," said Helen. "She seems a privileged character."

"She is, indeed; but tell me whom you saw, dear; and, for the love of Heaven, do not go out alone! That wretch would kill you if he could, and you must not interfere, dear Helen,—promise me that you will not!"

"Oh, I will not, indeed," said Helen; "I see that we are all slaves. I looked into a cabin from which I heard sobbing, but they warned me away immediately, and I hastened home."

"I told the man in charge last night to leave the door of Carlo's cabin open for air, that his poor wife might have the refreshment of it, and Jacobo's wife wanted to stay with her. Usually they are all locked in. I hope no harm will come of your looking in there. This creature must have heard you go out, or have been prowling round there herself. I do not know how she could get out, or how she dared to, but they have their own ways of circumventing us."

"My dear Isabella, do forgive me; I will make no more ventures. I see that I did wrong, but it is so hard to learn about such different customs that perhaps you can forgive me. Heaven grant that I have brought no one else into trouble. I do not know but it would kill me if I thought I had."

"I think Camilla could have had only a good will in warning you," said Isabella, "and she knows enough to know that it would be dangerous to herself if it were known that she was out, so I trust there will be no consequences to your imprudence; but you must be prudent, dear."

"I will be,— but don't you think the negress who warned me away might have told Camilla with the purpose of giving me a warning through her? It was Carlo's wife, and she could have had no desire to injure me."

"You are right, and I think that must explain it. Camilla has seen them this morning, for I sent her there."

This calmed Helen's fears, and she resumed her play with the children, who had begun to listen, and were troubled by the interruption. But it was difficult to rally herself as the horrors and dangers about her accumulated, and she soon told her friend that she would try to go to sleep, for she was not fit company for the children.

Just at this moment, Carlito appeared, led in fresh and blooming by the good Mrs. Warwick, who had watched for his awakening, and dressed him with her own hand.

It was the first time any one had done this but his own dear mama and his slave-nurse, from whose affectionate but uncultivated ministrations he had, unhappily, not been saved. Carlito, who was only six years old, was very precocious, and, in spite of his inheritance, a lovely child. He was his mother's boy, and thus far, at least, the hard heart of his father had not shown itself in him. Happily, the father was rarely at home long, and Carlito's little life had been passed in kindly offices to the poor victims of pillage and oppression, who were well treated in his father's home, not from motives of humanity, but purely from self-interest. Carlito was not yet old enough to understand this, but he had just taken one degree, and as soon as he learned that there had been a punishment of a slave on the plantation, he too looked grave and preoccupied. Children invariably sympathize with "the people," so far as not to betray them; and it is their first lesson in disingenuousness, but evidently sanctified to them by the motive that inspires it. The innocent prattle of the little girls charmed him into frequent smiles and sallies, and it was not long before he too had a Guinea-grass horse and trotted down the piazza with his steed. The Rodriguez children were never left in their babyhood without the superintendence of their mother or their nurse. Manuel had but lately emerged from the nursery to ride with his father and Ludovico, who were equally careful to keep him from contaminating exposure. It takes but a word or two of an uncultivated nurse to put an image into the mind of a child, as Helen was made aware that day, when Carlito asked her why that lady up in the sky, that took care of God, did not take care of Dolores and Pedro, whose fate still weighed upon his spirits.

"When I asked mama, she cried, and when I asked Tulita she said I must not talk so. I should not think God needed to be taken care of, but I think people do sometimes."

"My darling boy, who told you a lady in the sky took care of God?"

"Francisca told me."

"Who is Francisca?"

"Francisca is my nurse."

"Is she a kind nurse?"

"Yes, kindissimo," said Carlito, if we may translate literally his strong expression.

"My dear Carlito, Francisca may be very kind, but she is very ignorant — you must not believe all she says."

"She says Padre Jean told her so."

"Did you quite believe it?"

"Yes, I thought Padre Jean would know."

Helen could hardly rally her thoughts to answer such searching questions, but she felt how important it was to Carlito, in the present state of his feelings.

"Oh, if men only understood how to be kind to other men, always, then they would understand God better. God is not a man like us, dear; he does not need to be taken care of. Francisca is

so ignorant she could not understand what Padre
Jean meant. The people who go to church here
call Jesus Christ God, and he was so good there is
no wonder that they should think he was the
same, but he was the son of God, as you are, and
the Madonna was his mother. He was good to
every one — he would not have owned a slave,
because he would have thought every one must
own himself and could take care of himself as God
made him to do, if no one prevents him. Christ
taught men that they must love all men as if they
were their own brothers, and if they did there
would not be any slaves. We must all try to be
as much like the good Christ as we can. I should
not like to be a slave; would you?"

"No, indeed; but Tulita says it does them good
to be brought here, and papa says so too."

"It might do them good, if people would treat
them kindly and teach them something."

"Won't you let me go home with you when you
go," said Carlito; "Tulita says there are no slaves
in your country."

"There are none in the part of America where
I live, but in another part there are," Helen replied, sadly.

"I wish I was dead," said poor Carlito, who
saw no way out of his misery, and he began
to cry.

Helen drew him into her lap, and told him that
perhaps he could do some good to the poor slaves

when he grew older. "Once," she added, "there were slaves in New England, where I live, but the people there gave them all their liberty, and then they went to school and became as good as any one else, and, even in that part of my country where there are still slaves, people sometimes set all theirs free and send them away where they can be happier. When I first came here and saw a man punished, I thought I could not stay, but must go right home again; and then I thought to myself, 'No, I will stay and learn all about slavery, and perhaps when I go home I can make more people give liberty to their slaves. Now, perhaps you can do a great deal of good when you grow up, and I would think of that rather than of the sufferings you see. I think your mother will send you out of this unhappy country when you are old enough to take care of yourself — that is what Manuel's mother means to do."

"Oh, that would be good. I'll try to wait for that."

"And let us go now," said Helen, "and find Manuel, and try to make him feel happier, for he has seen a kind servant punished when he did not deserve it, and is very unhappy about it — as unhappy as you are about Dolores and Pedro."

A fresh burst of sorrow was his answer, but he was soon ready to go to find Manuel; and, when they went out upon the piazza, Manuel's pretty pony stood by the steps, and Ludovico and another horse were also waiting to give Carlito his first ride.

"You shall ride my pony," said Manuel, "for he is very gentle, and if you should fall off he is so low that it would not hurt you."

"I will walk you round at first," said Ludovico, who saw that Carlito was a little timid.

Thus reassured, Carlito allowed himself to be placed upon the pony, and a happy hour or two passed with this experiment, so that he returned in good spirits, and played cheerfully with the little girls. In the afternoon they all went to drive with the nurse, Manuel and Ludovico accompanying them on horseback, and nothing was said of the late sad event, for the Marchioness had prohibited all farther mention of it before the children, enjoining silence especially upon Camilla, on pain of being expelled from the house. Camilla knew very well that the housekeeping could not go on without her, but by keeping to the letter of the law she found many opportunities to give expression to her excited feelings. We will hope she did not enjoy the catastrophe too much, but the jealousies between household slaves are only held in check by the fear of severe punishment. The rule of the plantation is that if any strife occurs between them, both parties are punished, without any questions being asked. There is not even an attempt at judgment. Earlier in life, Camilla had had her share of suffering from this cause, for her domineering spirit needed to be checked in the bud. At present the quarry at which she struck was one far above her, where she knew she should not meet with the retaliation she deserved.

CHAPTER VI.

THE MARCHIONESS.

The Marchioness of Rodriguez had spent most of her childhood in the United States. A good education for a young girl was unattainable in Cuba at that time, especially upon the plantations, which were not connected with the cities even by highways passable at all seasons, and no judicious parents would send their daughters to the boarding-schools or convents of the city. The usual custom was to hire men to instruct in families, and these were in so subordinate and toadyish a relation to the family that they could only be called upper servants. They were expected to perform many services besides teaching, and were in no position to command respect from the young. They were also, very frequently, sources of absolute corruption. American governesses were not then, as later, the fashion.

The mother of Isabella was not qualified to give or even superintend such an education as her father was desirous of affording her. He had been educated partly in Spain, partly at a polytechnic school in France, where his native mathematical tendencies were stimulated. He had tasted the pleasures of knowledge sufficiently to crave it for his only child, and even had an ambition that she should be one of the women whose names were known in the intellectual world. He had not experience enough to know that only peculiar circumstances like those of some famous French women, Madame de Staël and Madame Roland for instance, were the educating forces that brought women occasionally to the front, and that the rule must be mediocrity while education for women remained on so low a plane as the usual one. Even Fénélon thought it best for women not to know too much.

Modern science was unknown in Spain, but Napoleon had opened the way to it in France, and the Marquis of Ramonte was imaginative. He was induced to send his daughter to Philadelphia by the fame of a certain boarding-school where other Spanish maidens had been placed, and had returned home able to speak a little French, which really stood for education in those days, not to say in later ones. There his child learned English by the natural process, enough French to prattle it a little, embroidery, dancing, a little arithmetic, a few geographical items, and a good deal of fashionable nonsense.

Helen Wentworth, left an orphan at fifteen, was sent to the same school by a New York aunt into whose care she fell, and whose highest idea of education was fashionable manners and French.

Philadelphia was the only city at that time where the two things were supposed to be combined in the same institution, and Madame Le Blanc's fame was widespread, for she was a good woman, and gained the affections of her pupils, the surest passport to their intellects.

Helen Wentworth was a Massachusetts girl, and the child of an educator who had advanced ideas upon that subject, so that her daughter was put in possession of her faculties early in life, and nurtured upon the trials, sacrifices, and conquests of the early Pilgrim history, which has made New England what it is. Helen's more puritanical manners and higher culture had developed a superior nature, which even a French boarding-school could not fritter away. She soon became deeply interested in the little Spanish stranger, whom she begged for a room-mate, and over whom she watched with sisterly care during her three years' residence there. In the summer vacations she was even allowed to take her to the home of a Massachusetts uncle who lived among the Berkshire hills, where they spent happy holidays, running freely over hill and dale, and drinking in the spirit of freedom and independence which characterizes northern society wherever it is lucky enough to escape the narrowing effects of a bigoted creed, which it happily did in this case, for Helen's family circle had emancipated itself from that bondage.

When Helen finally left Madame Le Blanc's school, she took the position of a teacher in a New England establishment, and the Marquis of Ramonte was but too glad to place his daughter under her care. The bond of affection between them was an indissoluble one, and when Isabella, at the age of eighteen, returned to her father, her mother having died while she was in the States, Helen promised to visit her before many years should elapse. Circumstances had prevented the fulfilment of this promise till now, and the intervening years had been passed in severe and useful duties, which had strengthened and deepened her character. Afflictions graver than bereavements of friends had purified and ennobled her affections, but had somewhat impaired her health; and she resolved to recruit her forces by a visit to her friend, with whom she had, meantime, kept up a lively correspondence in both languages.

Isabella had become a wife and a mother, and her outward and inward life were known to her friend as far as the exchange of letters could make either known, but Helen found herself in a new world, whose very forms of thought varied from those of her own corner of creation as much as the features of the scenery around her. Vegetation clothed the earth there as here, but here its rank luxuriance, where untamed, typified the unbridled sweep of human propensities, while the curbs and restraints that a certain measure of civilization imposed upon it only concealed the fens and marshes that were the product of a decay as pestiferous to the physical as the corruptions of the heaven-born passions are to the moral atmosphere. Life had given Helen an early maturity, that made her instinctively weigh all shows in a just balance, and, without destroying her faith in man's high destiny, which was anchored upon a rock, she keenly separated the true from the false in her estimate of values. Her own intimate history was of a nature not to be communicated to the nearest friend, for her highest happiness was denied earthly form, but the consecration of her affections was such as to act reflectively for the happiness of others, and she sometimes felt as if she were looking on life as a disembodied spirit might look upon it, interested in it, but no longer of it.

When Isabella first returned to Cuba, she was plunged into scenes and modes of life which she had wholly forgotten, and with which time only made her familiar again. If it had not been for her constant intercourse with Helen, her American life might have become to her as a dream, but it had been passed at a susceptible age; the bent had been given to her character, and its beneficent influences had been perpetuated by the friendship she had formed, and the fact that Helen had continued to be the sole repositary of her new life.

Her father had felt the growing distaste to the thought of slavery when he had visited her from time to time, although it was before the days when that subject was specifically agitated in the States, and when she returned to him he carefully guarded her from the worst aspects of it. When she married the Marquis of Rodriguez, he favored her in the same manner. Both the father and the husband were kind masters, up to the average of a slave-holder's possibility, and had seen enough of European life to be willing to disguise the most revolting aspects of slavery to Isabella. And Isabella soon learned not to inquire too curiously.

It is astonishing to observe how people can shade their own eyes from what is around them. But Isabella's heart was a tender and true one. She was a conscientious and considerate mistress, sacrificing much of her comfort and convenience rather than recurring to her overseer for aid when her people tried her patience and even endurance, as they often did. This leniency subjected her to many impositions, but she soon surrounded herself with affectionate servants, made so by her kindness. She had grown up a Protestant, not of the protesting kind, for she had been educated among liberal-minded Americans, who valued the substance of religion as exemplified in the life, rather than its forms and creeds.

When children came to her, she taught them to feel, because she felt it, that every child has a heavenly endowment that can make him a Christ child in his own sphere if he but obeys his conscience, which is the voice of God within him. This is all the religious instruction children need, and is adapted to every emergency of their lives, as this good mother found.

After Isabella became a mother, she gave up the half-yearly city life which is customary with every planter who can afford to spend the winter in the city, and her husband yielded willingly to her desire for an American nursery-woman. Helen had sent her an excellent one, not an uneducated servant, but one who could intelligently assist her in the early training of her children, as well as take care of their infantile wants. Mrs. Warwick had lived with her ever since the birth of Ludovico, and the children's nursery was a spacious apartment which was the children's home when they were not with their mother. Mrs. Warwick's superintendence necessarily made English the language of the nursery, and this in itself was a protection. The Marchioness had not followed the usual Spanish custom of assigning to each child a little slave to be its servant, so fruitful a source of corruption in a slave community. Her children were never left to their companionship nor allowed to domineer over them.

The nursery over which Mrs. Warwick presided occupied the largest room in the mansion, next to the great hall. It was a little heaven to Helen, and she passed much time in it. The Marchioness devoted some hours of the morning to the instruction of the children: and Helen now participated in this pleasant duty. She also taught them innumerable pretty works, and many songs, for she had a delightful voice, and the musical little Spaniards were never tired of hearing her sing, and of learning them from her lips. The children passed most of their indoor life in this charming room, which contained not only everything that could amuse and interest children, but lovely works of art; and Isabella liked to have them live as much out of the influence of guests as possible, so corrupting is the ordinary conversation of idle-minded people. Especially at this holiday season, and, indeed, in all the dry winter season, the country is full of city people, and Spanish hospitality must keep open house.

Mrs. Warwick was not made a drudge. Isabella insisted upon her retiring to her own apartment when she herself "kept school," as she called it, which she did early in the day. Mrs. Warwick often walked out by herself at these hours, and the Marchioness knew very well that she visited the chicken-house, and the hospital, and any cabins that she pleased. She never asked any questions, but listened when Mrs. Warwick had anything to communicate, and by this means had many more opportunities to relieve suffering. If Camilla had anything to say upon the subject, she peremptorily silenced her, and Camilla had long since resigned herself to the fact that Mrs. Warwick enjoyed a confidence she did not. Of course, she avenged herself whenever she could, and found plenty of ways to do it; but Mrs. Warwick saw that she was no more of a victim than the Marchioness, and knew that both had a champion in the Marquis when things came to an extremity. A word from him arrested Camilla's tongue, as nothing else did; and her tongue was her chief instrument of vengeance, though she did not hesitate to use other means when she could. She was not allowed to invade the nursery, and the children never came out of it unattended either by Mrs. Warwick or their mother. There are even Spanish mothers, exceptional cases, who devote themselves personally to the education of their children. In such cases, they are usually sent to the States or to France as soon as they are old enough to be sent from home; and when this cannot be done, the resource seems to be to teach them to look upon "*la gente*," or "the people," as upon a race of inferior beings, not to be imitated in anything. The strongest expression of disapprobation is: "Do you wish to be like the people?" who are a synonym for all evil. Even Manuel thought of them as *people* (in contradistinction to *the people*) for the first time, when Helen suggested the idea. He liked to talk to her about them, since his own sympathies had been so strongly excited; and so did Carlito, who often followed her to her own apartment after he became well acquainted with her in the nursery, where he was always perfectly happy. She had checked him in speaking of "the people" before the little girls, who were still in the heaven of unconsciousness upon that fearful topic.

It is astonishing how long people can live on the surface of a volcano without realizing its dangers. We turn away from the contemplation of evils that are inevitable, and, when we veil them from our sight, they are to a certain extent non-existent to us. Manuel had never actually witnessed the punishment of a slave. He had heard the noise on that fearful night of Helen's arrival, but he had been lulled to sleep again as the other children were. This could not have been done if the house had stood on a level with the ground, as most of the Cuban country-houses do, but the abode of the Marquis of Rodriguez might be called a palace, and twenty or thirty steps led up to the apartments of the family. The rooms of the household slaves were below, with other domestic offices. Manuel knew that punishments took place, but this was the first revelation to him of their violence. The former overseer was not passionate or cruel. Manuel did not know that he was forbidden to visit the punished slaves because they were left such cruel spectacles (they rarely emerge from the hospital under a month). He had an impression that punished slaves, as part of their punishment, were not allowed to partake of the nice viands his mother sent and carried to the sick.

He knew enough to prevent him from betraying a slave, but this was his first acquaintance with the whole truth, and it was a lesson he never forgot. Good, kind old Carlo he loved very much. Carlito had been much shielded also, for in the city the slaves are sent to the public stocks to be punished. It is not a scene for "ears or eyes polite." In private families, however, the ladies often keep a private whip, with which they slash their maids across the face and neck when displeased with them. Carlito's kind mama was not a lady of that order, and hitherto, when the fresh cargoes were sent from the family hospital to be sold, Carlito heard no more of them.

Helen's heart fainted within her, when she thought at what a cost these tender-hearted children were taught the sin of slavery, and she threw herself into the work of ameliorating the lesson to them as far as possible, without losing sight of the reactionary effect that she hoped and felt sure would follow. When the field slaves were absent at their labor, she and the Marchioness took the children out to play upon the driers, or to gather flowers in the gardens and hedges and portreros, as the woods were called. The flower circles practised in the hard floor of the piazza were tended chiefly by Juanita, who called the little naked children, that were constantly running about, to bring her water in their gourds; and this was a pretty scene, which the children could watch from their nursery windows, without coming in actual contact with the little darkies, to whom they threw confectioneries and lumps of sugar. Then Camilla would come with her tubs of water and her drying-women, and her endearments and droll sayings (well watched and guarded) were a great source of amusement, which, strange to say, she rarely abused. She probably had wit enough to know that she would lose her chance of seeing them if she was not watchful of herself; and, amid all her oddities and vices, she did love children, especially *white* children.

"She would have been an ornament to society," the Marchioness said, one day, "if she had had the opportunity."

"Such activity must have a field," Helen thought to herself; "it is not her fault that she has not a good one."

God leaves man to man. He does not interfere arbitrarily, even to do justice. You are your brother's keeper, he would signify, and he who runs may read.

The Marquis had assisted his wife in his children's education, and Ludovico was a young man of cultivated tastes and extensive reading. Generous childhood always takes the part of the oppressed, where any chance for the development of sentiment is afforded, and an early repugnance to slavery had manifested itself in

Ludovico, in which his mother inwardly rejoiced, while she was cautious not to impair his respect for his father. It was the Marquis' intention that he should go to France, as he had very decided scientific tastes, having inherited something of the Marquis of Ramonte's mathematical genius, and his mother hoped he would never return to the life of a planter, even if she was actually separated from him. But she knew that he was too affectionate a son to lose his allegiance to his parents, and a dim hope sometimes took possession of her that he might be the means of freeing them all from the life of bondage — for the bondage of the master is as veritable a fact as the bondage of the slave; the one being a moral bondage only, while the other is both a moral, an intellectual, and a physical one.

Thus far, Ludovico's existence was but a luxurious dream. He had not approached the solution of the great problem of slavery. As yet it was only his instincts that were arrayed against it. It was a subject never discussed, rarely touched upon, and the customs of the society around him were such that the germ had not yet expanded. Except in his father's house, books and literature were subjects scarce alluded to. The best standard works, and all the periodical literature of the day, were at his command, and he lived with his mother in a world of intellectual beauty. Life itself had hitherto been enjoyment enough, in that most delicious of all climates, surrounded by every luxury; and Ludovico had scarcely yet separated himself from balmy air and soft skies, nature in all its loveliest aspects, happy affections, and gratified wishes, and become a conscious, independent existence. Passion had not yet awakened into being any unsatisfied cravings, for his mother had never left him to prey upon himself, — but Ludovico's slumber was nearly at an end.

All development in those genial climes is premature. A youth of sixteen enters society on a certain footing of equality with older men. There is no boy-life, such as prevails in communities where they are thrown together in schools. Low and degrading pleasures; hunting, and card-playing that has no intellectual excitement in it, cockfighting, idle visiting, and dancing, and some cultivation of music are the chief diversions of country life. In the cities, bull-baiting, cock-fighting, and the opera are the chief amusements. In most houses, one sees no books but "Don Quixote," and no one can understand every-day Spanish conversation who is not familiar with this work, for a proverb from it finishes off nearly every remark that is made. Helen was so puzzled by it that her friend told her she must surely read "Don Quixote" if she wished to take part or even understand common Spanish talk.

Drawing and painting were special accomplishments of the Marchioness. She had studied botany with Helen, on Massachusetts' hills and in her valleys, and had imparted her taste and knowledge to Ludovico. Music is in the air in Cuba, and it requires little training to confine it within the keys or strings of an instrument. Spaniards are musical, negroes are musical, and the very air is musical. Isabella played skilfully, and had instructed her children. Ludovico had heard the best of Italian music all his life, sometimes at the opera in the city, and by the regimental bands, that had little else to do but practise it; and always in private life, for that and dancing were the only accomplishments there. European musicians always visited Havana, and the prevailing music of the hour was repeated on every plantation, with more or less skill. The Marchioness remarked to Helen one day that she could hardly produce so fine an effect as the young men who visited them, and who could *sacar* the music, as they called it, from a piano, with *two fingers*.

The vices that deform society are chiefly found in married life. I leave untouched the deep degradations growing out of the corruptions of city traders' life, where young men from the old country form temporary connections in the families where they apprentice themselves for a few years, to make money in a way they are too high-born and bred to do at home, leaving often large families of children and forsaken wives, who have cherished secret hopes of being taken to Spain into higher stations than their own, and confine myself now to the upper classes of Cuban society, whose vices are *sui generis*.

Marriage in these classes is but a nominal thing, and if these ties are violated within the circle of one's visiting cards little opprobrium is attached to the violation. The social position is in no wise altered by it. Lapses from virtue in unmarried women are considered disgraceful and are of rare occurrence, and therefore no unmarried woman must be left alone with a male friend or a relative farther removed than parent or brother. Indeed, no unmarried lady can keep her father's house alone with unblemished reputation. Not even with a priest would a careful mother leave her daughter for an hour.

It is true that women so corrupted are not received in high society, but the fact that left-handed families bear the sobriquet of *Holy Families* shows the average morality of society in the colonies, with perhaps some distant conception that there is something sacred in true affection.

It is impossible not to be aware that the institution of slavery deepens and extends these social evils in all communities. But where married women are obliged to reconcile themselves to the facts of concubinage, prevalent in all slave communities, and this, of course, even without the excuse or sanction of affection, perverted though it may be, the fountains of all virtue are poisoned, and it is only because the average civilization of Christendom is higher than that of savage life, and that some measure of intellectual cultivation withholds mankind from the last degradation, that society does not lapse back into barbarism. It is indeed only barbarism a little refined and gilded, and the remark may be hazarded that where suffering woman has any access to the founts of Christian truth, however muddy with superstition, redemption is always possible, and not infrequent. The very slaver's wife has her faith in God, though she sees man, who is made in his image, subjugated by her own husband. This is fact and not fiction. But female slave-holders are sometimes more refinedly cruel than men.

Such were the reflections of Helen, as her occasional conversations with her friend unfolded the true condition of things around her. The confidence between them was such that no concealment was attempted. Helen's only consolation was in seeing that the Marchioness' heart was still the loving and kindly one she had known it to be in her childhood, and that she suffered from slavery more than she was willing, for her husband's sake, to acknowledge. This was an earnest of higher internal life than a more comfortable apathy and acceptance of the evil could have been. Her personal happiness was in the affection of her husband and his warm appreciation of her.

CHAPTER VII.

THE DINNER.

Isabella and Helen had sank into their boutacles in the hall to rest a little before the visiting hour arrived, for the country was at that season full of company; Camilla rushed into the hall, so suddenly that Helen was alarmed.

"Ah, my lady! ah! gentlemen coming! Ave, Maria sanctissima! the niño Fernando! ah, yes, yes, see him, the niño Fernando and the niño Pancho in the country, too. Ave, Maria sanctissima! and there is the niño Pepe." Here she twitched off her shawl, and began dusting.

"No dusting at this hour, Camilla," was all the Marchioness had time to say before the young men had jumped from their horses and run up the steps. Camilla rushed forward, and called out from the piazza, "José! Tono! Pablo! come take the gentlemen's horses." The gentlemen greeted her as she passed, which was evidently what she wished for.

"Ay! good day, niño Fernando, many thanks, many thanks, very well, very well — and you, too, niño Pancho! my life! my soul! and niño Pepe!

José! Tono! Pablo! are you sleeping? bad boys! Canailla! why don't you come?"

"Camilla, go and find them, and make no more noise," said Isabella, not quite so patiently as usual.

"Ay, yes! my lady, going, going — yes — poor Carlo! — poor Jacobo! — poor Maria! Ah, yes — the dogs, the dogs! — did you see the dogs, niño Fernando!"

"Camilla, go instantly!" said the Marchioness, with all the sternness she could command.

"Camilla seems more lively than usual to-day," said one of the gentlemen, who had in the meantime greeted the ladies. "Has anything unusual happened?"

Camilla, hearing her name, had stolen back, and was seen peeping from behind the door.

"Oh, yes; poor Carlo! poor Carlo!"

"Camilla, be silent!" exclaimed the Marchioness, though in despair.

Camilla again moved slowly away, with her head sunk upon her arm, the picture of mock-woe and discomfiture; but she was not sufficiently afraid of her mistress to be obedient — indeed, it was one of the trials of her mistress' life that this woman was upon her hands, though she always declared her to be a genius in her vocation.

The young men who had called this morning were intimate friends of the family, and understood both parties perfectly. Don Pepe, the youngest of the brothers, enjoyed nothing more than playing off the old orang-outang, as he always called Camilla, and the Marchioness rather dreaded the encounter to-day, for the theme was too sad a one for sport, and she would willingly have kept it wholly in the background. There is no such thing as privacy on a plantation; the negroes are rapid means of communication, and a disaster on any plantation is soon known far and wide, and often with many exaggerations.

Isabella now presented these friends to Helen, with whose name they had long been familiar, and their warm welcome was very courteous and cordial. When she answered it in good Spanish their delight was boundless, for a visitor with whom they can talk is a boon on a plantation, which becomes a very tedious residence to young men and women, unless enlivened by entertaining company, for the Spaniards have few resources within themselves. The ladies embroider muslin for the dresses of the Christmas holidays, and the gentlemen hunt a few small game, make calls when the roads are good, get up dances when they can, even in the morning call, and, if it rains so hard that they cannot go out to ride, go to bed and endeavor to sleep away the time. They do not even indulge in the solace of a book, but are never tired of playing cards or billiards. Scarcely a family on the island was so cultivated as that of the Marchioness, whose literary resources made her a favorite in society, and she had a happy faculty of drawing out what intelligence existed in the brains of her visitors. An introduction in the home of a friend puts an end to all reserve at once in a Spaniard, and the guest is adopted as one of an intimate circle, without farther preliminary acquaintance. When a Spaniard tells a stranger that everything he has is at his disposal, and wishes him, at parting, to live a thousand years, it is very difficult not to believe him sincere, such is the potency of beautiful manners and the music of the language. "May God have you in his holy keeping," means no more than the French "à Dieu" or the English "Farewell"; but when such benevolent wishes are enforced by the most ardent gestures, one feels as if Christian love and community of interests were ingredients of the atmosphere.

The Marquis and his son now entered from the gallery. The sound of their voices again brought Camilla from her little pantry, which stood adjacent to the dinner-gallery, and from which she could always see or hear what was passing in the hall.

"Camilla, sugar and water," said the Marquis.

"Ah, yes, mi alma! Ludovico, my life! apple of my eye! core of my heart! welcome home!" Then, crossing her hands upon her bosom, she turned her head on one shoulder, and laughed foolishly to herself. "French ladies walk! dogs very bad! poor Carlo!"

"Silence, fool!" exclaimed the Marquis, in a voice that made Camilla disappear from the scene without farther word or pantomime; and when she returned with the sugar and water, she came with noiseless tread and downcast eyes. Upon her arm hung a long linen napkin of the finest cambric, deeply embroidered, and edged with lace, upon which the gentlemen wiped their fingers and mouths after sipping the sugar and water. Don Pepe thanked her with much solemnity, but not a motion was apparent in her now stony countenance, and no sound issued from her lips. The stage effect with which she threw herself into each rôle that she assumed would have amused a light heart, but Helen could not smile to-day unless her thoughts were diverted from that element of the society in which she found herself, and of which she found it a constant component.

It was not long before Camilla reappeared, with a huge tray of oranges, peeled and halved, stacked high, and a pile of napkins on a small tray behind her, that was borne by a little barefooted, half-naked negro boy. The company sucked the juice from the oranges, and threw the skins upon the floor, which were seized and borne away by the little fellow after he had handed the napkins. He soon returned and gathered the napkins.

When the gentlemen walked away to the other end of the piazza, in conversation with the Marquis and Ludovico, Helen asked the Marchioness if this was a common exhibition of Camilla's.

"Oh, very common; but it is not often that her master speaks so sternly to her. Probably she will not speak again to-day; neither will she do anything. We shall all have to suffer on account of her discomfiture, particularly as these young men are here. Fernando is very discreet, but Pepe has no consideration for me, and cannot resist playing her off. Sometimes she gets up some rare dish for them, but if she is displeased with me, she knows she can annoy me by having a very meagre dinner, or by spoiling whatever she touches. I am her slave, I assure you. If I go to make any inquiries, — about the dessert, for instance, — I shall only make the matter worse. I shall try hard to keep quiet. If I can privately communicate with Tom, the cook, who is as good-natured as she is ill-tempered, I shall be sure to have his part of the dinner in good order. They are sworn enemies, and she will do everything she can to defeat his plans; but it will be a comfort to have good meats and vegetables, if we cannot have good puddings, sweetmeats, and fruits. Perhaps Juanita will come in again, and she can sometimes outwit her. But Juanita is much out of spirits to-day, as we all are."

The gentlemen, now possessed of what happened the night before, of which they had heard rumors on the way, expressed great sympathy for the sufferers.

Helen's heart warmed up immediately to Don Fernando when he exclaimed, with much feeling, "Ah, la Marquesa! what a sad thing this slavery is! I wish there was no such thing!"

"So do I," said Ludovico. "I am going to the States to live; there is one part of them at least where there is no slavery, and I will brave the cold for the sake of turning my back upon it. I would not stay here if I were you, Miss Wentworth. I know you think we are cruel and wicked people. *I* do."

A look from his father silenced Ludovico as effectually as it had Camilla, but Don Fernando went on: "It is a sad inheritance. I sometimes wish I had never been out of the country, that I might not draw parallels. I think all the world that I have seen is pretty bad, but this is the worst that there is."

"Are you not talking dangerously, Don Fernando?" asked the Marquis.

"I don't know who there is to make me afraid," replied Fernando.

"But do you not risk promoting insurrection?"

"My people know just what I think, but I am not afraid of them."

"You have an excellent overseer."

"If he is as good when we are absent from the plantation as when we are here; but he keeps very good order without severity."

"Your slaves are not new like mine."

"I know I have that advantage, and Doña Josefa is a very gentle mistress. The people all love her well enough to obey her. They see that she has a fellow-feeling for them. You have good people too, Marquis. This accident must not discourage you. You have not so many deadheads to look after as we have had. They make the most trouble on a plantation."

All this was music to Helen's ear. It renewed her confidence in her friends, who must not suffer injustice from her because a bad man had done a bad action.

Still, the view she had had behind the scenes, in both her experiences, stamped the institution of slavery with the character it deserved.

Helen would fain have enlarged upon the subject, but she saw the turn the conversation had taken was not agreeable to the host. Other guests came, and all was hilarity.

The recent death of Ferdinand of Spain had suppressed all the public festivities of Christmas the preceding year; a decree went forth, as part of the public mourning, that there should be no public dancing for six months. No other observance of the national loss (supposing it was such) could so effectually have saddened the countenances of the pleasure-loving Spaniards, to whom music and dancing are as nectar and ambrosia were to the gods of Olympus. Outward rebellion was impossible under a despotic monarchy and its despotic representatives; but the spirit of the decree was thoroughly evaded by a proportionate increase of private music and dancing. The holidays were near at hand, the pressure would be lifted this year, and the proprietors of the plantations, most of whom lived in the city, were flocking to their country residences accompanied by troops of friends. Every day of the holidays must be spent in festivity and visiting. This was as much a part of the national religion as the observance of the festival days of the Church. Indeed, in Cuba the festal celebrations of the Church were still religiously observed, while the fasts were wholly dispensed with, for, since the license that had prevailed in the colonies at the period of the Constitution in Spain, religion had been but a nominal thing except in the hearts of some devout women and aged men.

Village balls were to occupy every evening of the coming holidays. These take place in some public home of the village, and are supported by the gambling tables. Few skilled games are played in Cuba, but the guests bet upon the number of spots upon a card, and then fall into the dance in another apartment, in the intervals of which they go to learn the fortunes of the game. Estates often change owners under the tremendous excitement of the play — not an intellectual excitement as in other regions, but strictly a moneyed one.

As Camilla was to all intents and purposes, through perverseness, off duty to-day, and as Carlo's family, the usual house servants, were disabled, the Marchioness was obliged to superintend in person the arrangements for a large number of guests, which number was liable to increase till the last moment. Tom was equal to all demands in his department, and the resources of the plantation in meats, fruits, and vegetables were inexhaustible, and sometimes Tom got up the best dinners when he was most intoxicated, but some exceptions to this always made his mistress tremble. Drinking was forbidden on this well regulated plantation, but Tom was the *chef* of a deceased relative, who had bequeathed him to the Marquis, and his equal was not known in the neighborhood, so that his delinquencies had to be winked at for the sake of his services. Besides this, Tom was the kindest, lovingest, and most faithful of servants, barring his infirmity. Camilla hated him because of his successes, but he did not hate any one, only coolly baffled her schemes, and, if she were off the ground from ill-temper, he would even venture upon her department and send in from his cooking cabin the choicest of pastry. This possibility was the only check upon Camilla's disloyalty to her kind mistress. If there had been no one to take her place in emergencies, the Marchioness would have been a more unhappy victim then she was. The expenditure of talent in the art of tormenting on Camilla's part was worthy of study. She was never so happy as when others were unhappy; the greater confusion, the higher her spirits rose. If she felt good-natured, if her inexplicable vanity was gratified, she could do wonders. The Marchioness rejoiced to-day that Don Fernando and Don Pepe were there, for they always praised her for her achievements, and she took pride in calling forth their commendations, not realizing the degree to which they amused themselves by playing upon her weaknesses. What she might do to-day no one could conjecture. If she would not speak all day there would be great rejoicing in high places, for this passive form of revenge was the least harmful under the present circumstances.

When the young people began to dance, which Ludovico promoted as soon as possible, Helen was rejoiced that there were enough dancers without her, and declined many urgent invitations to partake in the amusement. Her puritanic education did not admit of waltzing, but she could have enjoyed the poetry of motion as exemplified in the southern contra-dances, if the music and the gayety had not on this occasion seemed to her like heartless mockery. She would gladly have retired from the scene, but social life on the plantations does not admit of that degree of self-indulgence. Every one is expected to do his part, by presence at least, especially in the country, where solitude is the rule and society the exception.

The beautiful Juanita, who had attracted her attention all day, moved slowly round among the company, bearing oranges. Her beauty and her tasteful dress attracted the attention of every one. Her features were very soft, though their contour was lofty, and the rich brown complexion was set off by a highly colored muslin handkerchief, that was twirled into a becoming turban, — a costume that prevailed among ladies as well as among slaves, differing only in the costliness of the material. There was not a lady in the company whose grace of motion, clearness of complexion, or dignity of mien surpassed hers. She lifted her eyes to no one, and no one addressed her in the presence of her mistress. A simple muslin dress, cut to her throat, with short sleeves that left exposed an arm that would make a sculptor rave, set off her singular Moorish beauty, which bore no trace of the negro.

The dinner was a success, in spite of Camilla's perversity. Tom was sober that day, and realized the importance of his position. It was even supposed that Camilla sometimes smuggled into his cabin a bottle of liquor, to defeat any plans he might form to baffle her. She could not make him quarrel, and did not dare to find fault with him aloud; for Tom was one of the Marquis' pets, and of the Marquis she stood in awe. She had been known to make his nice viands disappear mysteriously, at the very moment they were wanted. I say "had been known," but mumma Camilla was too skilled a diplomatist ever to have been detected in such practices. It was only by inference that such things could ever be laid at her door,— circumstantial evidence, whose weight she was herself unable to estimate; sudden access of good spirits; preternatural activity to supply the deficiency, or pretended eagerness to discover the culprit, laying the charge, perhaps, to some unfortunate individual who had offended her, or even to Tom himself. No missing spoons were ever found in her baskets, but she would sometimes produce them with: "Does any one know how to find lost things like mumma Camilla?" And, if asked where they were found, she would shake her head mysteriously. "Poverecita (poor little one)! Canailla! we will not tell this time; it will never be done there again. My eyes are open now, and it would be hard to punish her the first time!" When pressed, as had sometimes been the case, punishment had been administered in the wrong places, and her mistress preferred, upon the whole, to pretend belief in the old hag's superior knowledge and benevolence, especially if things came back in due time; and she found that their reappearance was invariably in the inverse ratio to the anxiety she expressed.

Tom was the most kind-hearted of human creatures. He could not wring a chicken's neck without turning his head aside. He made toys for the children, cages for their birds, nets for catching fishes from the lagoon, and traps for game; brought them flowers from the forest trees, and birds' eggs from the deserted nests. It will be seen that Tom was not wholly consistent in his benevolence, but he would not rob a mother-bird of its eggs. His good offices were not confined to his mistress' children. All the little darkies on the plantation were his friends. He bound them to him by bones from his stews and cooked vegetables from his kettles. They brought him wood from the portreros, vegetables from the garden, windfalls from the orange-trees, eggs from the hens' nests, when they could steal them slyly, — but hens were negro property, and woe be it to them if they were found out! — such eggs were always ostensibly from stolen nests. Through the children he undoubtedly obtained the intoxicating draughts that were his passion, but no investigation had ever come to the bottom of this mystery. Tom was the only safe transgressor upon the plantation, for careful restrictions were, in other cases, well enforced upon this point.

But Tom never allowed the children to step over the threshold of his cabin, nor, indeed, did man or woman ever venture so far. He was lord and master of that domain. His cooking cabin was about twenty rods from the mansion, and he also appropriated twenty feet in circuit around it for his various kettles, for his culinary apparatus inside (I do not know the nature of it) did not accommodate all the varieties of Tom's cooking exploits. Don Pancho, one of the present guests, had been known to put his head into the door occasionally, to request Tom not to put pepper into the food that day, for he had been in France and had acquired the notion that pepper was not good for himself. From some unaccountable reason, supposed by the imaginative to be a golden reason, which could be transmuted into comforting beverages, Tom did not resent this intrusion, but it was the solitary exception known. Helen took a great fancy for peeping in one day, but the Marchioness described Tom's idiosyncrasy upon the subject, and also advised her not to do it on her own account, if she ever expected to relish her food again; so she gave up the attempt and endeavored to forget that she had ever thought of it, although Isabella ended her remonstrance with "Fire purifies everything, you know."

When the company was fairly seated at table in the open gallery behind the saloon and shaded from the sun by the linen drapery, which at a subsequent hour was raised for air and for a view of the splendid flower-border that separated the house from the coffee-driers, flagons of cool water standing in saucers and wreathed with flowers (a peculiarity of Spanish tables), with which Juanita had decked them to please Ludovico, for she cared little that day to please the company expected to the dinner, Camilla opened the door of her little pantry and came slowly forth, her face wrapped in a huge layer of cotton batting, and established herself with her dish-tub on the upper step of the gallery, where she was accustomed to wash the plates from the table as they were rapidly changed for the different courses. Her mistress would gladly have dispensed with this spectacle, though there was a certain satisfaction in seeing one's plates so thoroughly washed as mumma Camilla was in the habit of washing them, but she dreaded the display and the noise that would probably accompany it. Camilla walked slowly back and forth several times in pursuit of her soap and her cloths, her arms hanging lifeless as it were before her, her head drawn a little aside, apparently in pain, and her eyes red and swollen with weeping. When several of the company who knew her and had often been amused by her spoke to her, and expressed pity for her pain, she answered them only in pantomime, pointing with solemn gestures to her face, shaking her head, and drawing deep sighs.

"Mumma Camilla has the toothache," said Don Pepe to Ludovico across Miss Wentworth. "Shall I send her a dish of soup?"

It is a Spanish custom to send tidbits to friends across the table.

"Ay, Pepe! if you have any pity upon us, do not take any notice of her," said Ludovico. "There are strangers sitting by mama, and I am afraid the old creature will do some ridiculous thing."

"For my part," said Don Pepe, "I am never satisfied till I have had a little fun with mumma Camilla."

Camilla's eyes were not so swollen that she could not see that Don Pepe was ready for a frolic, and, catching the sound of her name, she sat down on the steps of the gallery, and began to wash some plates just taken from the table.

"Ay, no! mumma Camilla, do not sit in that wind; it will make your toothache worse."

A solemn shake of the head and a furious clatter of plates was the only notice taken of this kindly warning, nor could Pepe, by all his arts, elicit a word. If crockery could speak an intelligible language, it would have been all-sufficient, and the din waxed louder and louder, till the Marquis uttered in a loud voice, "Silenzio! go to your pantry, Camilla."

There was no appeal from this, and slowly and despondingly Camilla obeyed — but before long she emerged with a young assistant, who took her place at the tub, and every time she made the slightest noise with a plate, Camilla warned her with a sign from her finger. She watched the Marquis' eye, and if it turned to the other side, she indulged in frantic pantomimes of pain — but she was vigilant enough not to let him catch her at that amusement. She took no notice of Tom's wonderful performances in the way of pastry, but Pepe did his best to praise them and to send tidbits of them to his friends around the table, for each of which Camilla was called upon for a plate. Fernando turned his reproving eye upon him several times, but he was as incorrigible as Camilla herself, and did his best to make a sensation.

When the meats and pies were disposed of, the Marquis gave a signal, and the company rose and walked out upon the piazza on the other side of the saloon for refreshments, while the fruits and sweetmeats and some light wines were set upon the table, when the company reseated themselves, changing their former places for variety, and sat an hour longer. The party broke up after another dance, and the wearied hosts separated, hoping to rest after their thirty-six hours of excitement.

And every day was a partial repetition of similar scenes, till the holidays were over.

CHAPTER VIII.

THE DRIVE.

The quitrin which was whirled to the door after the departure of the guests was a volante with a movable top which can be thrown back like an old-fashioned English chaise. The calesero was in his gayest holiday livery, for he had been in attendance at the dinner table where the coachmen even of the guests wait upon their masters.

The harness was of burnished silver, polished to its utmost brilliancy, and the liveries were slashed with blue, and embroidered with silver lace. Long blue ribbons floated from the steeple-crowned hat of the calesero, with gay cockades to match, fastened upon the side of the steeple with large silver buttons. The blue silk linings and curtains of the quitrin were trimmed with deep silver fringe. There was not a more tasteful carriage in the island.

"This turn-out is especially in honor of you," said the Marquesa to her friend. "I suppose Pope Urban, as we call him, thought the carriage should match the liveries to-day, and every slave on the plantation knows that you are my particular American friend. Pope Urban has almost given up driving, since he has grown so old, but I understand this is a compliment to myself."

Before Helen was aware, Pope Urban had deftly lifted and deposited her in the sky-blue quitrin, and then performed the same office for his lady.

"I have had many a ride in a basket on Pope Urban's head. He considers me his especial property, and was a present from my kind father on my marriage."

One horse was placed between the shafts, the other outside, and the latter Pope Urban bestrode, with much grace, holding the reins almost at arm's length.

"What a fatiguing mode of guiding the horses," said Helen.

"Yes," replied her friend, "the caleseros do not generally live to be as old as Pope Urban. The position in which they drive soon affects the chest. But this old man has been favored. He superintends the younger caleseros, and rarely drives now. But I always feel safest in his hands. The boys have great command over the horses, with whom they are brought up as daily companions, but they are so careless that I never ride without trembling,—and indeed I rarely take out the children without my husband is with me, and he uses reins and an American bit to please me. This bit which Urban uses does not pass through the mouth, but only above and below it, and it never seems so safe to me. Pope Urban is always prompt too. I did not expect to see the volante for an hour to come. One New England domestic will do the work of half a dozen slaves, and in half the time. But it is a sad pity that you are plunged at once into this painful subject. I hoped to veil it from your eyes for a long time. Indeed, this dreadful occurrence is the first experience of the kind since my marriage. My husband has been so careful, and our good overseer never exposed anything to me."

Helen wondered if he was good to those below him as well as to those above him.

"Camilla was spoiled before I came to La Consolacion. A former overseer ruined her, and they became such tyrants together that the whole rule was taken from the master's hands, till on one occasion they ventured a little too far, and he was dismissed, and Camilla sent into the field till her proud spirit was humbled a little. Since my régime she has taken me for her slave; but she is so useful I cannot do without her, and when my children are ill she is like one inspired. She is never so well content as when the power is all in her own hands."

"You are under bondage, indeed, dear Isabella," exclaimed Helen. "Forgive me for reproaching you this morning."

"Oh, yes, dear, fully. To tell the truth, there

was a certain satisfaction in listening to your indignation. But my husband does the best he can. Many of these people are raw Africans. The cholera desolated this part of the island last year, and we lost more than half our people. It is very difficult to break the new ones in."

As the Marquesa spoke, the horse in the shafts gave a sudden start, and nearly disengaged the reins from the hand of Pope Urban. But, though unprepared, his presence of mind did not forsake him, and he drew him up strongly, directly opposite the object of his terror, judging, doubtless, that if he left it behind, he should not be able to restrain his flight. The sharp prickers on the bit penetrated his flesh above and below the mouth, and the blood spouted forth. This arrested his progress, and he suddenly stopped, trembling violently.

A little old man, frightful enough in aspect to have terrified man or beast, rose from the brink of a large marble basin to sue for money. He did not mean to frighten the horse, and probably a chicken in the hedge would have produced the same effect upon the noble animal.

"What are you doing here, José?" said the Marquesa.

"Dead fish kill fish, — take out dead fish," he answered, in broken Spanish.

"Go to the other side, away from the park, for fear of frightening other horses. If Pablo had been driving, we should have been run away with."

"Much sorry, lady — good lady. Urbano know horse, — horse know Urbano," he added, and, seeing the blood flow from the horse's mouth, he dropped his gourd into the water and put it to the poor beast's mouth, and then threw the remainder over his head. The grateful animal, quite tamed down, acknowledged the kindness with expressive motions of his ears, and they rode on in silence for some time.

"You see they are not all Urbans, dear Helen. That is one of the bozals that came last year; he is a cripple from some cause, but was bought in a large coffle, and has never been put to hard work."

Helen did not wish to know how he had been reduced to such a hideous semblance of humanity, and only replied : —

"He has a kind heart left."

"Oh, yes," said the Marquesa, "they are a kindly race; but let us not talk of them any more now. I am afraid you will not observe all the beauties around you. Is not my rose hedge beautiful?"

The hedge was about three feet in height and now in full bloom of clustered roses, as delicate and almost as small as the Multiflora. It looked indeed like a bank of roses.

Helen had not been unmindful of the stately

palm-avenues she had threaded the night before, but even the rosy sunset did not make them glorious to her to-day. All was darkened to her vision, and the long avenues, imposing as they were, no longer seemed to her living pillars of beauty, spreading their tufted foliage as an expression of their own inward joy for the fulness of life; for here the very plants of the earth seemed to breath consciously, from the spiritual night-blooming cereus — which expands after the sun goes down from bud to flower, before the astonished gaze of the beholder — to the more homely grain, which springs from the rich earth the very day after it is planted.

The mysterious shadows of the cocoas, which the day before looked like the guardians of hidden coolness, as they interposed their rustling shields between her and the burning sun when the horses' heads were turned into their friendly avenues for rest and refreshment, now cast a melancholy veil over the earth they shaded, and the stiff leaves whispered sad secrets of wrong done and unredeemed. The Gothic arches of the bamboo alleys were in consonance with her feelings. The deciduous leaf, which is constantly falling, forms a thick russet carpet under the plumy foliage of these gigantic tufted grasses, whose tops, interlaced in an impenetrable roof, give no access to the sun, and impart the sensation of a cool grotto. Every pore is sensitive to the influences of nature in this delicious climate. Each plant and tree tells its own tale, awakens its own analogy with life; but these analogies are but echoes of the soul that lays itself open to their influences.

When they emerged into an open plain and she saw groups of palm-trees in the distance, where they stood, in their native wildness, struggling up to the sky for light, it seemed to Helen that they were stretching away from the earth, lifting their tufted heads to the heavens to call down mercy upon the wretched world beneath them.

The negro gang was just crossing the plain, on their way home from a wood where they had been cutting brush, and as they passed the ladies they greeted them with the usual Spanish salutation, "May God have you in his holy keeping!" which probably many of them did not understand themselves.

A single garment constituted the dress of each. The men wore duck pantaloons, the women a short-sleeved, low chemise, fitting rather tight. Neither sex had any protection for the head, but had worked all day under the eye of the overseer, in the burning sun, scarcely daring to raise their heads for fear of the impending lash of the exasperated wretch, who was obliged to superintend more closely than usual, since he had disabled his negro driver. The superintendence consists in working all equally, whether able or not, and quickening the laggards by the application of the whip. Is it surprising that when their tormentor has to turn his back upon one gang, to visit another at some other spot, they all rest and even play, driver and all, for the ten or fifteen minutes of exemption? Yet a certain amount of work must be done, or the punishment comes at the end of the day.

On this afternoon, to close the day's work, they had been sent to cut brush, and were returning, unusually wearied and heavily laden and foot-sore. There were brawny men and stout women among the recent bozals, but others were bent and feeble.

Over the sad faces of many a gleam of sunshine passed, as if of remembered kindness, and dazzling and angelic must have been the vision of their lady in her splendid vehicle.

One tall, slender, but athletic-looking young woman raised her eyes for a moment but passed on without bending her head or uttering a word, or making a gesture of salutation.

"Did you remark that girl's eye, Helen?" said the Marquesa.

"I did indeed," she replied. "She looks like poor Dolores," was the passing thought.

It was indeed poor Dolores, though Helen did not realize the fact.

"I never saw it before, but I am glad she has looked at me at last. She is a recent bozal, and I have never before seen her but with downcast brow and eyes averted. No one has ever elicited anything but a monosyllable from her, and she has kept very much to herself, the women tell me. I have tried some of my arts to engage her attention, for I found Pope Urban much interested in her. She is a native of the same tribe as himself, and the only one he has ever seen. I am afraid this wicked overseer has not treated her well, for I am sure those eyes were more like the eyes of a wild animal than of a human being."

"The expression was indeed fearful," said Helen. And again she saw the resemblance to Dolores, but, not thinking it likely to be she, she could not bring herself to tell that sad story.

As they crossed from one plantation to another, they passed deep forests whose verdure was festooned together by giant vines, that often had smothered and hugged the life out of the trees that supported them; becoming in their turn the supporters, and flourishing upon the juices of the trees embraced, they had usurped the domain of earth and air, which were the original possessors of the trees. One, more remarkable than the rest, had been chosen as the entrance to the avenue of a splendid domain, and Urban had purposely brought them that way to show it to the "Americana," and now drew up his horses under the wonderful natural arch. Two giant ceyba or cottonwood trees that stood at the distance of thirty feet from each other, had, early in their growth, crossed their branches thirty feet above the head of a tall man, and both trees had continued to grow, had become encircled with an enormous vine, and now presented a symmetrical and perfect pointed arch. The two had then shot up straight into the air, joining their trunks and forming a double column. The intertwining had not checked their growth, but both had prospered.

The ceyba tree, whose roots appear above the ground, and seem to support the shaft, shoots up to an immense height, and is surmounted by a crown of leaves of very delicate form and texture, so that it traces a fine net-work against the sky. A huge vine of the boa-constrictor species had grown up by the side of this one, laying its own roots parallel with the enormous cordages thrown out from the broad spread trunk, which balanced the mighty top, and thus enabled the shaft to resist the sweeping tornadoes, which would otherwise tear it from its bed. The vine had seemed to respect the picturesque arrangement of nature, for it did not begin to twine around the tree till it had grown above the archway, and then it wound its huge spirals about them both, bedding itself firmly in the bark as it grew, till the enormous trunk had withered in its embrace, so that one side of the arch was hollow to its very peak. The delicate foliage of the vine, adorned with pale yellow flowers, crept over and around the branches of the original tree, mingled itself with the few remaining living twigs of one portion of it, and hung its luxuriant tracery in the most graceful drapery over the whole. Our stateliest hemlocks hardly compare well in height with this tropical tree. Once in many years it bears flowers and fruit, which latter is bedded in a pod of the softest and silkiest down, not yet brought within the grasp of machinery, but used for beds and cushions. Just after the dropping of the pod, the tree loses its foliage for a time, but its symmetry is so exquisite that even in its nakedness it is sublime.

La Ascencion, where the Marchioness proposed to make a call, was the residence of Count von Müller, one of the few Germans to be met with in the island. The approach from this unique gateway was through an avenue of mango and tamarind trees, that skirted a deep wood on either side. The mango trees, somewhat resembling the horse-chestnut in form, were weighed to the ground with the brilliant scarlet and orange, pear-shaped fruit, a great favorite with the islanders, when cooked as a sauce. The long, shining, lanceolate leaves are not unlike those of our mountain-laurel. The feathery, acacia-like foliage of the tamarind contrasts finely with these. Under their shade grew many delicate plants, and among the rest was cultivated, carefully, one that is generally found only in wild woods: the Campanula, a shrub surmounted by large, white, bell-shaped flowers of the frailest texture, half a foot in length, and of exquisite symmetry of shape. They looked like spiritual bells, too large for fairies, but too delicate to be handled by mortal hands.

In a circle of tea-roses, all in rich and fragrant bloom, stood the house of Count von Müller. Behind it stretched away extensive stone coffee-driers, skirted in their turn by clay cottages, of tasteful form, the habitations of the negroes.

When they drew up to the door, a huge turbaned head, surmounting a plump, handsome mulatto face, of proportionate dimensions, was thrust from a window, and as quickly withdrawn, but not till the beholders had had a full view of massive gold ear-pendants and necklace.

In a few moments, the portly dame, arrayed in a flowing robe of fine white linen, richly embroidered, and trimmed with lace, stepped upon the gallery. Count Von Müller was not in the house, and a rabble of naked, black children, who ran across the gallery, were bid to seek him. As they stood gazing at the splendid quitrin, the portly negress enforced her words with a stamp and a slap or two, and drove them before her like a flock of geese, or, rather, black swans. They dived, jumped from the gallery, scampered through the hall, and fled in every direction; but no sooner had the ladies alighted and seated themselves in the cool and comfortable boutacles, than they saw woolly little heads peeping in at doors and windows.

' The portly mulatto sauntered out into the gallery to enforce her authority, and this time the warning finger was accompanied by a threat which sent the naked little blackies scampering over the coffee-driers, as if to seek some place of safety.

"Count von Müller rules five hundred slaves, and Mariana rules Count von Müller," said the Marquesa, by way of explanation, during the absence of that potentate.

"Has he no family?"

"Yes, if you can call half a dozen of these little yellow things a family. His lawful children are in Europe for their education, for his wife died before he came here, and he came to make money for them. But I doubt if he ever returns, for he has become quite a creole in his domestic habits, and prides himself upon his model plantation."

Shocked as Helen was by what these habits appeared to be, she was glad to hear of a model plantation, and pleased herself with the hope that a man born outside of slavery institutions might have better conceptions of humanity than even an honorable Spaniard had risen to.

The return of the mistress of ceremonies, followed by servants bearing golden panetala (the very ideal of sponge cake) and oranges, already divested of their yellow skins, cut short farther conversation between the friends.

In a few moments the Count von Müller

appeared, a stocky, dumpy German, with bald head and blue eyes.

The Marquesa was a great favorite of his, because she admired his plantation, and was in the habit of bringing her guests to see his improvements.

The main building ran all round a quadrangle, and they immediately began their walk through it, as there was much to be seen which Isabella justly thought would be pleasing to Helen, and which she unfortunately could not exhibit at home, for Spaniards follow in the beaten track, and even her own household ameliorations had broken in upon time-honored customs.

Adjoining the mansion was a large, latticed hall surrounded by a balustrade, and the ends of the gallery that ran on two sides of it were secured by wicker gates. In this hall stood innumerable baskets, fitted with clean cloths, on which reposed the future coffee-pickers of the plantation, and naked children of all ages above these babies were trotting about under the care of two nicely dressed negro women, who patted the babies kindly, and fed them out of civilized bowls. Next to this hall, which the Count facetiously called the crying-room, and where a good deal of that sort of music was going on, as is the case even in nice nurseries, was the picking-room, a long corridor with glass windows on each side, an almost unheard-of luxury on Spanish plantations, even in the apartments of the family. Down the centre of this corridor ran the plank tables, with benches on either side, for the sorters of coffee. This work is usually done in the open air, but the negroes suffer much from the heavy dews of the island in their early morning labors. Then came the packing-room, in which innumerable empty bags were stored, this not being the packing season.

Farther on, and nearer to the family mansion, on the other side, was the hospital, with numerous appliances for the comfort of the sick. There were many patients in this hospital, and it was frequently suggested by the Count's friends that if all his plantation arrangements compared well with the hospital, there must be less occasion than in ordinary cases for feigning sickness. Helen was glad to see coarse straw hats on both men and women; the Marquis' negroes working bareheaded.

When the ladies ascended the extensive driers that lay beyond the mansion, they had a fair view of the neat habitations and gardens of the "people."

It was plain that the Count pursued a different policy from the ordinary one of the colonies in regard to his negroes. Yet his wealth was the envy of all.

As the party turned towards the house again, they passed the ample stables. Planters pride themselves upon the number and beauty of their horses, and no one surpassed Count von Müller in the possession of fine animals of the noblest breeds.

Helen was a horsewoman, and knew how to appreciate this taste. But, as she turned the corner, a scene characteristic of slave institutions, even under the mildest regulation, burst upon her.

A group of colored men and women were standing under a tree, to which was chained an infuriated blood-hound, from whose sides blood streamed upon the ground. Two negroes, also attached to a post, at a little distance from the dog, by long ropes, stood bleeding and apparently exhausted; one held a whip, which was stained with the animal's blood, and which he had just lifted to inflict another blow, when the overseer, seeing the company, arrested his arm. But he could not prevent the blood-hound from springing and gnashing his teeth at the negroes who were within reach of him, and who had evidently been tormenting him.

"I beg your pardon, ladies," said the Count, "but you know, my lady," he said, apologetically addressing la Marquesa, "the white man is never bitten on my plantation. This training must be attended to."

The whole truth dawned upon Helen in a moment. The next, she fell heavily upon Isabella's arm, and slid to the ground in happy unconsciousness. It required little of the German's superabundant strength to lift her from the ground and carry her in his arms to the house, where he laid her upon a couch.

Isabella, scarcely more able to walk than Helen, sank into a chair and covered her face with her hands.

Mariana and other women brought water and wine, and did their best to restore the horrified visitors. Soon the room was partially filled with curious lookers-on, of all ages and complexions, but a furious stamp of the Count's foot and a threatening gesture of his uplifted hand cleared the space of intruders at once.

Isabella had never beheld this revolting sight before, though she well knew the mode of training the blood-hound to his work. As soon as Helen opened her eyes, her friend begged the Count to place her in the carriage, for she dreaded the repetition of the faintness, or the burning word that might burst from Helen.

"Your friend is a stranger, I see, my lady. I regret this accident very much," were his parting words, to which Isabella made a faint reply. She felt that she had no right to reproach him.

The fresh air and the motion soon restored Helen to full consciousness, and when they had driven from the door she was relieved by a violent fit of weeping, in which Isabella joined her.

It was long before either spoke. At last the Marquesa broke silence.

"Ah, dear Helen! what can you think of us? I hoped to give you a pleasant picture to counterbalance your sad introduction to Cuban life — and this most shocking of all the horrors of slavery," and Isabella wept again convulsively.

Helen could not raise her eyes during the ride home. She did not wish to see the skies, so desecrated by the earth, over which they hung so lovingly in their twilight beauty. Isabella tried to persuade her to look at their surpassing colors, "for, as I often remind you," she continued, "it is God's world still." But Cuban skies, palm-trees, bamboo, and all tropical glories, were inevitably associated henceforth in Helen's mind with the unutterable woes of humanity, such as they must be where the first principle of brotherhood is violated.

The words of the great preacher rang in her ears — "The sum of all villanies."

When they arrived at La Consolacion, she begged the Marquesa to excuse her to the family, and went at once to her own room.

The Marchioness had admired Count von Müller for his benevolence, with apparent justice. But how can benevolence comport with the fact that a man brought up in free society goes to a slave-holding country for the purpose of making money at such a cost? The Count's policy, as we have said, was to take care of his people's health, for he thought that paid better in the end, and his benevolence to white men induced him to have his dogs well trained so that they need not fall upon any one but a fugitive; but the rules of his plantation were very rigid, the work he exacted very severe, the punishments for delinquency very terrible when they came. With true Anglo-Saxon sagacity, he saw that slackness of government produced slackness of service in the gentle race he domineered over. If he had tried the plan of giving them some interest in their labors, he might have struck something out of human souls, which hold all germs of motives, that would have made them labor with a will and serve his interests too, but he had not made that innovation with the rest, and even comfortable hospitals and picking rooms did not preclude the necessity of using force to extract the amount of labor he required. There is no North Star to a Cuban slave, but there are mountain fastnesses where they can hide and even intrench themselves. He boasted that he never punished the same individual twice, but what did that imply? The blue eyes could look soft and amiable upon an admiring friend, but they were pitiless when they looked upon the chattel whose blood and sinew he would transmute into gold.

Blood-hound training, it may be said, to the credit of most masters, is not usually done upon the plantations, but the cruelty is only once removed by being perpetrated elsewhere. It belongs to the institution of slavery, and no sophistry can evade the imputation, whether such dogs are trained by the overseers in Cuba, or by professional negro-hunters in the United States.

CHAPTER IX.

JUANITA.

ONE day when they were alone, Helen begged her friend to tell her the history of Juanita, who interested her deeply by her sadness and her beauty. The whirl of events had prevented her from coming much in contact with her, but she often saw her bending over her work, in the Marchioness' apartment, or occupied about the little children in the nursery, and she saw Ludovico apply to her as to a sister to supply his little wants.

"Juanita is so different from the rest of the people, I do not wonder you ask," said the Marchioness.

"You do not mean that she is a slave, Isabel," exclaimed Helen, almost gasping.

"Yes, dear Helen, it is even so," said the Marchioness, rising to close the door into her apartment, which Juanita at that moment entered.

"Juanita is a Moor," she continued; "you perceive her straight hair and her beautifully chiselled features. Her grandmother was purchased by my father-in-law in a coffle of slaves, of which she was the only Moor. They are not often enslaved. They have little resemblance to other negroes; indeed they are not negroes. Juanita's mother was the daughter of a white man, and that bleached her complexion. Juanita's has been still farther changed by a similar parentage."

"Horrible!" exclaimed Helen.

"Ah, yes, dear, the fate of such beautiful girls is sad indeed, but not so in their eyes. They would no more take a negro for husband than you or I would, but have a pride in such connections as they form, that seems incredible to us, and yet I do not know why I should say so. They see that white men are superior in civilization; they learn to be ashamed of their African origin, which they often deny. Civilized life is so above their own degraded condition, that it is not strange that they wish to ally themselves with it. My father-in-law gave the mother and child to me when I was married. The boy was as beautiful as Juanita, but we were obliged to send him away, for his independent spirit brooked no control."

"What has become of him?" inquired Helen.

"I presume he is in the city, but I have not heard of him of late. He was named Juan de la Luz (John of the Light.) He was my father-in-law's special pet and attendant. He was full of ability; was a good locksmith, kept all the machinery in order, and contrived, no one knew how, to learn to read. Probably through this, or possibly in the city, where he often accompanied my father-in-law, he learned of the English treaty by which all slaves brought to the island after a certain date were truly free. This he communicated to his mother, and Juanita undoubtedly knows it. If all who are free by that treaty knew it, we might be overpowered by their combined action; but the whole community is so ignorant, the standing army so numerous and strong, the government so despotic, that it is, to all intents and purposes, null and void. The Captain-General has his royalty upon every slave's head, and he is too powerful to be thwarted. The English commissioner, who resides in Havana, told me himself that his office was a sinecure, and always would be while the Captain-General chose to connive at slavery."

"What corruption!" was all Helen could ejaculate.

"Yes; there is no such thing as fathoming it. He told me that, if he confiscated a vessel and threw the captain in prison, in a few weeks the surgeon of the prison would report him ill, and request a permit from the Captain-General to send him into the country for his health. Soon after, he might meet him in the streets of Havana, pardoned, and ready to sail on the same errand again, in a new vessel. Usually, the landings are made on unfrequented parts of the coast, but the coffles are openly marched through the country, and the planters purchase many on the way. The rest find their way to the city, or, rather, they are smuggled there under false pretences, and are thrown into the slave-pens, where old slaves are constantly exposed for sale. These pens used to be within the walls of the city, but they are now outside."

Helen shuddered at the recollection of all she knew on that fearful subject, and would fain have asked her friend if she knew no other family in Havana to whose kindness she could have commended her on her arrival; but she forbore, and only asked : —

"Where is Juanita's mother?"

"She pined away and died of a broken heart after the sale of her son, for the separation was necessarily a final one. Every means had been taken to break Juan's proud spirit; but he was vain — he loved dress, and lavished upon his handsome person the money guests lavished upon him. He looked like a prince in my husband's splendid livery. He bought fine shirts, rings for his fingers and trinkets for his ears, and put on such airs that he was unendurable. He was proud of his nationality, and his mother cherished all these feelings in him. Wherever Juan goes, he will make trouble with the slaves, and the worst fate awaits him if he does not get to the mountains. I do not know but he might become a chief among the fugitives there. They often 'come down upon the plantations at the foot of the mountains, and help themselves to whatever they wish for."

"So there is no defence against them, on the plantations?" inquired Helen. "I should think they would be very dangerous."

"There is no defence but the blood-hound and guards, that take care of the plantations at night, and the guards themselves are slaves. They are a timid race, and a few resolute persons can intimidate them. They will make an alarm if any one comes to steal the horses, but they would be afraid to oppose these marauders, who bring their own dogs, and spread terror wherever they appear."

Helen breathed more freely. She was glad God had made mountains.

"How can you make a distinction between Juanita and the other slaves?" she asked.

"Oh, that has taken care of itself. Her mother was my mother-in-law's maid, and always lived near her person, as such girls do, and was accomplished in every pretty and useful art. In almost every family you will see one of these girls attached to each child, but it is a source of great corruption. I have known of unmentionable evils growing out of it. My children have had no pets or servants of that kind but Juanita, who is thus far, I am sure, as good and pure as any of us. She was a happy, merry little thing, till her brother was sent away and her mother died. She always learned everything Ludovico learned, as she peeped over his shoulder at whatever he was doing; and very early she showed a wonderful genius for painting. I say genius, for the word talent does not describe it. She drew beautifully, and when I gave her colors she was like one entranced. You will find the night-blooming cereus, our gigantic ceyba tree, and, indeed, all the peculiar tropical plants, in her portfolios. The walls, as I have told you, are ornamented by her brush. She copies from nature with her needle, as well as her pencil. She has always slept in her mother's room, adjoining mine, and you will find every inch of it covered with her productions. She has always heard me read to Ludovico, — indeed, she is scarcely less well informed than he is.

"Perhaps I have done wrong to bring her up so; for, if I should die, her fate might be very sad. But I am sure Ludovico would protect her even from himself, and so would my husband as far as he could."

"She ought to have her freedom," Helen ventured to say.

"Yes, and she shall have it. My father would never free them, though they often begged him to do it, but my husband has promised to do it. It would make but little difference in her happiness, except perhaps in her imagination."

"And that is everything," exclaimed Helen. "She would tell you differently if she dared, I think."

"Perhaps so, but I have never asked her. While her mother lived and Juan was here, she seemed happy. She is not so now, I know. She would be far better off to die, too, for there is no career for freed women but what you and I should call infamy."

"They would at least own themselves. Do not the other slaves in the house envy her position?"

"Oh, yes, indeed! and Camilla began to exercise dominion over her as soon as she was old enough to help her; but I put a stop to that at once, and she only torments her as she does me and every one else."

"Why do you keep Camilla in your household?"

"Because she knows how to do everything, and I cannot keep house without her. That she knows this, is my misfortune. She has a true genius for organization, and is accomplished in every household art. She has her corps of sweepers, house-washers, dish-washers, laundry-women, errand-boys. She is the queen of pastry-cooks. In that little pantry from which you see her emerge, she performs miracles of that sort. It is a small place, but everything in it is kept in neat order, and out of it come the rarest viands, cakes, custards, tarts, sweetmeats, candied fruits, and all the devices of French and Spanish cooking. She can always judge of the quantity of food to be provided for any occasion, and has her reserved forces for an emergency — saves all her nice scraps for the hospital, and never is so completely in her element as when there is too much to do. We all have our greatest immunity at such times. It is in the long leisure days, when the country is deserted, that we suffer most. Her activity has then no other objects on which to expend itself. I see her now prowling. This long talk, of which she knows herself to be the subject, makes her uneasy. I will send her away on some errand. Camilla," she continued, as the old woman approached, "go and inquire for the new baby; — perhaps you can bring it over for us to see."

"Yes — my lady — yes — new baby" — laughs to herself — "very pretty, very pretty," and she slowly descended the steps.

"She does not wish to go. She suspects that it is only to get rid of her that I send her."

"What a life of slavery it is for you!" exclaimed Helen.

"Yes, it is for all planters' wives except those who leave everything in the hands of the overseer; but that involves much unjust treatment, and often cruelty. If you were to see my life in the season of sewing-work, you would not call this slavery. For three solid months I cut out and superintend the making of these people's clothes. The women sew on the gallery, under my supervision. If left to themselves, the work would occupy the whole year."

"Cannot Mrs. Warwick relieve you of this care?"

"I tried it, but they will obey no one but me. They know the overseer stands at my right hand, if necessary, and they are afraid of him though not of me, but my personal superintendence precludes the necessity of his services except on rare occasions."

"I understand you," said Helen. "Other women do not always stand between them and punishment, I fear."

"Many do. But it is more economical to have the work done as quickly as possible, that the women may be ready for other uses. The field hands always come in to share the work, and that gives me an opportunity of contact with them all."

"The voice of kindness must be a balm to their souls for three whole months," said Helen.

Camilla now appeared with a pretty baby, wrapped in her shawl, which she laid on the Marchioness' lap.

"Oh, take it up and wrap it up again — it will have the lock-jaw. Why did you not bring it in a cloth?"

"Lock-jaw in the sunshine? no, lady — lock-jaw

in the dew — morning — evening — no lock-jaw in the sunshine!"

"I believe she is right," said the Marchioness.

"Is lock-jaw common here?" asked Helen.

"Very common, and in that way mothers dispose of many children, if they are not watched."

"Isabel! I cannot believe it — and yet why not? It must be to save them from a worse fate."

"Undoubtedly. When I first learned the fact, I could not believe it. It seemed to me too unnatural. Even animals passionately love their young when first born. When I was convinced of it, I resolved to be present at every birth. My husband laughed at me, and said it would make no difference; that at any time within three weeks the mothers could effect the object by laying the naked child out in the heavy dew for a few moments. Planters resort to every sort of punishment to save life, though not for humanity's sake. My husband promised a reward to every woman whose child lives, but nothing broke up their habit of putting an end to them till he had a wooden babe bound to their backs, and turned them out to work with it for six months. Since that time the practice has been checked. Slaves live so short a time that their lives are very valuable after they come to working age, and it is cheaper to rear them on the plantations than to purchase them."

"But, Isabella, how can you bear it? Why do

you not persuade your husband to leave such a country?"

"Ah, dear Helen, you do not know what a Spaniard is, when you ask that question. We are not very wealthy, and where would be our means to do it? I have the kindest, the most devoted of husbands. I know he is virtuous, and I must be satisfied with that. Every reasonable wish I have is gratified, — many wishes are anticipated, — but he would be out of place elsewhere, unless he could take with him all the means of luxury he enjoys here. We may be called rich here — elsewhere we should really be poor."

"I fear it is hopeless, indeed," said Helen, "but I must thank God that I am under no such necessity."

Camilla wrapped the babe in her shawl again, meanwhile, and carried it away, muttering, "No lock-jaw in the sunshine! dew in the morning, evening! God takes the babies, poor little ones!"

"That is what they always say," said the Marchioness, — "'God takes the babies,' — and I assure you I never mourn for them. Camilla says that, wherever they are buried, their bodies go home to the old country. This is said to be an African superstition, and there must be consolation in it."

"Perhaps they believe in the worship of their ancestors, like the Eastern nations in general," said Helen.

CHAPTER X.

CAMILLA.

ONE morning, Helen, whose northern habits made her an early riser, came out of her apartment a little after dawn to enjoy the pure, dewy breath of Nature on the open piazza. Several rows of bed-chambers skirted the salon at either end, all opening on one or the other piazza. Helen had never ventured abroad alone again, and had returned so late from the evening balls during the holidays that her usual morning habits had been much broken in upon. She now approached the salon, where she encountered Camilla and her satellites making ready for the day. It was one of the scenes of Camilla's daily enjoyment, because it was an occasion of exercising power, and the appearance of Helen added zest to her display.

"José, come quick! Wash this floor the very quickest! José, pour a tub of water over it!"

Enter Francisca with another tub of water on her head, which she too pours over the floor.

"Quick, Fisca, quick! here is the lady!—yes, there she is!—wants to sit down!—all water!—don't drown the lady!"

Enter Solidad with another tub of water. Helen turns back.

"Ay, here's Solidad, too — more water! Ave, sanctissima! Spiders, lady! ants, lady! much dust! Where's Maria? Where are the cloths? Lady cannot sit, must walk. No, no more water! No, José! did you not hear? I said no more water! Canailla, don't you see the lady? She'll be tired walking."

"I do not wish to sit down," said Helen. "I prefer to walk," and she sauntered down the piazza. But, when she came round, Camilla was ready for her.

"Ay, yes, lady! not been sleeping? French ladies walk — no dogs on the piazza, lady." (Laughs mysteriously, then suddenly drops her head on her shoulder.) "Poor Carlo! poor Jacobo! poor Maraquita! How do you feel this morning, lady? Are you well? Very glad, very glad! Dance much? Not at all! Ay de mi! not dance!" (Runs in for a chair.) "Here, lady, here's a chair." (Dusts it with her shawl.)

"I prefer to walk, thank you," said Helen.

"Walk? Ay, French ladies walk. Poor Carlo! poor Jacobo!"

"How are they?" Helen ventured to inquire.

Camilla stopped, looked mysteriously, put her finger on her lips, then whispered, "Bad; very bad!"

At this moment a boy came up the steps with

a tub of water for the piazza. Camilla arrested him. "Bad boy! Canailla! See the lady? No water here!" (Strikes him with her broom.)

"I will walk round the other side," said Helen.

"Oh, ay, thanks, lady, thanks! ready soon, ready soon. Here comes Josefa with the cloths. Where have you been? sleeping? eating? Take that!" (Strikes Josefa with her broom, and snatches the cloths from her.)

"Go in now and wipe the floor; lady walking — wants to sit. Sun is up. Lazy people! Where's Cecilia? feeding pigs? hunting hens? Tell her to come and wipe the floor quick as possible," and Camilla continued to fly round among her subordinates, beating one with her broom, pushing another into the water, snatching the cloths away and throwing them about, when suddenly she heard the voice of her master, who opened his door and called out, "Coffee!"

"Yes, señor; yes, indeed. Ave, sanctissima! master wants his coffee! Yes, señor; yes, señor. Master calls — wants his coffee — going to ride — good master, takes care of the people. Canailla! not worth it! Cecilia, wipe the floor! What are you standing there for? I can't do everything. Master in haste — wants his coffee — going to ride."

The Marquis again opens his door, and says "Coffee!"

"Yes, señor, yes, yes!"

Disappears into her pantry, and soon emerges with the coffee, which she carries to the door, wading through the water.

"Canailla, wipe the floor. See my wet feet! Now for the toothache!"

Manuel comes out of the nursery, and wades through the water.

"Ave, sanctissima! see the niño! Shoes all wet! Where's nurse? sleeping?"

"I want some oranges. I am going to ride with papa," exclaimed Manuel. "What do you have it so wet here for, you silly old woman?"

Enter Mrs. Warwick.

"Manuel! Manuel! come to me! Don't walk in that water! Now, I must change your shoes! How could you!"

"How could I help it? That silly old woman always floods the piazza just so. She is a great fool!"

He sees Helen passing by, and looks a little ashamed of his cross tones.

Helen held out her hand to him. "I would not call people fools, dear."

"People!" repeated Manuel, as he walked on with her. "Is Camilla a people?"

"Just as much as you are, I think. You would not like to be called a fool."

"No, indeed; but I never thought Camilla was like us. But then she is, only she has a black face, and is a stupid — I won't again. But see how they wet everything. I never can get out when I get up early in the morning to ride with papa without getting my feet wet. I used to ride with Carlo," and here Manuel's heart stopped him. He could only say "Poor Carlo!" and his lips quivered.

"Niño Manuel, where are you? Here are the oranges. Oranges, lady?" offering some to Helen.

Mrs. Warwick brought out a chair for Helen, who sat down and partook of the cool, sweet fruit, so different from oranges in the States.

"These people are so stupid!" said Mrs. Warwick. "Do look out the window, ma'am, and see those wenches drawing those cloths across the floor like so many pocket-handkerchiefs. That's the way they do things here. I tried to teach them how to wring them into the tubs, but it is no use. They never saw a mop, which might be such a saving to their backs; and they don't know when they have got enough water on. I believe that old woman calls for more and more tubs full, just to plague them and keep them at it two hours every morning, when it might all be done just as well in one; but it only makes matters worse when I meddle, so I say nothing; but my back often aches for those poor gals she totes round. I often wish I was out of it. I know that—"

"What would the Marchioness do without you?" Helen replied, soothingly.

"Oh, yes, I know it; that's the reason I stay. I would not see these children in their hands, for any money."

Camilla could not bear this any longer. She had been bustling in and out with oranges and golden panetela, and now she appeared — with José behind her, carrying a tub of water for that gallery.

"Pardon, lady! much pardon! Other piazza ready now. Time to wash — spiders, ants, much dust!" Takes up Helen's chair, and runs round the house with it.

"Mumma Camilla, that's my chair!" calls out Mrs. Warwick. But Camilla does not heed, and disappears round the corner with it.

"Plague on her! I shall not get hold of that chair again for a week. Oh, she is a trial!"

Helen follows the chair, after bidding Mrs. Warwick a kindly good-morning.

"Oh, you must see me mount my pony, Aunt Helen!" said Manuel, seizing her by the hand. "She is such a pretty little horse! Won't you ride with me some day? You can take mama's horse."

"I should like to very much."

José had waited respectfully till Miss Wentworth moved away, but Camilla hailed him from afar.

"Boy! lazy dog! put the water on!"

"Always scolding!" muttered José.

"What did you say? Take that, Canailla!" rapping him with her broom, and at the same time knocking the tub of water off his head, wetting him from top to toe. "Good enough for such! Work away now; soon the gentlemen will come out, and all wet and soppy. Cecilia! Maria! Josefa! bring your cloths; go to work. What are you good for?"

Mrs. Warwick appears at the door of her room, and, in a deprecating tone, remonstrates in broken Spanish against quite so much noise while the children are sleeping. Having given the hint, she closes her door again without waiting for a reply.

"Old Americana, keep in your own basket! Don't talk to me!" But nevertheless there is a lull in the confusion for a few moments; for the Marquis opens his door, and inquires for the horses.

"Less noise here, people! your lady is sleeping! Where are the horses? José, go for the horses! Have they been forgotten? I am in haste."

José runs down the steps.

"Ay de mi! The señor waiting! Urbano not coming! bad people! Canailla! no horses for the señor and the niño! Ave, sanctissima!"

"You confuse every one with your noise and your tubs of water in the morning," said the Marquis. "What is the need of making the floor so wet? It is not necessary."

Camilla began to excuse herself. "José, Pablo — two fools!— put on too much water!"

"It is no one's fault but yours, and don't do it again," replied the Marquis, as he walked out upon the gallery.

Camilla made no reply, but stood motionless, her long, orang-outang arms hanging limp at her sides, and her eyelids cast down, until he was fairly out of sight, when she disappeared into her pantry, leaving the women giggling to themselves at her expense, and José's mouth stretched from ear to ear.

But the next morning, salon and galleries were wholly unwashed, and great was the annoyance of ants, spiders, and dust all day. There was no time to ask explanations, and only Helen and Mrs. Warwick could account for the neglect.

So Camilla had her way, and after that the flooding went on as usual, with perhaps a little less screaming and bustle; for Camilla did care for being found fault with by her master.

CHAPTER XI.

THE CHICKEN-HOUSE.

THE chicken-house was a long cabin built of bamboo sticks, like the habitations of the negroes. It stood on the edge of a little pool of water, tinged deep red by the colored earth of the island, and had in former days been a home for turkeys and other fowl, whence its name. It was now used as a sort of nursery for the children of the plantation, where a superannuated negress took charge of the little ones, while the mothers were absent in the field. At nightfall they were again given in charge to their mothers.

Old Panchita, "the brooding hen," as she was called, was a woman of experience. She was one of the oldest inhabitants of the plantation, and in her youth had been a favorite house-servant and nurse, being both capable and amiable; but when no longer wanted to take care of her master's children, she had been installed as a nurse over the children of the slave mothers. A natural love of the young fitted her for this office, but it was a trying one, and mumma Panchita's patience was a little threadbare, and was not always proof against these trials. It was quite as much of a task as she was equal to to administer food to the babes, who were deposited in small wooden boxes about the edges of the building, and who lay pretty contentedly upon their backs if they were not hungry or bitten by mosquitoes and neguas, that infest the human foot in tropical climates. A good mother can easily judge how often these contented intervals occurred among forty or fifty babies under the circumstances of a mud floor and a neighboring laguna, and one old woman as feeder, besides having to spank into submission those who were old enough to crawl in and out of the cabin, or to pick them out of the laguna, into which some of them were always tumbling, and to threaten the still older ones with the lash of the overseer, which came quite often enough, under Don Ermite's reign, to make the threat overpowering — not that mumma Panchita ever invoked it — no! poor soul! She had given birth to and lost too many children of her own to do that. Some had been sold, others had died of hard work. She did not know where the living ones were. She often thanked God for having taken the others. Great vicissitudes had mumma Panchita seen. Once a petted servant, living amidst family comforts, then cast out into the negro quarters to take care of too many children, whom she must see suffer under her eyes, and she tender-hearted! Every woman who expected to bring a child into the world wanted her, because she was skilful and kind. At night, when the mothers took their children to their own cabin, she visited the sick who had sent for her, and shared their lamentations when they found themselves the mothers of daughters, and was not sorry when God took them by the lock-jaw. He would have taken them oftener, if the mothers had dared to let him do it! but a too frequent repetition of this permission was dangerous.

This habit of slave-mothers, which has often been adduced as a proof of innate depravity and barbarism, looks far otherwise to the philosophic mind. Enforced motherhood, which is the rule in slavery, has none of the holy sanctions thrown around it by human love, and yet so strong is the maternal feeling that when these children are old enough for natural interchange of sympathy and affection with their parents,— in short, when they have become persons, — the bond is a very tender one, and the poor slave-mothers' hearts are wrung with as bitter anguish at the sufferings of their children, or their separation from them, as those of happy mothers. The attachment of these people to the children of their masters, whom they nurse and fondle, shows the strength of the natural sentiment. It cannot be, then, that the slave-mother lets God take her child when it first sees the light, because the maternal feeling is not awakened with its new life, but because she dreads for it such a wretched existence as her own. Driven to her work as long as she can stand, before the birth, unbefriended in the hour of greatest peril and suffering, unaided and unsolaced in the early cares of her travestied maternal life, and so soon deprived even of the privilege of exercising that care, for she is immediately turned back again into the field, and only sees it when too wearied at night to enjoy it, how natural to wish the young creature safe in God's keeping — for these uncultivated savages really believe in a presiding deity, little as they see any outward testimony of his existence. The phrase they use about these mysterious deaths, so conclusively traced to their own act, proves this faith.

One of mumma Panchita's chief occupations was picking neguas out of the children's feet, which she did with a sharp thorn and hot grease (a darning-needle and some hot tallow are used in the upper circles for the same purpose, for the inmates of the great house are by no means safe from the invasion of this pest). This operation is not agreeable to the victim, but on its faithful performance depends the fact of having any toes left, and Panchita was partly responsible for the embryo slave having those useful appendages left, or even any feet at all, for, as soon as this little flea is imbedded below the third layer of the skin, it lays a bag of eggs, which incontinently becomes huge, and the progeny, instantly developed, eat their way still farther in, each laying her respective sack of eggs. This responsibility Panchita shared with the mothers, whose first duty on taking their children to their own cabins at nightfall is to see that the feet are safe, and the "brooding hen" is sure to hear of it if she has not done her work faithfully up to that time. The sounds that issued from the chicken-house made it very easy for any one to find the spot who walked that way. Just as mumma Panchita was performing a boring operation upon a little foot, Camilla made her appearance, and inquired for a little goddaughter of her own, whose services she needed in the absence of the members of poor Carlo's family. The little girl in question was one of the oldest children, and quite useful to Panchita, who was not willing to part with her.

"Ave, Maria sanctissima!" exclaimed Camilla, "are you killing that poverecita? poverecita, what a cruel nurse you have!"

"Cruel! what do you mean, you old monkey," said poor Panchita. "I am only saving the poor little foot, which is almost a honeycomb now — there, little one! now lie down and cry yourself to sleep; and if you cry yourself to death, so much the better."

"Yes, yes," said Camilla, "poor people! — poor people! — better let God take them! — poor Carlo! —"

"Hush, old fool!" said Panchita, "it is time for

Don Ermite to come — don't let him hear you pitying any one."

She had no sooner uttered the words than Don Ermite rode up to the door, and, with a flourish of his long riding-whip, which never spared old or young, asked, with a Spanish oath, if all the children were there.

"Yes, master, all," said Panchita. "Come here, children; here's the master!"

Suddenly, like a flock of partridges that had hid in the grass, the children rose up from behind cradle boxes, or dropped down from the roosts that still remained stretched across the chicken-house, or appeared from the high weeds on the margin of the laguna.

"What are you all hiding for? and whom are you afraid of," said the brutal overseer, accompanying his words with another slash of his heavy whip, which made many of the children scream out with pain.

"Hold your tongues while I count you, or I'll cut deeper," and with these words he made a second application of his lash, which hushed the terrified children into silence.

After counting the outsiders, Don Ermite descended from his horse, and entered the cabin to count the babies. Camilla had stepped out of sight, but he now saw her again, and recognized her.

"What are you here for so early in the morning, old woman?" he said, in a milder tone, for he was not pleased to see a house-servant there just after he had been in disgrace with the Marquis.

"I came to find Muerta-Viva, to help me in the pantry, mi alma," she said, humbly, for mumma Camilla was a little frightened.

"Muerta-Viva? who is that? where are you?" he said, fiercely to the frightened group of children.

A slender little girl of seven came timidly out of the crowd, and stood before him. She did not look as robust as the other children, and had a limp in her gait.

"What are you good for?" said the brute, "and where did you get that limp," he added, jerking her by the arm.

"Fell off the roost!" was the scarcely audible reply of the little cripple.

"Go with the old woman, and see if you can do something," he said, a little softened, not by humanity, but because he was disturbed at having been caught in his brutal treatment by such an important official.

Children are leniently treated on decent plantations. It is important to their future usefulness that they be well fed and propitiated, the latter being done with small coins and confectionery thrown to them. Under the former overseer these children had led a comparatively happy life, as happy as it could be with neguas in their feet and with mumma Panchita's spankings, which were 'frequent though not cruel, but she must train the older ones to help her take care of the little ones, and they did not always mind her the first time she spoke, any more than little white children in nice nurseries mind their nurses or even their mamas!

They were allowed to pick up oranges when they could get a run into the orange avenues; and now they joyfully ran to their respective cabins for the gourds, for Don Ermite's last words were, — "See that you water the new borders in the mango avenue before noon, or I'll give you all a lashing!"

Perhaps they should see Tom the cook, who often saved broken food for them; perhaps they should find some plantains! Don Ermite had gone to the field, and the naked little things swarmed like ants back and forth from the red laguna to the mango avenue by all sorts of circuits and winding ways, with the gourds deftly poised on the tops of their heads, on their return taking the great house on their way, scampering up the steps and across the gallery, peeping in at the windows, and watching the proceedings of the household slaves. Plantation manners are very easy in these points of taste, and strangers soon get broken in to the spectacle.

Mumma Panchita had a long interval of silence, for the care of her babes and other small fry not old enough to be watering-pots. They will be sure to come to their *bacallao* (salt-fish) when the bell rings at noon, especially as Don Ermite will then come from the field.

Mumma Panchita had much food for thought when she had time for it. She did not even hear the babies cry when she was thinking of her own lost ones. Her two pretty daughters had been sold for their beauty, to high bidders, to pay a gambling debt, and it was her grief at that event that had made her intolerable in the family, and led to her instalment in her present office.

"Where are they?" was her constant cry, and she had grown prematurely old uttering it.

Muerta-Viva, or Dead-Alive, was an unfortunate little girl, who one day fell from one of the roosts, where she was perched at play, and fractured her hip, which was never rightly cured, and she had been thus made a cripple for life. She was only three years old when the accident happened, and her father and mother had quarrelled and been separated, — as is often the case with the slaves, who are bound together by no marriage tie, and are not allowed to live together unless in harmony, for that would not be profitable to the master. The father always took Muerta-Viva at night, and was very tenderly attached to her, so that she enjoyed some advantages over the rest. He bought for her gay trinkets of the pedlers, often took her to ride with him when he watered the horses, for he was a calesero; and Camilla happened to have taken a fancy to her, so that she was often brought into the pantry for useful offices — such as beating eggs, running of little errands to Tom the cook, or picking up sticks for Camilla's brazier.

Muerta-Viva's father and mother had quarrelled for some domestic reason, unknown to the public. Each mother has a cabin assigned to her, in virtue of her being a mother, which cabin is her castle. The father had been turned out, and no objection had been made to his taking the little cripple to his own bosom at night; for the mother had other children to take care of, and her anger against the father extended to his favorite child. He could keep an eye upon her at all times of the day, as he was a calesero (coachman), and not on duty in the hated field, where neither men nor women owned even their own eyes, or the direction in which they should look. Since the cruel overseer had been on the plantation, Tono had suffered much; for he knew how brutally the wretch slashed his whip over the children's shoulders, when out of sight of the house, and he had begged hard to send this child to his mother, in Havana, when Carlo went for the American lady. Mrs. Warwick knew his wish, and would have taken kind care of it; and Tono had procured a nice little dress for her, with some of his chicken-money, and a sewing woman had made it neatly, and, dressed in this gown, and some red shoes and a shawl, he came to prefer his request. But, as Tono was a little pretentious, it was thought best to refuse this very reasonable request; his quarrel with his wife had also subjected him to punishment, according to the plantation rule. Masters cannot be disturbed by servants' quarrels, and servants' hearts are not supposed to be made of the same stuff as masters' hearts. A compliance with this request would have appeased the smarting pride of Tono, who could no longer boast of never having been punished; but the rule of action is, "Their spirits must be broken." The negro race is wonderfully forgiving, and susceptible to kindness, and, in this instance, certain little tender relations had been established between Muerta-Viva and the children of the family, as she was often allowed to come and assist Camilla; otherwise, Tono might have been a dangerous enemy. Helen learned the particulars from Mrs. Warwick, whose room was opposite Camilla's pantry. When the door was open, she could see Muerta-Viva perched on the shelf, where Camilla always kept her when unemployed, for fear she would run away. There her wistful eyes gazed at the children, with whom she was not allowed to play, but who would roll oranges into the pantry for her, and run to mumma Camilla's door with little playthings for her. Muerta-Viva had touched some tender chord in old Camilla's heart, and, when not occupied with teasing some one, she kept up a constant murmur of her instinctive enjoyment of this by-play. It was a blessing to the old soul to see this young life sporting about her. Tono, at such times, would lead his horses round that way, which pleased the little girls, and sometimes he made them baskets out of the wild plum-tree stones that grew in the portreros. Mrs. Warwick's heart was quite softened toward Camilla by this proof of her humanity, and she took care that the children should never annoy her. This relation also ameliorated the penalties Mrs. Warwick would otherwise have suffered for her somewhat anomalous position in the family.

Mrs. Warwick's kindness of heart had won upon "the people," who confided to her many of their sorrows, and, in the earlier days of her residence, she often communicated them to Isabella, who, in her turn, endeavored to ameliorate them; but this sometimes conflicted with discipline, and the Marquis had found fault with Mrs. Warwick for troubling his wife by making her a participant of these sorrows of the lowly. Mrs. Warwick had long since ceased to do it, but, in her own way, expressed her sympathy, and was beloved and trusted by the slaves, whom she never betrayed unless she felt it necessary for the family safety. When she first drove out with the children, the carelessness of the calesero frightened her to such a degree that she declined to go without the

Marquis or the Marchioness were of the party; and when she gave her reasons, it was made a special cause for severe punishment if any accident should ever happen during such drives. One or two had been barely averted, and it was on these occasions that Mrs. Warwick's confidence had been destroyed; for the calesero averred before her face that everything went right, when, in fact, the harnessing was so careless that he could with difficulty manage the horses. Being managed solely by fear, no trust could be reposed in them. Sad accidents often occurred from this cause, and it seemed but a just retribution to the masters, when they had destroyed, by their severity, the very germs of truth and fidelity.

Camilla had seized the opportunity that morning, as she passed Carlo's cottage, to gratify her feeling of sympathy, or curiosity, or both, and, during her brief visit, had been asked if the lady got safely back to the house. She could not keep Helen's secret, but undoubtedly discovered, by the quick sympathy of her race, that Helen had not made known her visit. Helen felt very sure, at the time, that she understood enough English to comprehend what passed between herself and Isabella, and for a long time Camilla lost no opportunity of reminding her of it, by cautioning her against the dogs, but never otherwise revealed the fact to any one in the house. Helen often found that many an earache and toothache were invented expressly to elicit kind inquiries for her, and often a song would suddenly change to a moan when she saw her approach. Helen's benevolence always gratified her by a sympathetic word. It was a mode of giving her pleasure, that could hardly be withheld from one to whom the voice of kindness was not a familiar sound; for Camilla's characteristics were not so amiable that one could form any attachment to her. She loved her master and mistress very much, but half her time was spent in making their lives uncomfortable, by the exercise of just so much power as her privileged age and her useful office gave her. Isabella understood her so well that she always made arrangements in reference to the possibility of her being off duty at the moment when she might be most needed. A deadly enmity had always existed in Camilla's mind against Juanita, not commencing with the latter, but dating far back, when Juanita's mother, who was a Moorish woman of great beauty, had excited her jealousy, not only by superior manners, but in her influence in certain quarters where Camilla wished to reign paramount. She never dared to express her enmity openly to the present Juanita, but the Marchioness had recognized and never lost sight of it, and, since the death of the mother, had kept Juanita near her own person, and more closely under her protection than she would otherwise have done.

CHAPTER XII.

THE AMERICANS.

"VOLANTES! quitrins! my lady! company coming! the Americans!" screamed Camilla, rushing up the steps.

It was, indeed, the Americans. The Marquis had had horses upon the road for a week, awaiting their arrival, and Camilla had seen the familiar face of Luis, the calesero in charge.

The Marquesa had invited no guests for the holidays; for she was in daily expectation of this party of friends from Philadelphia, who had sent her word that they were coming to bring home an orphan niece of her husband, who had been a resident of that city since her extreme childhood. Madame Le Blanc, a well known and distinguished teacher, had long since passed away, but an accomplished assistant had taken her place, and received many pupils from Cuba. The Marquis of Rodriguez had placed the little orphan girl in this establishment on the death of her parents. She had always been very happy there, but her health was delicate, and her kind instructress preferred to bring her to her native climate and to pass a few weeks there herself. They proposed to come before the holidays. The visitors to La Consolacion were therefore only day guests, which gave the family a few hours of freedom at early morning and late in the evening, and afforded Helen and Isabella some leisure to remember together the days of their early friendship. Unforeseen circumstances had interfered with the enjoyment of this leisure thus far.

Madame Cazneau, the accomplished teacher in whose school the little girl had been placed, had visited Cuba before, but had never been to La Consolacion until now.

Carolina Rodriguez was now eighteen, and a brilliant beauty. Her ecstasy at all she saw gave additional zest to the usual animation of her manner. Her complexion, though not so fair as the average American one, was still dazzling in comparison with the brunette beauties of the tropical island, and Ludovico, who had met and accompanied them to the door, was transfixed with his delight at her aspect.

Ludovico had few young acquaintances. He had rarely visited the city, and Spanish customs forbade all free intercourse of young people in polite circles. When Carolina frankly extended her hand to him, in American fashion, he took it mechanically, but hardly knew what to do with it, whether to shake it, to kiss it, or to kneel upon it. Carolina burst into a merry laugh at his confusion. She knew nothing of Spanish etiquette, and did not care much for any. An American boarding-school girl from one of our cities is never especially diffident, and Carolina was in all respects Americanized, for she had forgotten the land of her birth entirely. She knew the fact of being allied to high-born Spaniards, but it had never been a reality to her till now, when she saw herself surrounded by affectionate friends, and the picture was set in the rare and gorgeous beauty of tropical life. Her enthusiasm had been rising as she approached her destination, till she was quite beside herself. She threw her arms round Isabel's neck and devoured her with kisses, greeted Helen with scarcely less warmth, snatched up the lovely children, and gazed at them with undisguised admiration.

"Where is uncle — dear uncle?" she said, eagerly looking round.

"He will soon be here," said the Marchioness, "and how have you borne your drive, Madame Cazneau," addressing the benevolent-looking lady, who had stood smiling at her pupil's wild enjoyment.

"Oh, very well, madame — this dear girl has kept me in fine spirits all the way. I could hardly hold her in the carriage. Does she not look finely? The voyage has done her good, and I think we shall hear nothing more of delicate health."

"But where are the friends that were to accompany you?"

"We came alone, after all, unless we include Fanchon, whom I took the liberty to place in one of your carriages, as she never rode, and was afraid to mount either horse or mule. Fanchon is an old family servant of my mother's, who left service many years since, and has supported herself and a large family by making wedding cake; but when she heard I was coming to Cuba and needed an attendant, she insisted upon accompanying me. I was very ill when I came to Cuba before, and Fanchon professed to be a good sailor and was sure her care could spare me much suffering. I therefore took the liberty to bring her, — but where is she? I suppose she alighted from the carriage behind us."

"Mama," said Manuel, "she is sitting on the steps of the other piazza, and Camilla is talking with her."

"Camilla is talking French, mama," said Luise.

"Ah, then, Fanchon will be quite happy, for she cannot talk Spanish," said Madame Cazneau.

"Camilla's French is not very fresh," said the Marchioness, laughing; "we once had a French overseer, and she always picks up something. But Camilla is so secretive that we cannot enumerate all her accomplishments. I am glad, for Fanchon's sake, that she can talk French."

"Your nice servants looked so respectable, and were so attentive, that we needed no other escort.

I was assured it was safe to travel in your island now — so different from my last visit here!"

The Marquis now arrived, and welcomed his niece with much warmth, and then the ladies retired for bathing and rest.

"Miss Wentworth! how beautiful she is! don't you think so?" said Ludovico, waking from his trance.

"Yes, she is lovely," said Helen.

"She is divine!" he exclaimed, passionately.

"Oh, what a pretty cousin!" said little Pepita. "Has not she red cheeks?"

"She kissed me!" said Luisa.

"And me too," echoed Manuel. "Oh, won't she play with us? I'll show her my Noah's ark, that you brought me."

"And I'll show her my paroquets. They'll say 'Como Sta'; will she know what that means? Can she talk as we do, Aunt Helen?" inquired Pepita, anxiously.

"Oh yes! she is a little Spanish girl, that lived here when she was very small, and she can talk both ways."

"I like French best," said Luisa.

"But you cannot talk it," said Manuel, "and I think Spanish is the best of all. Get up! get up!" he vociferated, in that sonorous idiom. "Out of the way! Pepita, here comes Caravalle." And Manuel pranced across the salon upon his long Guinea-grass, which waved its graceful head like the mane of a steed.

"Oh where's Alezan?" cried Pepita. "Luisa, naughty girl! you are standing on my Alezan — oh! you'll break it."

"No, that's my horse!" said Luisa. "'Tis not Alezan; it's Rosillo grande!"

And the two little girls pulled at the long grass, which broke in two, at which Pepita wept loudly.

"Ay de mi! little ones," said Ludovico, "don't quarrel about the grasses. I'll get you five hundred if you will not cry, Pepita! Come, ride on my shoulder," and he snatched up the delighted child, and ran down the gallery with her. Luisa picked up the broken horse, but the plume was quite broken off, and she ran to tell Manuel, who always sympathized in her woes.

As Helen turned to throw herself into a boutacle, she saw Juanita leaning against the door, with a troubled expression of face. She immediately disappeared, but a chill struck to the heart of Helen, as she remembered the look of woe.

"I feared so!" she ejaculated, mentally. "How could it be otherwise! What infatuated blindness! Isabel, Isabel!" and she covered her eyes with her fingers, as she leaned back in the chair, as if that could shut out consequences.

That short meeting of the cousins was an epoch in two lives, if not in more.

To Ludovico it opened a new world of at least present happiness.

To Juanita it opened an abyss of woe into which her life was fated to descend — how deep?

Neither had had a conscious life till now in one sense. Juanita's existence was wrapped up in that of Ludovico, but she did not know it till she saw his meeting with Carolina, and heard his rapturous expressions to Helen.

Ludovico could hardly have told whether he was a bird, a flower, a favorite book, or anything separated from the nature which he instinctively loved and investigated. Juanita was a part of him, as his mother was, associated with all his childish plays and youthful enjoyments, and even intellectual pleasures. He knew she was a slave, if he had been asked, but he had never thought anything about it. She was nothing to him now — still less was she an obstruction in his way. Henceforth Carolina was all in all. "What a proud-looking creature that pretty girl is," said Carolina, the next day, to Ludovico; "who is she?"

"She is only my mother's maid," said Ludovico.

He had not looked at her — he did not know she was proud — he had not remembered her existence, even.

Juanita heard both question and answer. They stung her as keenly as if she had known herself to be Carolina's equal. She was, in fact, much her superior, for Carolina was frivolous and heartless. She had never really loved any one but herself. Juanita worshipped with all the depth of her tropical nature. To Ludovico she had been a part of nature, a thing of course, one who never thwarted him but obeyed his lightest wish. He had never tyrannized over her, but he had never questioned her allegiance. Every occupation had been in common. They had ridden the same pony when they were children; when they had driven in the volante, Juanita had been one of the party, to carry the shawl for his mother and to hold the baby. She had brought him the flowers from the garden when he painted; he had brought her the flowers from the trees in the woods when she painted. Having no other daily companions of his own age, she, ever present, had been his companion. It is true he had eaten at the table in the hall; Juanita had waited upon him, and had eaten at the table in the nursery. He had been guarded by an instinctive knowledge of his position and hers. She had worshipped the sun that had always shone upon her, never thinking to ask if she might worship. She knew all his thoughts, which he had never thought of concealing from her, but he did not know hers. She had never told him that she was legally entitled to her freedom, that she was an *emancipada;* and what difference would it make if she had, since the privilege was practically denied her? The ban of caste would also still have been upon her.

Within the last few days it seemed as if the

form of her brother Juan de la Luz was ever present to her. The shock of old Carlo's punishment had revived the bitter recollection of his loss, a loss due not to any fault of his, but to his beauty and the independent spirit which the history of his family had cherished in him. Only the presence of Ludovico had made it good to her; but Ludovico was, in truth, more her equal than the strong impatient boy who was her terror as well as her pride, — her terror lest he should bring down wrath upon himself, her pride in his beauty, and grace, and love for her.

In slavery, the heart and affections of the slave are not taken into account. "They do not feel as we do," disposes of all such considerations with the superficial and unfeeling, and better people try to think so. It is so easy to bear other people's burdens where there is no love. Juanita had not been the subject of any special neglect heretofore. In heaven's code of morals she had not been treated too kindly, but hers had been an exceptional case, wholly out of relation with what surrounded her. If she was neglected now, there was no tribunal to which those were responsible who might leave out of the account her possible human affections. Simply to ignore them was enough to make her miserable, and that misery she must bury in the depths of her own heart.

The next day was to be Sunday, when the negroes have a dance of their own by time-honored custom, at which they show forth all their sympathies, or want of sympathies, with each other. The distinction of caste is as marked in their low life as in that of high life. On New Year's day, a long table is spread in the dancing-room, and the aristocracy of the household department sits at the first table, and is waited upon by the "Canailla," as Camilla calls the field hands and other subordinates. Poultry and pigs are the sole property of slaves, except what articles of dress they are tempted to buy with their hoarded pennies from the pedlers, who are encouraged to come upon the plantations to prevent this hoarding of money. On the days of baptism, when they are allowed to go to the village church, they dress elaborately. This privilege, however, is confined to those employed about the house. The field hands are absolutely cattle, and their human relations are utterly ignored, the parental one being only recognized in their master's interest, for they no longer own even the baby when they have done nursing it. Their ordinary food is bacallao (salt-fish), jerked beef, cooked corn, and plantains.

These they cook, each for himself, and eat from gourds, sitting on their haunches, in the most convenient places; but on New Year's day they eat together, though in rude fashion. On the Marquis of Rodriguez' plantation they were allowed to have oranges and anything else they could find on the ground. After the feast, they fell into the wild dance which is peculiar to them, and which consists for the most part in violent contortions, accompanied with screaming and clapping of hands. Helen had already heard it on the Sunday after her arrival, but the impression it made was so painful, partly from her recollection of the wedding dance in Havana, and partly from the nature of the performance itself, that she had felt no curiosity to witness it. The beating of the hollow log that forms the rude drum of the negroes is so deep and penetrating that it seems to strike on the very heart of the hearer, rather than on the tympanum of the ear. From early in the morning till six o'clock in the evening one unremitting sound was kept up, and the various negroes fell into the dance at pleasure. When many were engaged together, the wild scream sometimes rose to a fearful pitch. It was not merry, but it was an unforbidden utterance, and to Helen's ear it was the sound of otherwise pent-up emotions, which made the best of this opportunity for expression. The drum had sounded all this day, and those not occupied in preparing the feast had danced outside of the dancing-house as they listed; but in the afternoon they formed in procession, and ranged themselves in a semi-circle on the lawn before the house. The dance began by the contortions of one man, who, after exciting himself to a sort of frenzy by his motions, dropped a hat upon the head of a woman. This was a signal for other men to throw themselves forward in the same way and challenge each another partner. Not more scrupulously do the ladies of a fairer hue wait for an invitation to dance than did these sable maidens and matrons. At last all were fairly engaged, and, as they whirled around each other, vying which should make the most display of agility and variety of motion and contortion, they accompanied themselves by throwing out their arms in rhythm with the drum, and piercing the air with their screams. One or two women, more tasteful than the rest, wound and unwound their shawls as they danced, but no one appeared to suspect this had any significance but Helen. When the dancers were exhausted, and some of them kept up their wild gestures till they fell to the ground, they gradually subsided into quietness, and the Marquis and Ludovico ended the sport by throwing out to them from the gallery handfuls of small coin. Manuel noted the absence of old Carlo, whose Congo nature made him a dancer even in his old age; and of Jacobo, who was one of the most celebrated performers. Their wives, too, were absent, and Camilla turned up her nose at such frivolity and such want of dignity as to dance with the "Canailla." Juanita was nowhere to be seen. She always hid herself on these occasions.

The guests looked on with wondering, and even with terror. The dance left no impression of joy, but only of mad excitement, and the party in the salon sat down in silence at its close. Even Carolina's gayety had a check for the moment, and when the dinner hour came, which was a little later than usual, the conversation was low and scanty.

At six all was hushed on the plantation, and the whole gang, except the household servants, safely locked into their cabins before dark. They were locked in every night after their work was over, and answered to their names from each cabin. On this occasion, more care than usual was taken to house them all, for the day had been one of unusual excitement.

"Two worlds existing side by side!" was Helen's mental ejaculation, as she threw herself upon the bed. "So intimately associated, and yet so apparently isolated. Does it never occur to these slave-owners that all are the children of one Father? — that similar affections and passions exist in each?"

CHAPTER XIII.

FANCHON.

FANCHON had been assigned to an empty cabin, with the usual accommodations, that is, a board and a blanket. But she was not locked up at nightfall with the other slaves, and had lingered on the gallery with those actively employed about the household, till some one should be at leisure to show her the place. When she was at length introduced to her night quarters, which were very near the house, she indignantly refused to occupy them. Pope Urban in vain endeavored to quiet her, and the family in the salon were startled by loud and quick voices at the foot of the steps.

"Where is Camilla," demanded Fanchon.

On hearing herself called thus, Camilla opened her door, which was below the piazza, under her own pantry. Her room was little else than a bunk, on the floor of which lay the board that shielded her from the ground.

"Let me see where you sleep," demanded Fanchon, thrusting her head into Camilla's dormitory.

"So this is the way human beings are treated in Cuba. I have lived too long in the world, among Christian people, to put up with a board and a blanket; but I could bear it better than this poor old soul."

And Fanchon ran up the steps to find her lady. The Marchioness and Madame Cazneau arrived at the spot as she gained the gallery.

"Madame Cazneau, is this the way I am to be treated? thrust into a hole with a mud floor, and made to sleep on a board? Ave, sanctissima!" for Fanchon was a good Catholic. "I knew there were slaves here, and my own mother was a slave, but she had a bed to sleep on, and here these poor souls have not even that comfort, Ave Maria! and are locked up every night like so many sheep. Madame Cazneau, can you have a bed provided for me? My old bones can't rest on a hard board any more than those of you ladies can—"

"Stop, Fanchon," implored Madame Cazneau, laying her hand on the woman's arm, which was raised in violent gesticulation as she spoke. "Be calm, you will make trouble—you do not know what you are doing—come to my room—" and she drew her away, followed by the Marchioness—who joined her entreaties with those of Madame Cazneau that she should be quiet and not disturb the plantation with complaints.

But Fanchon was not to be silenced.

"I have been talking with that old woman, Madame Cazneau, and I have been boiling all the evening—for I have been asking her questions, and I see what sort of a place this is. In our country it's bad enough. I have seen a good many runaway slaves, but I never saw one yet who had nothing but a board to sleep on. I never'll bend my back to lie down on a board if I never go to sleep again. I've slept on the floor in my day, and more than once too, and I can do it again if you are sick, or anybody else is sick, Madame Cazneau, but I won't sleep on a board for anybody's telling me to, nor on a mud floor—"

"Perhaps the lady will let a cot be spread for you here, Fanchon, for to-night."

"Certainly, if you wish it," said the Marchioness, and she left Madame Cazneau to calm the excited Fanchon, who, as soon as she left the room, burst into tears of rage and grief.

"I am sorry I brought you here, Fanchon,—I might have known you would not be contented."

"Contented! I hope not! If you had seen that wicked old overseer knock these poor creatures round when they came home from their work, you would not wonder that I am not contented. Camilla told me more horrible things in half an hour than I ever heard before in my life all put together. There are two people in the hospital that have been whipped almost to death because they would not be bitten by blood-hounds without trying to defend themselves. I'll go into every hut on the place and see for myself."

"I am afraid you will not be allowed to stay

here if you do that, Fanchon. You will see and know enough without going to look for it, and I must beg you to say nothing, whatever you may see or know, for we are guests here, and must make no trouble. Here comes Camilla with the cot. Try to go to sleep, and to-morrow I will see what can be done to make you comfortable; you know how much I esteem you, Fanchon, and how much I am obliged to you for leaving your nice home to come with me. But, for my sake, be careful what you say and what you do."

And, having seen poor Fanchon safe in bed, Madame Cazneau returned to the salon to make what apologies she could. But Fanchon was not to be appeased. She sprang out of her cot in the morning when the plantation bell rung, and saw the half-naked people shivering in the cold dews of the morning as they filed before the hated overseer, each answering to his name as he passed. She followed Don Ermite to the chicken-house, when he made his morning rounds and finally to the field.

Fanchon was a character. In her own sunny little home in Philadelphia, she was surrounded by orphan children whom she had taken from the snares and destructions of city streets to mother and to educate. She was not much cultivated herself, but she knew the advantages of even so much learning as the knowledge of reading and writing. She made wedding cake for her maintenance, and found it a lucrative profession. By frugality and industry she earned money enough to bring up several children, whom she sent to school, and, when they were old enough to assist her, she took more employment, turned her front room into a small shop, and became very well-to-do in the world; as her means increased, her little asylum grew. Black children and white children were equally objects of her care. They grew up side by side in her loving heart, and Fanchon showed wonderful sagacity in her disposition of them. She placed some in good families as domestics; others she put to trades. Two lovely little white girls of superior ability she destined for teachers, and, knowing the disabilities they would be under if they went to school from her humble roof, she sent them to a good boarding-school in New York, and furnished them with every advantage of dress and books enjoyed by the children of the great. Their origin she carefully concealed, and she had already had the satisfaction of seeing them in good situations, respected and admired for character and accomplishments. Nor did she ever let them know to whose bounty they were indebted for the remittances that never failed.

Fanchon is not a creature of the brain. She was a living reality. Her attachment to the mother of Madame Cazneau, who lived in St. Domingo and had been saved by the fidelity of her slave, Fanchon's mother, extended to her children, and partook of that enthusiasm which is so well known to characterize that abused people when they meet with real kindness. Madame Cazneau had aided her in all her labors for the orphans she had adopted, and had been the medium of her bounty to the two beautiful girls above mentioned. When that lady returned to the salon, she told this history to the family, and begged the Marquis to forgive her for so unwittingly bringing a troublesome guest. The Marquis courteously replied that if the woman could keep quiet, there would be no difficulty, but the event proved that Fanchon was an independent power, whom conventionalities could not rule.

Only a few of the negroes who attended to the cattle and horses had been taken out to work the next day, which was New Year's. Fanchon followed them and the overseer to the portrero, and during the amusements of the day she had circulated freely among them, but, when they were shut up for the night, her indignation again burst bounds.

The Marquis did not attend the evening ball in the village, and, after the rest of the family had left home, he sent for Fanchon, and told her to pack her box, for at daylight she must return to the city, which she would reach in time to sail for New York in the next packet. He would listen to no remonstrance, told her that she would be safe with his messenger, who was to go the next day, and bade her speak to no one upon the subject. He was afraid of such an inflammable torch in the present condition of the plantation, and had found it very difficult to pacify Don Ermite.

Fanchon went to Madame Cazneau's room and collected her things together. She was aware that she had trespassed upon proprieties, but proprieties seemed to her very trivial under these circumstances. When Madame Cazneau returned from the ball, she informed her of the Marquis' directions, and Madame Cazneau, though distressed and alarmed for Fanchon's comfort if not safety, could do nothing but comply.

Early in the morning a knock at her door roused her at dawn. The Marquis stood upon the steps when she went out. A mule saddled with a pillion, or basket, held by a negro, awaited her. "I cannot ride upon that," she exclaimed; "I never rode any beast in my life."

"You will soon learn," said the Marquis.

"Madame Cazneau, must I be treated in this way?" said the indignant Fanchon to her lady, who had followed her out. "Where am I to go when I get to Havana?"

"I am very sorry for you," said Madame Cazneau, composing herself with great difficulty. "My dear sir," she said to the Marquis, "I should not have done this, but is it not possible to send Fanchon in a cart?"

"It is not possible," said the Marquis. Luis is a careful man. He will soon teach her to ride the mule. Her box can be strapped upon another, and she will go safely," and Luis will put her on board the vessel, which sails to-morrow for New York.

Seeing that remonstrance was vain, Madame Cazneau said no more, but Fanchon's anger knew no bounds. Terror nearly deprived her of her reason, but she was obliged to mount, and left the plantation screaming with affright at the motions of the mule, and holding on his mane with both hands. How many falls and mishaps she had, no one knew, but Luis brought back word that he had seen her safely on board a packet for New York, and Madame Cazneau was obliged to bear her mortification and grief with a smiling face. She had consoled herself, as far as she could, by furnishing Fanchon with ample funds to purchase all sorts of comforts, accommodations, and immunities on her passage to the States.

CHAPTER XIV.

THE NEW YEAR'S BALL.

When Carolina heard of village balls she was all delight and ready to go on the evening of New Year's, which was a special holiday among the great as well as among the lowly. She had been terrified and somewhat depressed by the exciting dance of the negroes; but her spirits were restored by the prospect of the ball. She was there whirled in the waltz and led in the contra-dance by many strangers, for she was the object of attention to every one who could approach her. Ludovico had first led her out, and begged her to dance with him all the evening.

"Oh, but it will be such fun to dance with the Spaniards! I cannot do any such thing; indeed, it is too bad for you to ask me."

It was not selfishness that had induced Ludovico to make the request. He had never thought of the matter before, but he could not bear the thought that any of the voluptuaries who had access to the ball-room should touch the fair vision which filled the whole heaven of his soul. Carolina had pained her aunt all day by the ease with which she had accepted the flatterings of the guests who, among their other amusements, had visited her house that day; but Carolina showed no fine instinct that would have made a truly delicate-minded girl shrink from a strange hand Like a beautiful moth that singes its wings in the candle, she allowed herself to be made dizzy first by one and then by another gay cavalier, whose approach made Ludovico shudder. He stood still while she danced, and was rejoiced when the music ceased and the revellers dispersed.

"Are you affronted?" said Carolina, saucily, when they ran up the steps. "Why didn't you dance?"

Ludovico stammered out some reply. He hardly knew that he had not danced.

"I did not feel like it," was all he could say.

"I always feel like it," said the thoughtless girl, "and such splendid music! so different from Philadelphia bands! I do not see how you could resist it."

"She is so young and innocent, mama! Such men as Mirante and Remòn ought not to dance with her. Can't you tell her so another time?" he whispered to his mother when she bade him good-night in his own room, where she always made him a farewell visit.

"I will try, my son," said Isabella, "but young girls are so thoughtless. She does not know anything about our society, and has never been into company much, Madame Cazneau tells me. This is really her *début* into the world, and we must teach her how careful she must be of herself."

Isabella had observed that Ludovico did not dance, and could read his face so well that she divined all his thoughts, and saw that he was wholly unconscious of the remark he excited by not dancing. But she was more gratified than pained by this evidence of his delicacy for his cousin. She saw that his imagination was kindled, and only hoped that the unsullied purity of his nature would not clothe with ideal beauty any form of outward loveliness that would disappoint him or degrade his conception of womanly modesty. Ludovico had not the experience to detect frivolity beneath that fair and dazzling exterior which had already inspired him with the master sentiment of his hitherto slumbering nature. Nothing on earth is purer than the soul of an ingenuous youth when first waked by the touch of beauty and loveliness, which it never separates from the "perfect good and fair" till rudely waked from its first dream. The Spanish maidens whom Ludovico had known and danced with were gentle and friendly, and beautiful too; but the sparkling wit and sprightly gayety of Carolina fascinated and spellbound him.

After the guests had retired, Isabella and Helen sauntered upon the gallery a little while. New cares were dawning upon Isabella. Helen had drawn her attention to the new shade of pain on the features of Juanita since the arrival of the American ladies, and Isabella had for the first time admitted the thought that she had rashly exposed her poor heart to irremediable suffering. But she was still sure Ludovico neither imagined it nor shared it, and was not sorry for this engrossing interest in his cousin — provided that it did not go too far. But, again, she felt that she might not be able to control it if it did. Even if she found Carolina unworthy to inspire a profound sentiment, she might not be able to make Ludovico see it with her eyes. She was not the first mother whose heart had beat quick with such fears and hopes. Carolina had shown vexation and even passion when she heard of Fanchon's dismissal — not against her uncle and the cause of the ejectment, but against Fanchon herself, though she well knew her noble heart and disinterested life. Isabella wished Ludovico had seen it, but he was not there.

"It is selfish in me to be glad that you are here, dear Helen; but it is difficult for me not to be. I have never had any one to speak to but my husband before, and now I cannot speak to him, even of his own child, or of other things that pain me."

"I am glad too, dearest, if I can be any comfort to you — and am so glad you are willing to speak to me. Do not be too easily alarmed about Ludovico. It will do him no harm even to fall in love with Carolina, if he is as true and good as I think he is. He may suffer, but he will not be vitally injured. You must think of his escape from the other danger — there he might have inflicted injury upon another."

"Oh, do not say so, Helen! An insuperable barrier separates him from that race, however fascinating. I know that the first thought would have been the right one there. I have been wholly to blame, and I do not know what I shall do with that poor girl. She must know her place amongst us, but her heart may break," and Isabella's heart was all but broken for her.

She had trusted too confidently to Juanita's probable estimate of her "place," and had forgotten, as those of her caste too easily forget, that "all nations are of one blood," and that all hearts hold similar affections. The young do not reason about these things; they only feel.

The Marquis joined them, and Isabella dried her tears under cover of the evening shades, but not without realizing that a shadow had come between her and her husband, because she could not tell him of her pain. She feared for Juanita, and felt for the first time that he was the slave-holder. So apathetic do we become under an accepted wrong. Helen, and circumstances of unusual occurrence, had broken the spell, and revived all her youthful abhorrence of slavery. She could never "make the best of it" again, after looking upon it through

Helen's eyes, for her heart was a loving and true heart, and had been warped by affection itself, which blinds the eyes if it does not purify them.

The next morning brought Mirante and Remòn and many other cavaliers to call upon the fair "Americana," who was bewildered with this unwonted homage. It was not strange that she imagined herself all-fascinating. She did not know that a novelty, especially a *blonde* one, was the greatest boon idle and good-for-nothing Spaniards could see upon earth.

She could soon talk Spanish easily, for Madame Cazneau, knowing she would go back to her rich inheritance in Cuba, had had her carefully instructed in that beautiful language.

It was not till the holidays were past that Ludovico had her at all to himself; and no one knew all that he had suffered in those gay, festive days.

Ludovico had had no opportunity of seeing Carolina's character tested in such a whirl of pleasure, of enchanting drives, horseback rides, holiday visits; and, even when the excitement of city company was over, there was enough visiting possible for the winter season, when people can move about, to keep her amused. The young girls of the neighborhood, after the holidays were over, and time began to hang heavily, solaced themselves with preparations for the Easter festival, which was to come next, and this solace consisted in working new embroideries and making new dresses for the occasion, for it would not be stylish to wear the same again. The old ones were often disposed of to pedlers, who sold them at a distance, exchanging them for new material. The young girls borrowed Carolina's dresses for the fresh patterns — and she was equally desirous to vie with them in the richness of their embroideries.

"Do not spend your time sewing," said Ludovico, one day. "Juanita can do these things beautifully for you —" and his thoughtless remark involved Juanita in many a weary task, for Ludovico wished it, and that was enough.

She wrought in silence and increased despair. She saw and felt the selfishness of Carolina, the infatuation of Ludovico. She was no longer called upon for her sympathy, but only for her services. Indeed, he appeared to have forgotten her very existence except when Carolina had a wish to be gratified.

A generous heart may love a deserving rival, but not an unworthy usurper of one's kingdom of happiness.

Isabella felt scarcely less pain when she saw that her own influence was for the time being null and void. Carolina was far from docile to her warnings or instructions, in that care of herself which a virtuous woman must take in a society so utterly corrupt as that of the Spanish colonies;

and Ludovico thought only of ministering to her gratification.

"Remember, dear mama," he said to his mother, "she never had a mother to confess to and account to for her daily deeds — you must not expect prudence of her. She thinks everybody is good."

"I know it, my dear boy — I will do all I can to show her the proprieties of this society; but I am afraid I cannot take the place of her mother. She hardly remembers her existence, and still less what is the value of a mother."

Ludovico made no reply, for he felt it was too true.

It were vain to attempt to describe the state of Helen's mind. Uncertain when any change of overseers could be made, the family passed anxious days and fearful nights. Sufficient warning had been given to the negroes not to bring their complaints to the house; but the Marquis and his son passed little time at home during the mornings, riding about the ample domain that their presence might be expected everywhere and at all times. By noon, company demanded their presence, and all was outward gayety.

The Marchioness insisted that Helen should attend the village balls in company with her guests, and escorted either by her husband or Ludovico, one or the other remaining at home on some pretext. It mattered little to Helen, and she gave herself up to the tide of events. The music was so fine even at the village balls that it alone made the attendance upon them agreeable.

Helen's little maid Solidad was very anxious to array her for the ball, but she could not prevail upon her to adorn herself with jewels, for Helen's heart was too sore to enable her to wear finery. But when Solidad brought her a beautiful wreath of orange flowers, Helen allowed her to fasten them in her luxuriant hair. When she emerged from her apartment she was startled by the sight of a tall figure closely arrayed in white.

"Do not be alarmed, Helen," said Isabella, "this is the way in which we go to a village ball, for any other garb in which we might array ourselves would be sure to be stolen; besides which, we should be suffocated, and our dresses ruined with this red dust. Let Mrs. Warwick pin you up safely, and tie a handkerchief over your head, and then we shall be ready. All our guests have been made ghosts of, and gone before us. Ludovico waits for us."

The village balls were as peculiar to the colonies as all the other customs which arrested Helen's attention. They were held in a hall in a rustic village of bamboo houses, which looked more to Helen like a Hottentot kraal than anything else she had ever seen depicted. The houses were uniformly low structures, of one or two apartments, without windows or chimneys, with openings in the side wicker-work for light and air.

The company assembled in the dancing-hall was of a motley character. It was composed of the proud Castilian nobility and the guests who passed the holidays on their plantations, of country planters and mountain peasants, the latter of whom usually dressed in the pantaloons and embroidered shirt bound together by a showy sash that served the purpose of sword-belt and money-pouch. On this occasion they mounted a coat, and thus made themselves candidates for the hand of any lady in the room. Introduction was not necessary, but etiquette prescribed that if any lady refused the hand of any partner who invited her to dance, she could not accept another. Dancing commenced by one couple waltzing in the open area; others soon followed, and when enough were upon the floor, they resolved themselves into the form of a contra-dance, and continued their slow, poetic motion to the sound of the most ravishing music, played by a band of free negroes from the city of Havana. The plaintive wildness even of these waltzes went to the heart of Helen. The profound silence which is the accompaniment of Spanish dancing deepened the impression upon her imagination that this was a requiem dance over the woes she had witnessed. The dances were long as well as grave, and were enjoyed in part for the intrinsic beauty of the music and the motion.

The simple figures of crossing hands, right and left, dancing down the middle and down outside, which she had always seen in the dances of her own hills, were repeated here, as probably everywhere.

Helen resisted all entreaties to join in it, but gave herself up to a sort of melancholy pleasure in the spectacle, which she could not have endured if it had partaken of the gay and noisy character of American dancings.

When the music stopped, no conversation took place except a whispered one between the ladies in their seats by the wall.

In the intervals of the dances, the gentlemen usually disappeared to partake of another diversion, that ran side by side with it. In another hall stood gambling-tables, on which lay packs of cards. These gambling-tables were hired of the owners of the premises, and the fees given by each player paid the expenses of the dancing-hall and music. Indeed, the Spaniards of the colonies would have felt it to be an indignity to be called upon to pay for the privilege of dancing, until they were in danger of losing that pleasure; but when part of the six months of mourning prescribed by the Governor for the death of King Ferdinand was the prohibition of gambling, an enterprising American gentleman ventured to solicit a subscription for the dancing, and, contrary to his own expectation, was met with so favorable a result that a very goodly company met and danced on that new basis. The dancing was but a by-play to the more important and momentous transaction of bartering away estates, even homestead and the inheritance of their children, which is frequently done in this outwardly quiet but inwardly passionate mode of gambling.

Helen occupied herself in observing the countenances of both dancers and gamblers, and the multifarious fashions of dress that met her eye. The pretty brunettes of the plantations floated in fairy-like tarletans or soft mulled muslin, or delicate linens ornamented with rich embroidery, which had been the work of their hands, for many long months, for these express holidays, for they must be renewed every year.

The Russian ambassador's wife sported a deep green velvet, trimmed with ermine, to the astonished gaze of the islanders. It mattered not that it was wholly out of keeping with the scene and the climate. It made the lady more conspicuous than the costly jewels that flashed on her arms and in her hair.

Gray-headed ladies danced solemnly, as over their own graves, in short-sleeved and low-necked dresses, trusting to their pearls or their diamonds to take attention from their wrinkles, or, when portly, as many were, from their graceless motions.

The mountaineer's long sword dangled at his

side, as he awkwardly carried the unwonted coat that hampered his otherwise graceful bearing. The city gentlemen danced in heavy broadcloth, but the plantation lads, who knew better, and had a cool country fashion of their own, quite as genteel because they were so themselves, wore light seersucker jackets, and had a good time, instead of perspiring under imposing dresses.

The Russian ambassador and his wife, at the earnest entreaty of some Spanish gentlemen, consented to give a specimen of the German waltz, which proved so distressing a performance, under the velvet and ermine, that, after a few of its rapid whirls, the lady fainted in her husband's arms, and had to be carried from the hall into the open air. Then came a requisition for the French quadrille, one set of which formed in the centre of the area, the Spaniards standing round it, and clapping their hands at every figure; but they did not venture to emulate it, and the few individuals who knew how were very glad to fall again into the majestic national contra-dance.

Helen observed among the guests who were only spectators, like herself, a splendid-looking woman, who looked like a Jewess, with a young lady by her side, who was evidently her daughter, only more beautiful because more youthful. The passionate interest with which the latter looked upon the dancing, and the expression that crossed the countenance of the elderly lady as she occasionally looked upon her youthful companion, excited a deep interest in Helen. She observed that no invitations were offered them, although no proud dame glittered with more unmistakable diamonds than those which adorned these silent partakers of the festivity. Could they be Jews, and could that be the reason of their exclusion? Helen was not aware of the Catholic prejudice against them, or she would not have asked herself the question, for they would not have been there.

CHAPTER XV.

COCK-FIGHTING.

WHEN Carolina found from the Sunday visitors, who were always numerous, that it was the custom even for ladies to go from the morning Mass to the cock-fighting ground, she was very desirous to do the same. But the Marchioness spent Sunday morning in a very different way. Her religious education in America had not been Catholic, as Carolina's had nominally been. When she married the Marquis of Rodriguez, it was inevitably by the form of the Catholic Church, but her husband knew she was not of that faith, and the Cuban gentry had ceased to make any religious observances obligatory, so that toleration was a fact, though not a principle, and, unless circumstances raised a question upon the subject, none were enforced. Shortly after her marriage, one of the Massachusetts Unitarian clergymen visited Cuba in pursuit of health, and was sent to La Consolacion by friends of the Marquis to whose kindness he had been consigned, because they knew his wife was conversant with the English language. They probably did not know she was not a Catholic, however. This gentleman carried with him a great many books, and passed several months at La Consolacion, where his superior mental and moral endowments made him a welcome guest. While there he was invited on Sunday mornings to read from the religious literature he brought with him, which were the sermons and writings of Channing and other Unitarian writers. The Marquis listened to this reading, and was interested in it. It was ethical, not controversial literature, and the Marquis' European education had exempted him from any allegiance to the Catholic priesthood, and naturally from any bigotry. His admiration for his wife was a much more potent influence. After the departure of their clerical friend, who left all his books with them, and as long as he lived sent them fresh works of a similar kind, their Sunday morning readings were continued, and Ludovico had thus been educated religiously in the spirit of enlightened Protestantism, without any special efforts at proselyting. He had never attended Mass, nor the Sunday cock-fights, although he always heard them discussed and described with all the heat and passion with which Cuban society pursue their sports. Every young man Ludovico knew owned a favorite cock, and sometimes brought it under his arm when he made a Sunday call. Madame Cazneau expressed her pleasure that her young friend was not exposed to the barbarizing influence of such a sport, and was happy to listen to the reading of the Marchioness, and to hear of the clerical friend who had left such a deep impress of his character and culture. It happened that the rite of the communion service was the subject of the sermon read that day, and Madame Cazneau, who was an ardent Catholic herself, a lady bountiful and much revered for her benevolence in the Catholic church of Philadelphia, and to whose school many children besides those of the Catholics were sent, remarked that it always had seemed to her that the Unitarians were the most consistent and reasonable of all the rebellious daughters of the church, and she wished Miss Wentworth would tell her their precise views in regard to that special rite, for, if they did not believe in transubstantiation, what did they believe in?

Miss Wentworth replied that they observed it as a memorial rite, not as one of any supernatural influence.

"There is some sense in that," the lady replied, "and now I understand it."

But Carolina was not interested in the conversation. She evidently preferred the license of no belief in anything that would interfere with her amusement, and, as soon as the reading was over, which every one else had enjoyed, she sauntered out of the room in evident displeasure, and was only restored to good-humor by the arrival of guests full of excitement. Here was another pleasure which she was evidently to be forbidden, and she did not hesitate to express her regrets for the loss. The Marchioness was so highly respected that none of her visitors were disposed to take exceptions to any of her proceedings, and she had never been annoyed by any questioning of them. But this rebellious little inmate was introducing new sentiments into the family circle, and the Marchioness was very glad to have Madame Cazneau's sympathy on this particular subject. But no one's opinion influenced Carolina, and Isabella's heart sank within her when she thought of how potent it was likely to be in quarters where her own had never yet been disputed.

CHAPTER XVI.

THE CACTUS. — THE SLEEVE OF WIND.

As the rainy season approached, the visitors, and even the owners of the plantations, found their way back to the city, where they prefer to pass the summer months, during which, from May to September, the heavy tropical rains prevail, rendering locomotion almost impossible.

Horseback rides were now all the rage with Carolina, and Helen was always glad to make one of the party; for she had been a natural horse-woman, as it were, on New England hills, where girls ride as if by instinct, without any need of riding-masters. Helen had often dropped from the branch of a tree, in which she used to get her lessons, upon the back of a favorite pony that would come at her call, and gently trot her round the fields, as she clung to his mane.

One evening, as the party was returning from a ride through a fine wood, an oppressive odor of living sweets elicited from Ludovico the exclamation: —

"The cactus! the cactus!" And, guided by the perfume, they soon stood before a vine that resembled a dried corn-stalk in texture, and wound in huge contortions round a knotted stump.

"It is the glory of the world!" said Ludovico.

"What do you mean? Where?" said Carolina. "Is it this dried-up old vine?"

Helen had once seen the vine in a northern greenhouse, and had a distant view of the flower over the heads of a crowd of visitors, assembled to behold the rare wonder. She at once recognized it, and the next moment saw eight or ten large buds standing erect, ready to expand.

The riders alighted from their horses, to watch the process of this prodigy of nature, and, for the moment, she forgot everything painful in the contemplation of the living, breathing miracle. The expansion of the flowers began slowly, but perceptibly. The pedicles, nearly a foot in length, stood erect upon the vine. As Helen gazed into one of them, she saw life, — it seemed to her that she saw intelligence, and felt the breath of a sentient being. The long filaments, that had reposed upon the delicate lance-shaped petals, were gradually rising from their bed, and clinging round the pistil, which rose in the middle of the flower. It slightly resembled the pond-lily of her native lakes, but was at once more gigantic and more delicate. A gleam of green and golden sunlight, as it were, streamed up from within the long tube of the pedicle. The light in the sky was fading, but enough remained to show the rich brown tint of the calyx, which softens off through every shade of that color to the dazzling whiteness of the inner petals, which gradually fall back, as it expands, and form a large disc. It seemed as if that stiff brown stalk communicated at its base with some hidden sun. The gleam that struck up from below, and illuminated the interior of the flower, was as brilliant and as soft as the light of an unclouded evening sky, after the sun has sunk below the horizon. But whence streamed the radiance that gleamed on every petal? What was the inexplicable motion that ravished her sight? Is beauty indeed motion? she asked herself. As she watched the now rapid expansion, which seemed to be accelerated by some hidden force, she was aware that the appearance of life and light was the result of the motion of the filaments, as they altered their position. And Helen took heart of hope, as she saw this supernal light stream from the dry stalk of the cereus vine, that lay prone for many yards around, its stars gleaming forth upon the night. Flowers had always spoken to her heart like intelligent beings. This most glorious of all flowers, shining out upon the dark night, brought back her old faith, that God had not forsaken even the land of the slave, and the clear stars of the upper firmament, which had of late been dimmed in her eyes, again poured down their radiance upon her.

As the party turned their horses homeward, a

roll of distant thunder warned them of a coming storm. As they approached the house, which was not far distant, they observed a crowd of negroes standing in the dusky twilight at the foot of the steps. Helen's heart sank within her, for she apprehended some new calamity, and immediately she saw a tall, stout negro, with his hand hanging by the skin from his wrist, severed from the arm and spouting blood.

Don Ermite, the overseer, was inquiring for the Marquis, and the household servants were running to and fro in pursuit of him. He soon appeared and retired to his apartment with the overseer.

The story was soon told. Don Ermite had returned to the field to recall one of his dogs whose bark directed him to a hollow tree, which proved to have been the place of concealment of a fugitive slave from a neighboring plantation. The negro had been surprised out of his hiding-place by the dog, who attacked him, and he was now defending himself with his long *machete*, or weeding-knife, for their daily task of weeding is performed by the slaves in a stooping posture, by the aid of this rude weapon of husbandry. He had severed the hamstring of the dog in his attempt to save himself from being torn and mangled, an operation which these fierce animals achieve in a few moments.

Don Ermite, enraged at the act, drew the sword which always hangs at the overseer's side, and

with one blow cut off his hand. He had no
sooner done the deed than the consequences
flashed upon him. He knew too well the danger
he incurred, for he did not doubt that this was the
fugitive who had been in vain hunted for several
weeks, and who belonged to a neighboring planter
of great cruelty, — and, what was more important
to him, an enemy of the Marquis of Rodriguez.
This enmity had been excited by Don Alfonso's
knowing that the Marquis was acquainted with a
case of very atrocious cruelty that had occurred
on his plantation, several years since, one of those
cases so heinous that planters of decent character could not pass over it in silence if it was
once made public. He had been heavily mulcted
for it, and from that day had been the sworn
enemy of several of his neighbors, who had in-
dicted him for the offence. The circumstances
were well known in the district. He had never
yet paid the fine, and was known to have sent
away his coffee by night ever since, to escape the
possibility of its being seized for the debt. No
one ventured to interfere with this proceeding, for
he was the terror of the country; and such is the
corruption of the judiciary in the Spanish colonies,
that a moneyed man can act with impunity as long
as he can offer bribes of sufficient magnitude.

When the Marquis and the overseer emerged
from the house, the former gave the order that
the wounded man should be sent to the hospital,

and the overseer, after seeing it done, mounted his horse to seek a physician from the nearest village, three miles distant.

The poor fellow was laid upon the gallery of the hospital to await the return of the passionate wretch who had injured him, and who was to have the sole care of him, that the Marquis might not be drawn into difficulty. No aid whatever was allowed the sufferer. No friendly negro was allowed even to bind up his hand. If he should die of bleeding, the responsibility must rest with the overseer.

No entreaties of Isabella's could alter her husband's determination upon this point, for he too well knew what the consequences would be to himself and his fortunes. No pains would be spared by the owner of the slave, as Isabella assured Helen, to draw the Marquis into the case, and, in the legal processes that would be instituted, he might be stripped of all his patrimony, for his estate was a coffee estate, which was not protected by statute like the sugar estates.

This was all the defence that was offered to outraged humanity.

The Marchioness was too much occupied in quieting the agitation of her children, from whom this sad outrage could not be concealed, to talk long with Helen. Ludovico was endeavoring to excuse the transaction on the plea of necessity, to which Carolina listened very quietly, not shocked, as Ludovico really was himself, and fondly imagined her to be, but quite ready to admit the plea.

Helen saw that the corruption of the noble young man had commenced its work, but could she speak against the parent?

A startling peal of thunder and a crash of rain brought every one to his feet, and it was followed in quick succession by another and another.

It was the first shower that had occurred since the arrival of either of the ladies, and one of unusual violence. The lightning appeared to enter the house and play round under the chairs and tables, and its flash was of a deep red hue, that looked as if the very atmosphere was in flames. For a few moments the thunder rattled in the tiles of the house, as if imprisoned there. Carolina fainted with terror. The servants of the house, and, indeed, many from the quarters, rushed in to the hall as if they could find greater safety in the presence of their superiors, who allowed them to crouch around them while the fury of the storm lasted. Its extreme violence abated in about twenty minutes; but, from the steady howling of the blast, and the continued illumination of the atmosphere, produced by the whirling of the red powdered earth, upon which the lightning, now one sheet of uninterrupted flame, shone and was reflected, gave evidence that it raged at least as fiercely not far away. The lawn was soon turned into a laguna, and if the house had stood upon the ground, as most of the Cuban country-houses do, it would have been in danger of floating from its moorings.

The war of the elements, however, was rather congenial than otherwise to Helen, in the high-wrought state of her feelings this evening. It was not her nature, hitherto, to rage; but indignation boiled within her at these accumulating and ever recurring horrors, and she hardly knew herself. She saw how the terrors of the storm paralyzed the weak natures around her. Perhaps she gave them credit for more sympathy with the moral tempest that raged within herself than they merited. They cowered at the roar of the elements, while she stood aghast at the depravity of man. Their childlike confidence touched her. They sought refuge and protection near that very master who held usurped possession of them. She had become aware before this time that the slaves looked to the master for protection from the immediate agent whom he sets over them, and this fiction of their imaginations had been more pathetic to her than any direct appeal they could make, when they fled from the terrific dogs of the present incumbent of that dreaded position. She credited this homage of their hearts to the instinctive feeling with which men look up to what is above them. They trusted till their 'faith was broken, even hoping for protection against hope. Their mistress' kindness was all the providence they knew, and every human soul believes there is one standing over it. It is the soul's birthright, and is only transferred, never lost.

"Poor man drowned, lying on the gallery! bleeding! bleeding!" whispered mumma Camilla to another negress, who stood near Helen.

"Was he not carried inside?" asked Helen, in the same tone.

"Ave, Sanctissima! no, lady! no! lying on the gallery! dead now perhaps! May God take him!"

"May he take him indeed," murmured Helen.

The lightning continued to flash, and the thunder growled unremittingly in the distance; but the violence of the rain had in no measure subsided when the Marquis ordered the domestics back to their quarters.

Camilla had assisted Ludovico in the care of Carolina, who now lay quietly upon the sofa, thinking more of her own fears than of the wrongs of others.

Good Mrs. Warwick had done her best to help the Marchioness soothe her children, who now began to prattle their fears.

"Papa, where's that poor man?" said Manuel.

The Marquis made no reply, but continued to pace the salon.

"Oh, Manuel! don't talk about that man!" sobbed little Pepita. "Mama, when will the doctor be here?"

"Isabella," said the Marquis, approaching his

wife, "that man must be sent for. Who can go? we must send some of these people."

"This terrible night, dear Hernando! I do not know who will dare to go — these people are such cowards."

"We must insist upon it; everything depends upon it. We must protect them from the storm as well as we can."

The most experienced coachmen were summoned, and, contrary to all expectation, were willing to brave the dangers of the night for the sake of finding the overseer and bringing the doctor. The former motive was doubtless the stronger, for they knew perfectly well to what penalties he had subjected himself.

"I shall be glad if he has not escaped to the mountains," the Marquis remarked to his wife, as the men rode from the door, well mounted, and well protected by blankets.

Helen retired at last to her apartment to pass another wakeful and feverish night.

Towards morning, the negroes returned with the tidings that Don Ermite had been detained by the storm, but was coming soon with the physician. Many hours of anxious suspense followed, during which the mangled negro lay untouched upon the hard floor of the gallery, without being approached by a human being, but his groans gave evidence that he still lived. The hospital was sufficiently near to keep all the household cognizant of the sad fact. It was high noon before relief came, and then it was not relief, but he was moved by Don Ermite and the Spanish physician out of the burning sun into the interior of the hospital, the hand was spliced to the wrist and bound up in a bag, and an opiate administered. When the effect of that was over, he waked to suffer again, and several weeks passed in alternate ravings and uneasy slumbers; the slumbers being the only relief either patient or listeners enjoyed. Every day fervent prayers went up from many hearts for his release; but nature weathered it out, no one could tell how.

Meantime, the runaway slave's owner was not idle. On that very day had arrived a party of ten, justices and lawyers, to investigate the circumstances. This investigation consisted in taking depositions from every party in any way concerned in the case, and here the Marquis' precautions were justified by the event, as far as events could justify them.

The great bell summoned all the negroes from the field, and for the time the salon was transformed into a court of justice. But no one could make any deposition but the Marquis and the overseer, for no one else had been allowed to speak with or to touch the wounded man. Day after day this party returned with the object of involving the family in the quarrel, and Isabella was obliged to preside at the table and exercise all the rights of hospitality to the very courteous individuals who were employed to harass her and her family, the owner of the slave not once making his appearance. At last the persecution was withdrawn, and the overseer cast into prison to await his trial. No movement was made to return the slave to his owner. He was of no use, and was abandoned to the mercy of the Marquis of Rodriguez, who no longer prohibited Isabella from giving him the care and attendance she had so long wished to bestow.

When the excitement of this visitation was over, the Marchioness fell into a condition of weakness that alarmed all her family. The events of the last few weeks have been but partially told. All that we have noted was on the surface, but are there not two worlds on every plantation?

The family of the overseer, who were peasants in the mountain district, came down to the plains to rescue their brother from the law. They were well off in worldly goods, for they cultivated good *sitios*, or farms, guarded by dogs, and were the natural enemies of the negro, and, therefore, the natural allies of the planters in case of insurrection. They had a right to expect aid in their object of saving their brother from rotting in a wretched jail, which was his probable fate; but the Marquis refused to take any part in the matter, and sent them to plead for themselves before Don Alfonso. Angry, and swearing revenge, they left the plantation, and Isabella now felt anxious in the fear that they might execute it with violence, negatively if not positively, for the peasants form a very distinct class, and much care is taken to keep them on friendly terms. Overseers are chiefly furnished from that class, also, a sturdy race of mountaineers, descendants of the old Spaniards and the Indians of the island. It might be difficult to supply Don Ermite's place, and slave-gangs will not work if not watched. Anarchy soon reigns on a plantation if it is not thoroughly and resolutely managed, and these were chiefly bozals who took the places of the victims of the last year's cholera, and were not yet wholly aware of their limitations. The prospect was an appalling one.

But Isabella said nothing of these dangers to her friend.

The overseer of a neighboring plantation, who had charitably helped the Marquis take care of his slaves the year before, when cholera visited them, gave what assistance he could to the Marquis in this emergency.

CHAPTER XVII.

PEDRO AND DOLORES.

LET us now look into the lower world of La Consolacion a little more closely.

When the "Justicia" came to the plantation to make their investigations, the startling sound of the great bell, rung at an unusual hour, caused every negro to pause and wonder before he dropped his working tool. They had gone to the field under a temporary leader, selected from their own number, and the work of the day had gone on without noise, but with less constraint than usual, not so much because the overseer's eye was not upon them, as because each one was occupied with his own reflections upon the accident and the storm of the night before, which, to their simple apprehensions, were intimately connected in the relation of cause and effect.

Enough of them had seen the bleeding man, and recognized in him one of Don Alfonso's negroes, to comprehend the whole affair, and they had communicated to each other all they knew before the summons came. A common hatred of the tyrant overseer made them rejoice in his expected ruin, and they hastened to answer the roll-call. A short examination was all that was held on that day, as no one could give any information farther than that they had seen the man brought to the house by Don Ermite on the night when he had returned to the field to seek his dog.

Every negro answered to his name but one. One girl was reported sick, and was found in her cabin raving with fever, and incapable of giving any evidence.

No importance was attached to this circumstance. On ordinary occasions she would have been carried to the hospital, but no notice had been taken of her absence at the morning roll by the man who took the overseer's place, who was no other than Pope Urban.

The fugitive negro was no other than Pedro, who had been purchased by Don Alfonso, as he was familiarly termed, the Marquis' vengeful foe. To escape the vigilance of his various creditors, the law that had mulcted him among the rest, Don Alfonso had had his coffee conveyed away at night for many years; and, to effect this, his negroes were subjected to double tasks. He was a cruel master at best; but the night work brought unusual suffering upon his slaves, who were always ill fed, ill housed, ill clothed, and savagely punished.

Pedro had found no interpreter upon the plantation, but was soon made aware that no mercy was to be expected either of master or overseer.

The coffee was dried by artificial heat in pits prepared for the purpose, instead of being dried in the sun, and was then buried with much secrecy, to be transported from the plantation at night in bags upon the shoulders of the slaves, who carried it through a wood to deliver it to a man who was employed by Don Alfonso to receive it. Few persons knew the means employed or the details of the suffering involved, for furious dogs guarded the plantation; but it was well known that Don Alfonso's negroes occasionally escaped, and that those recaptured were terribly punished.

Pedro did not wait to learn the difficulties of the attempt, but soon took advantage of the night-work to hide in the woods and make his way from the earthly hell in which he found himself. No fate could be worse than that. He had suffered one terrible chastisement for remissness in the work assigned him, and had then been set to work upon his hands and knees, not being able to support himself upon his feet. He could not escape to any distance, but had hidden in a hollow tree on the plantation of La Consolacion, and had there fed upon plantains and oranges, gathered at night. Strict search had been made for him on the Marquis' plantation, but in vain. Growing a little more courageous by degrees, he had punctured a small hole in the tree in which he had taken refuge, and from this he could watch others without being seen himself. He had no plan of 'escape, he knew not which way to go, and was too lame and sore to attempt farther flight for many weeks.

It happened that one evening, after the slave-gang had returned from work, a girl was sent back to find her machete, which she had left. She took a shorter path than the avenue through the coffee squares, and, as she passed the hollow tree, was transfixed with astonishment at hearing her own African name pronounced in a low voice. No one knew that name but Pedro, for this was Dolores, who had been purchased for La Consolacion shortly after the sale of Pedro.

She stood for a moment, every sense transmuted into that of hearing. She heard the same word again, and now perceived that it came from the tree. A few suppressed words told her the whole story, and the next moment she heard the call of the driver, and plunged through the coffee in search of the knife, and immediately rejoined the gang. The driver saw her breathless and excited, but, supposing it was only from the haste of the search she had made, and the fear of punishment, took no farther notice of it. It was with difficulty she controlled herself to stand in the mustered row and answer to the roll-call. When she was shut into her cabin at night, she threw herself upon the ground, and rolled over and over in strong convulsions, from which her night companion found it difficult to restore her. The next morning she was reported for the hospital; but, strange as it appeared to others, who sought excuses to be put into those comfortable quarters, she preferred to go into the field. Dolores' fits, as the other slave called them, were so frequent at night that at last her companion begged shelter in another cabin, and she was left to pass her nights alone. She had become an altered creature from the time of the fearful discovery. Her hitherto listless demeanor had given place to a fiery energy and restless activity which completely transformed her. It was this change which the Marchioness had noticed when she met her on the evening drive. Subsequent events had banished the young girl from her thoughts. But Dolores had one friend.

It is customary for the slaves of a plantation to gather round a new-comer to ascertain if he is one of their own tribe; for fresh importations are so constantly landed on the coast of Cuba, that unexpected meetings sometimes take place, and the same dialect, even of strangers, immediately forms a bond of union. Dolores had found but one fellow-slave who recognized the language of her tribe, and that was Pope Urban.

Pope Urban was one of that band of young men who had left the valley of the Ayete to see the world, and had been seized and sold, and therefore never was heard of by its inhabitants again. He was overjoyed to recognize a fellow-countrywoman in Dolores, and was the only person with whom she had ever held communication. Urbano had never confided her story, which she told him, to his kind mistress. No temptations are offered for such confidence. But she had noticed his interest in Dolores, and knew that he understood her dialect.

Dolores was glad to be left alone at night, and no sooner was she sure of this immunity from observation than she determined to venture out under protection of the darkness. She had heard of the danger from dogs; but she was young, and took no counsel of prudence. She did not think long, but began at once to remove — with her long knife and her hands — the clay floor of her cabin, and to burrow out under the bamboo stakes that formed the structure. She did this noiselessly, and, after it was completed, she waited long enough to be sure that every one in the neighborhood was asleep. The cabins of the slaves stood upon the edge of a coffee square. The dogs watched upon the piazzas of the house and the hospital, and upon the coffee-driers that stretched behind the latter building. She therefore made her way out on the other side, and, skirting the edge of the plantation, penetrated the distant squares to the hollow tree. Many times she stood still and held her breath, but at last she reached the spot, and tapped lightly upon the tree. There was no answer, but the next moment Pedro emerged from a coffee square and stood before her. He was as much terrified as gratified to see her, and, after a short, convulsive greeting, he told her of his fears lest any attempt at escape should betray him, and of all he had suffered since he had parted from her at the sale in Havana. She told him of Urbano and of his kindness, and asked him if she might tell him where he was. He consented, and they then parted, after another wild embrace, both trembling for the possible consequences of this meeting. But Dolores gained her cabin in safety, and soon removed all vestiges of her means of escape from it.

When Urbano heard the story of the hidden man from Dolores, his terror knew no bounds. He had long since reconciled himself to a fate he found inevitable, and which he had ameliorated by rendering himself worthy of offices of trust. But the thought of the youthful chief of his tribe in such danger restored fire and vigor to his old limbs, and he revolved every possible means of aiding his escape, even if he must accompany him in flight. He restrained Dolores' impatience as well as he could, but she repeated her nightly visits many times, and gradually a plan had been arranged by which the three should escape to the mountains. Urbano had been into the region with his master, and knew the way. He had entire command of the horses, and only awaited some favorable opportunity to give a preconcerted signal to Dolores and

Pedro. The mountains once gained, they were safe. He knew the dangers, but had resolved to brave them.

On the night of Pedro's capture, Dolores rent the air with wild shrieks of distress. Urbano knew that it was not the terrors of the storm that brought on the "fits," as the negroes called them, and when he was called the next morning to take the overseer's place, and was obliged to repeat Dolores' name at the roll-call, it was with difficulty he could utter the word. But the report of "sick" was accompanied by no evidence of her having revealed her knowledge of Pedro, and he simply omitted any directions for her removal to the hospital, glad to have her left to the solitude of her own cabin, where he meant to visit her on his return from the field.

Luckily, mumma Camilla was so aristocratically inclined that she knew little of the events in the cabins of the field hands, unless something excited her curiosity. But Urbano had begged Pazienza, the wife of Jacobo, to look in upon Dolores, knowing that she could not understand any words that might fall from her, and Pazienza carried the case to her kind mistress, who had been to see the poor girl and sent her food from her own table, as she was accustomed to do to the inmates at the hospital. Urbano had suggested that she should not be removed there, while Pedro filled the air with his groans. When Helen heard of her illness, she begged Isabella to let her accompany her, and as she stood over the poor girl, she opened her eyes and fixed them upon her. The moment she had done so, a piercing shriek burst from her, which startled Helen almost from her self-control, for had she not heard that sound before? Another glance, and she was sure the truth had flashed upon her. This was the Dolores she had seen married, and might not the wounded man be Pedro? Her first impulse was to recognize her and communicate her suspicions to Isabella, but she hesitated, not knowing whether it would be for Dolores benefit or not. As she stepped aside from the board that served Dolores for a bedstead, her foot plunged into a soft hole in the earth.

"The rain, lady, the rain," said Urbano, who caught her as she was falling.

"The people often burrow into the ground to make sleeping places for themselves," said Isabella. "I suppose this poor creature did so."

"It is a softer bed than a board," thought Helen.

This was only her second visit to a negro cabin.

"Urbano is an excellent nurse, and understands this poor girl," said Isabella. "We can do nothing better for her than to leave her with him and Pazienza. She is in a burning fever, and seems to take no comfort in seeing me, as many of them do. I sometimes think they like to be ill, but it is no matter of choice with this one. What do you think of her to-night, Urbano? will she die?"

Urbano shrugged his shoulders. "If she's not better soon, my lady. She has much fever—much strength — sometimes she runs out."

"Why do not you put her in the hospital?"

"Man makes too much noise there — could not sleep."

"Let her go out into the shade if she wishes to; it is better than to be shut up here," said Isabella, and, with this advice, the two ladies walked sadly away, but Helen often went over to inquire for Dolores, and to take her an orange or some little tidbit. The convulsions returned frequently, and then would follow an interval of entire prostration.

Helen was resolved to visit the hospital after the "justicia" left, and satisfy herself upon the point of Pedro's identity, for she thought she should know him. She remembered the meeting with Dolores on the day of her first drive with Isabella, and also her momentary thought of the resemblance, which she now wondered she should have forgotten, but it had not occurred to her at the time that Dolores was just as likely to be sent to La Consolacion as elsewhere. She did not lose sight of her purpose, and it was not long before the desired opportunity offered.

CHAPTER XVIII.

DOÑA JOSEFA.

"Who is Doña Josefa, to whom Don Fernando referred?" Miss Wentworth asked one day.

"That involves a sad story, that will shock you almost as much as the knowledge of our peculiar institution," replied the Marchioness. "These young men are the sons of the most influential man in the island; the one who has most to do with the Governor-General, and without whose counsels I suppose nothing is determined upon. He is a Marquis of S., a man of great legal acumen, but a proud Castilian noble who would on no account demean himself to practise law, but is brains to several lawyers, who pay him largely for his opinions. He has ten children by his legal wife, who is now dead, but with whom he did not live for many years previous. They quarrelled, but they lived in the same house, the husband in one part, the wife in another, and had not met for many years, but the children passed to and fro at will. His two daughters are well married, and are fine women. Whatever these two ladies do is thought to be the right thing.

They are really leaders of society. Their five brothers are younger than themselves, and I know of no young men who bear such unspotted reputations. I have often thought in their case of the wonderful compensations we sometimes see in life. They have suffered pain and mortification for their father's character, and their mother, who was deserted by him, was a very noble woman, and her memory is held in great reverence by them. She lived on very small means, and since his death they have had to practise great economies, and have passed much time on the plantation near us, which belonged to their mother, and is their only inheritance. Since the husband and wife parted, he has been devoted to this Doña Josefa, who is a woman of fine education, but has a taint of negro blood in her, which is sufficient obstacle to his marrying her legally as well as socially, but he built her a house and lived openly with her, and has had ten more children, of whom she is the mother. One of these is a beautiful daughter, and such is his social position that he could marry her to any man in the island, but his death wholly alters their position. They are no longer eligible to society. Such families as these are called "Holy Families" by a strange sarcasm. But the strangest thing is that these young men live on the plantation with Doña Josefa, and thus condone the whole situation. The daughters never come, and the Holy Family lives in a different set from the one in which these young men move. This is the first time I have ever heard Doña Josefa alluded to by them. The father died a few months ago, and since that event the sons have had to do something for their own support, and are obliged to live outside the walls of Havana, instead of in the city, which is a great mortification, as the walls are locked at a certain hour, which obliges them to leave company or the opera earlier than their city friends do. Now their father is dead, his vices are freely spoken of, though never noticed in his life. He was poor; the salary his lawyers paid him no longer continues, and Doña Josefa had to sell the beautiful house he built for her, and come into the country to live. She and her sister, another capable and well educated woman, have educated her family rather above the average of Cuban society.

"There is something revolting to me in the whole thing and I have never visited them. Yet the Marquis visited my husband."

"What strange customs!" exclaimed Helen.

"Yes — and I never heard one of the young men speak of her before. It makes me feel that she must have some claims to respect, after all. A wholly unprincipled or unfeeling woman would not show sympathy with slaves, for fear of being more closely identified with them. The colored woman whom you have seen, and who inherited all her owner's wealth, is not a kind mistress to her slaves, if I am rightly informed."

"What a chaos all these things make in society!" exclaimed Miss Wentworth. "I do not wonder you live so much apart from it all."

"Yes. I have always made the most of my explanation that I attend personally to the education of my children, and I know one other mother who does the same, whom I should like to have you know, but she lives so far from here that I rarely see her."

"Are none of these brothers married?" asked Helen.

"No; they are as proud as they are poor. I am sure you will appreciate one trait in these young men. They know the history of Juanita, and yet they never have spoken to her, or given me the least uneasiness about her. They evidently feel that she is to be guarded, and though they admire her talents they treat her with entire respect, never praising or noticing her. They are the only men she is not afraid of. She knows they were very friendly to her brother, and have befriended him since he left us, but they leave her entirely to her reserve."

"The noble life you lead, dear Isabella, will have its reward in your children; but it is sad to have them pass their lives here."

"Yes; and I do not mean that my sons shall do it, even if I have to part with them, but I must not think too much of that, till time makes it inevitable. Meantime, I try not to forget that it is all God's world."

Company interrupted them, and Helen had begun to feel that the distraction this afforded was necessary to her friend sometimes, for her trials were thickening around her with the growth of her children, and strength to bear them might fail.

As Helen pondered upon this domestic history, she asked herself if it was possible for these young men to live on such an intimate footing with their father's paramour without being demoralized by it. She evidently had some claims to respect; but, when the first principle of family life was thus openly violated, on what could they base morality? They had kindly feelings towards their slaves, but no convictions about human rights that suggested to them to turn their backs upon it, and see if the world did not offer something better. They had some education, but literature did not seem to interest them, as it did Ludovico, or to offer them any resource for the failure of their domestic life. How far did they criticise their father, she wondered. Probably not much; though there was something in Don Fernando's manner that made her feel that he was not happy. She could only hope he was not, for she saw no way out of the dilemma they were in except to suffer, and custom lays such a weight upon the soul that man turns away from suffering that does interfere with personal comfort. Upon the whole, her reflections left her content that her friend was not as happy as she deserved to be, and her children bade fair to be still less so, for she saw in the near future that Isabella could not live long.

CHAPTER XIX.

LA MODESTIA.

When Carolina saw the freedom of life which a married woman enjoys in Cuban society, she longed for the day when she might throw off the restraints of girlhood, so rigidly enforced by her friends. The general elevation of society in the northern and middle states of America, which allows great freedom to young people, can only be rightly estimated when compared with an opposite state of things, where public morals are so corrupt that no one can be trusted.

Carolina was now anxious to visit her paternal estate, which was not far distant, and the magnificent domain made her heart swell with pride and ambition. The solid weather of the season — if one may so express the nature of a climate where the season determines the weather, as in the tropics — makes an ordinary expedition a fiesta, and the whole family accompanied Carolina in her visit to La Modestia.

During her minority, the plantation had been left in the care of an elderly French gentleman, who was a naturalist and nothing but a naturalist. M. Larimon, doubtless, had his reasons for banishing himself from society, and the custom, prevailing in that region, of not prying into personal affairs, shielded him from idle curiosity.

Carolina found every apartment converted into a menagerie, except the old gentleman's bedroom; and there he not only slept but ate, when he could not do the latter outside of the house, for want of room elsewhere. In the grand salon were pens for gazelles, cages for birds, parrots, rabbits, and other small game. Shelves laden with alcoholic specimens were hung in all the bedrooms. Glass cases contained collections of insects. Minerals were piled in corners. Shells were stacked on marble-topped tables.

The long white hair of the serene philosopher floated over his shoulders, and his mild blue eyes surveyed the party that suddenly descended upon him, as if they were only specimens of another genus of animals.

Not so old Celia, the housekeeper. She well remembered the little niña, who was carried to the States after the death of her parents, and she wept and laughed alternately to see her again, a beautiful lady.

And where could she spread the dinner, or ask the company to sit down? She brought chairs to the piazza, for there was positively no other place. She lifted the little girls, who enchanted her, into the low hammock of M. Larimon, that swung in the gallery. She brought fruits, oranges, *cau sucré*. And when she had blessed and seated and oranged and sugared the party, which latter she did in tiny cups and saucers filled with the hot juice from the boiling sugar-vats — for this was a sugar plantation — she begged the keys of M. Larimon, and opened chests that were only opened now to have their contents aired and sweetened, and saved from cockroaches' nests. From these she drew the finest and most highly ornamented napery, and spread them upon a table, which she drew upon the piazza from some hidden recess. In vain the Marchioness told her they needed no dinner or lunch, for they were not far from home, and she did not wish to disturb M. Larimon with entertaining guests elaborately; but Celia remembered that she reigned triumphant in that department, and, while the children amused themselves with the animals and other curiosities, chickens were killed, eggs were fried, plantains, yams, and tomatoes were prepared, fruits were gathered, and, amid volleys of apologies, the party were at last called to partake of a delicious but impromptu dinner, which Celia deprecatingly called a "little lunch."

M. Larimon entertained his guests with the utmost nonchalance. He was too much a man of the world to show that he was disconcerted, though he was caught in undress; but, in truth, he would have been glad to have known beforehand that he was to have so distinguished a visitor, and so well attended. He might at least have cleared the grand salon, and would perhaps have retired to his own pavilion, on the other side of the *bassey* or square in which the house stood; but that had been filled with his collections long ago, and, like a true philosopher, he thought it just as well to make good use while he might of the ample apartments of the grand mansion.

He did not even know Carolina was expected home.

Ludovico was a great favorite of M. Larimon. It was Ludovico who had planned the surprise for him, for he did not wish to disturb the arrangements of the good old man. Ludovico knew every item in Monsieur's collections, and was the solitary individual who had the freedom of La Modestia. Of late, since Manuel had learned to ride on his pony, he had sometimes accompanied Ludovico, and been introduced to the manifold treasures of the place; and it was now his delight to show them to Carlito and his little sisters, for it was their first visit.

A little whitewash and paint, great factors in a Cuban house, would soon make all right again. Celia had taken good care of the nice furniture, which was stowed away in various places. What would she have done with her otherwise useless life, if she had not had this to do for the young heiress, who would come home at some future day? She was much disappointed to find that

Carolina had forgotten her and her tender nursing, and the old home, and could remember nothing distinctly that preceded her life in the States. Celia had lavished all her movable affections upon M. Larimon, who had been a kind master to her, if not to all "the people." He had simply neglected them, except to ride round every day with the negro driver, who was a capable assistant and understood the making of sugar, which M. Larimon did not; so that, after a general inspection, he would retire to his beasts, birds, insects, fishes, and books.

Carolina, who did not care for the curiosities, wished to see the process of sugar-making. The season for the work was at its height, and, leaving the children under the care of Celia, the party ascended the steps of the sugar-house and saw its deep vats, its huge cylinders for pressing out the juice of the cane, the roaring fires beneath, into which whole saplings were thrust at once, the branches only being trimmed so far as to allow them to be pushed into the mammoth ovens.

The cylinders were kept in motion day and night by oxen who were driven in an eternal round by — could it be? — by little children from four to six years of age, who excited the animals by a sustained, monotonous cry, in which the wearied little voices struck mournfully on the ear. A driver stood over them, and whenever a little voice relaxed its song, and the ox stopped in consequence, his lash reminded them of their duty.

It was a sickening sight. Helen's vision was dimmed for a moment, not by tears, but by a sudden blindness as the blood rushed to her brain at the sight of this new atrocity.

"How cruel! horrible!" exclaimed the Marchioness, in French. "Why is this, M. Larimon? It is the first time I ever saw children at this work. How can you allow it?"

"The cholera killed so many of the people last year, madame, that there are not enough to keep the mills in motion unless they are so relieved."

"But does my husband know of this?" she asked.

"Yes, madame; it is done upon all the sugar estates this year. Last year's losses were very great, and the gangs have not yet been replenished."

"But are there not older children than these babes, who could be used?"

"Many have died this season, madame," was his reply.

Carolina heard this conversation, and knew that this sugar estate supplied the wealth that she enjoyed, but she made no remark.

They passed into the next department, where the negroes were stirring the boiling caldrons with mammoth spoons. The clay floors were hot to the feet. The naked forms of the workmen dripped with perspiration. They looked gaunt and thin.

"They look as if they were hungry," exclaimed Ludovico.

"The supplies of corn have not been as good as usual this year, and there have not been enough hands to plant rice," said M. Larimon, "but at this season they are nourished by the sugar-cane, of which they eat all they want."

"We do not care to go any farther," said the Marchioness. "Let us go into the air."

Helen cast one more look at the wretched creatures that rolled their eyes up at the party. They looked more like demons than like human beings.

Had the fair vision that looked down upon them come as their redeeming angel? Alas! they had never yet seen any earthly representative of the Holy Virgin to whom the white man prayed.

From this hell they passed into the bland and perfumed air of the gardens, where fruits and flowers of all kinds abounded for the white man.

M. Larimon was a horticulturist as well as a zoölogist. He found no difficulty in keeping his grounds in order, though the gangs had been thinned by the cholera.

"If it was my plantation, the mills should not be kept going at night," said Ludovico.

"That would make a great difference in the income," said M. Larimon; "the fires are not allowed to go out during the sugar-making season."

Carolina made no comment upon this, either. Could she have been unconscious that a word from her might have stopped all this cruelty?

The Marchioness listened in vain for a word of feeling from that frivolous heart.

With pride M. Larimon now introduced the ladies into a green labyrinth of his own devising, and proposed that each one of the party, entering a separate alley whose shrubbery was too high and thick for any intercommunication with other paths, should meet together in a tall summer-house, whose minaret could just be perceived in the centre. Soon each one was at a loss, and no one could emerge from the bewildering mazes, till M. Larimon stood upon the tower and directed the lost wanderers whether to turn to the right hand or the left. The whole party at last gained the tower, and behold! not far distant the glorious sea.

Helen could have knelt in worship to it, for was it not the only path by which she could regain the lost heaven of home, — a home which now seemed to her the very vestibule of heaven. Carolina was charmed, for would she not have a yacht and sometimes sail upon the silver sea!

M. Larimon led them out of the "Labyrinth of Ariadne," as he had named it, and for many hours they wandered through his parterres into which he had gathered all the plants of the West Indian islands. One pathway led to the "silver sea," that bounded the plantation on one side. Carolina's delight was not to be expressed in words. She shouted her girlish transports, and chased Ludovico over the shining beach, and gathered tropical shells and sea-weeds like the child that she was.

Helen loved the sea, but the childish voices that sounded across the cane-fields from the pandemonium of the sugar-house drowned to her ear the gentle plashing of the waters on the beach, and she only wondered that the caleseros, who sat upon the horses waiting to take them home, could be so amused by the thoughtless girl as their broad smiles testified.

"What a splendid home! What a good steward you have been, M. Larimon!" Carolina exclaimed, as he handed her into the volante. "I hope you will live with me when I come, and you shall have a house for all your pets. I will draw the plan of it myself."

The tropical sun lighted up the sea and the heavens with indescribable glory as they drove homeward, bathing the landscape in celestial, rosy light, kindling the palm shafts, penetrating even the gloomy arches of the bamboo avenues, and touching every coffee-berry with such brilliancy that each one looked like a living carbuncle. On this moonless evening, without the interval of a perceptible twilight, all this changed into a darkness that would have been perceptible had not the glorious, starry arch above them reminded them of its great author. The southern cross was a new object of interest to Helen. It rested nearly on the horizon. The little girls would have gone to sleep if they had been permitted, but the evening dews are heavy, and that is not allowed.

"The gentle but heartless naturalist! The sum of all villanies" — these were Helen's thoughts. "But the stars were set by God's own hand."

"Vengeance is mine," saith the Lord.

"He will surely take it," was her mental ejaculation.

Does he not take it every day and every hour that we desecrate the nature he has implanted in us, negatively if not positively? God's negations are his severest punishments, for in them souls may sleep the sleep of death till roused by the vision all divine with which they must compare themselves.

There will be a waking, and God's light will penetrate every dark shadow, but not till every crime committed on the earth's surface has been expiated. That is what forgiveness means. Its popular meaning hides the true one, and men think they can lie down at last and find themselves forgiven without expiation. What a waking it will be when the truth dawns upon us, let it be in what world it may!

Carolina was now ready to throw herself away

upon the first suitor who should admire her or her inheritance and give her liberty! There were plenty of such admirers. But it was the duty of her uncle to see that she was not sacrificed to a gambler or an adventurer, and why not secure to his own son such worldly possessions, when his heart was all ready to give itself into the keeping of his cousin? He did not feel "justified," as the phrase is, in withholding his consent to his son's imperative pleadings, though he regretted the relinquishment of all his plans for the completion of his education; but Ludovico promised to visit France after his marriage, accompanied by his wife — if such she would consent to be — and it was not long before the prize was sought and won, there being very little heart in the matter on Carolina's part; but there was not a handsomer cavalier than her cousin, who had grown from a boy to a man in the few last weeks, and she could not hope to find one more devoted to her every whim and wish.

After the betrothal, which carried sorrow to the loving heart of the mother, it required no little remonstrance to teach Carolina the proper etiquette to be observed by a *fiancée*. She must no longer dance with any gentleman but her accepted lover, and in a thousand ways she felt herself fettered and annoyed. But her uncle was very peremptory. Isabella saw too well that after marriage she would fall into all the dangers of that corrupt society, and she hoped Ludovico's eyes might still be opened; but Helen saw more clearly that the spell was riveted by his inexperience and his generous love. He was perfectly unsophisticated, and Carolina was not. Her caprices, which others saw arose from selfishness, were all graces in his eyes, and his devotion was unwearied.

The fame of the pretty Americana and the betrothal spread rapidly and brought many visitors. Young girls were curious to see her beauty (indeed, a stranger in that isolated society is considered a public prize), also to be numbered among her acquaintances, for she was a wealthy heiress soon to be established in their neighborhood, and unnumbered fiestas were looked forward to. Mothers came to accompany their daughters, and Spanish cavaliers found her American manners and gay spirits a source of endless amusement. The months of the dry season were quickly passing, and Carolina had become the star of the plantations, and had transformed the society around her in many ways. She played and sang well, and, even among the musical Spaniards, was an admired performer, especially by her Italian singing.

The Marchioness tried to love Carolina, and to find in her what she craved for the wife of her son; but in vain. And Ludovico seemed to be lost to his mother. Helen looked on with a sad heart.

She saw no evidence of character in Carolina that would finish the good work that had begun in Ludovico. On the contrary, he too had become selfish for his idol, and offered no defence for his old and tried playmate against Carolina's caprices, for she took pleasure in tyrannizing over Juanita. Silently Juanita did her bidding, but Helen could see a growing aversion to her new tyrant. Carolina's tyranny consisted in regardlessness of her fatigue or her feelings, and in unreasonable requisitions of all kinds. She took up easily her latent character of slave-holder, taking slavery as a matter of course, and proud of her own human possessions, over whom she was soon to preside.

Madame Cazneau, delighted to leave her charge with such good prospects, lingered longer than she had intended, but at last returned to her duties at home, promising Carolina a visit when she should have a home of her own. Carolina was rather relieved that so much guardianship had departed, for she could now give herself up more than ever to the novel enjoyments and triumphs of her position.

Ludovico made no confidante of his mother of his occasional jealousies and heartaches. His infatuation was so great that he rather blamed himself than Carolina if any clouds came between them, and attributed to her want of knowledge of the world many departures from true delicacy which even her guarded life gave opportunity for.

Among all the cavaliers who visited the house, Don Fernando was the only one whom he liked to see approach Carolina, for he was the only one in whose character he had any confidence, and there was a dignity in Don Fernando's manner that even Carolina did not invade, though she preferred his admiration to that of all the rest. Ludovico did not acknowledge to himself that his hold upon her was slight, for it would have pained him too much to dwell upon such a possibility, but his friends saw it, and no one more clearly than Juanita, who was as much a part of the family circle as ever, though downcast and proudly humble where she had once been confiding. The extreme suffering of such a position as hers was fully appreciated by her sensitive nature, but others knew it only by her varying countenance, for a slave has no freedom of speech, no right to complain except to an equal, and she had no equals. Other favored servants of her class, the personal attendants of members of families, and who often have far more grace and attractiveness than their mistresses, and who receive and minister to guests, and take pride in their vocation, pass their lives in adorning the persons of their mistresses, holding their fans, picking up their handkerchiefs, combing their hair, and waiting upon their caprices; but she had been the indulged companion of intellectual and artistic pleasures that had elevated and refined her, and was now for the first time treated as an inferior.

She sat apart in Mrs. Warwick's room, the home of the children, where the family passed much time, pursued her sewing or her painting, ministered to the children, and never intruded the services she was always ready to perform when called upon. Hitherto they had been rendered for love, and gladly. Now they were those of the slave.

CHAPTER XX.

THE TURTLE DOVES.

One day there came a messenger from La Modestia with a present to the little girls of four beautiful turtle doves which they had much admired.

Tom, the cook, was summoned to make them a cage. He was so busy with company that he could only fit up a large basket that day, but in the course of two or three days he constructed a very elegant one, of delicate rattans, open work on every side, and with slivers of corn-stalk made a nest such as the turtle doves make, and fastened it securely, as he thought. The cage was five feet square, and stood upon the piazza, not far from Mrs. Warwick's room, in order that the little children should enjoy the sight of the beautiful birds. Carolina thought at first that she must always feed them herself, but this grew very tedious, and Manuel was only too glad to have that pleasure. It was several days before a sound was heard from the doves, whose mournful cooing is very musical. One day one of the birds approached the basket nest, and shook it with her beak. It did not prove satisfactory. She was evidently afraid to get into it, and after due consultation it was taken down to be remodelled. Some of the corn slivers were left upon the floor of the cage, and before the new one was put in and made irreproachably secure, which Tom was very careful to do, Mrs. Turtle-dove had arranged a few of the corn shavings in one corner, and laid a beautiful egg upon it. The children were transported with this proceeding, but the egg was small and fell through one of the squares which the corn shavings were too frail to floor securely. The father-dove from his perch near the corner where the egg was deposited had done melodious homage to it, thus proving his parentage, by the most musical sounds in his beautiful throat, bowing his head to his pretty mate, inflating his breast and prolonging his cooing into a song of triumph. The accident hushed his pæan in a moment. But the next day the mother-dove climbed into the new nest, and laid another lovely egg, over which he rejoiced in the most exultant manner. The whole family gathered round it, and the children were made happy daily by the devotion of the father-bird who brought worms and grains to the sitting mother, and who would bow before her, and throw back his beautiful head in an ecstasy of joy. Tom soon constructed another nest in another corner, but the other pair of doves took no notice of it. So the watching and the feeding went on till the bird was hatched from the egg, and then followed the curious spectacle of the mother-bird first taking the corn into her own crop, and feeding her little one from her own bill. The baby-bird grew and waxed strong, and when it could fly would pursue its mother round the cage, till the sympathies of the beholder were quite excited for her, for she evidently did not wish to feed her babe as often as it desired it, and the little one grew to be quite a tyrant. It was decided at last to let the mother-bird out of the cage for a little while every day for relief and refreshment, and Manuel learned to perform the operation very skilfully, though it was rather difficult to do it without letting out the young bird too. The mother always came back after amusing and exercising herself on the rose-bushes that grew in the gallery, but did not seem disposed to forsake the neighborhood of her little one. One day, however, she flew into a neighboring tree, and did not return at nightfall. There was great lamentation among the children who were allowed to sit up later that night, awaiting the return of the mother-bird. But she did not come, and the guard that always watched upon the piazza was enjoined to open the door of the cage if she did return. The next morning, when Manuel stepped out upon the piazza, the first sight that caught his eye was that of the head of the mother-bird, which lay upon the floor of the piazza, with many beautiful feathers scattered around. A cat had been prowling round the house, it seemed, all day, and, meeting the bird on its return, had ruthlessly devoured it. Loud and long were the cries of the children, to whom the birds had become so dear. The little one soon began to peck at the corn, and gradually grew and flourished. The father-bird, who had always been allowed to fly since his mate sat upon her egg, brought the baby worms, and did his best to supply the place of the lost mother.

But the cat had tasted of a dainty morsel, and one evening a loud noise of beating wings was heard by the company that sat upon the opposite side of the house, and a general rush was made, every one exclaiming, "The doves! the doves!" And it was the doves indeed. The cat had broken the bars of the cage and seized upon one of the birds. The bird had thrown up its wing, and the cruel claws had torn its side, which was bleeding profusely. The noise of footsteps had frightened away the cat, and, after a while, the ruffled wing had been closed over the wound. It was proposed to wring the bird's neck, but Tom declared it would get well if not touched, and so it was left; and it did get well. But another of the birds had been so frightened by the assault of the cat that he would occasionally throw his head back as he sat on the perch till he would lose his balance and fall backwards from it. This was repeated many times, and at last Tom proposed that he should be put carefully into a basket and carried to the woods, and placed upon a tree, that he might have the pleasure of dying in the open air — for die he must, since he had ceased to eat. The next day, Miss Wentworth and the Marchioness, accompanied by the children, took the poor bird in a basket to a pretty little wood where they often went to gather wild flowers, and set the bird upon the branch of a tree. It remained quiet there for a long time, and at last spread its wings and flew to the top of the tree, and from there to another, till it was quite lost sight of; and Tom, who had accompanied the party, predicted that it would get well in its native woods.

The guard who watched on the piazza that fatal night had doubtless fallen asleep, but, luckily for him, that had not been thought of. The cat suffered the penalty of her assault, though Helen exhausted her eloquence to make the children feel that the deed was no crime on the part of pussy, who only followed her instinct in catching and devouring the beautiful turtle dove, and she did not rest till she had made the children acknowledge that it was as innocent a deed on her part as the killing of a mouse, which they would not have found fault with. When the wounded bird could again jump up and down upon the perch, they carried it also to the woods, and Tom made a new cage for the other birds; but it was not long before the children wanted to free the others, who had seen the carnage the cat had inflicted, and must, they thought, live in constant fear. Helen was on their side, and Carolina concurred, for the mournful cooing wearied her. They never saw their beautiful pets again, though they often looked for them when they walked in the woods, for they probably made their way to the other side of the island, their original home.

As they strayed homeward, they saw a spectacle to be seen only in the tropics, the native region of the tarantula, which is a gigantic spider, as large sometimes as the palm of the hand, its huge legs and head fiercely bearded. One was lying in the path, apparently dying; but at a little distance stood a beetle on long legs, just preparing to make a dash at the spider. The party stopped to gaze, when the beetle darted forward and thrust its sting into the unprotected part of its victim's body, now too much exhausted by repeated attacks to defend itself by assailing its enemy. The battle never ends but by the death of one of them. The beetle had the advantage this time, and its assaults seemed so cruel that Manuel suddenly picked up a stone and threw it at him, breaking his stiff wings and legs. All were relieved at the release of the poor spider that crawled away, perhaps to recover by some process of nature, but apparently almost disabled. The little girls were much agitated and afraid of the great spider, but their mother assured them that there was no creature on the island whose bite was poisonous, or whose venom could not be cured by killing and cutting it open, and laying it upon the wound. This was a great comfort to Helen too, who had been so often startled by a rush of insect life, the darting about of lizards, — pretty creatures though they are, — or the stalking about of scorpions and centipedes. One day she had taken her towel from the bracket to wipe her neck, and been stung by a scorpion lurking in its folds; but Camilla, who heard her give a little scream, ran to her aid and performed the cure in a few minutes. Another time she was bitten by a land crab that laid under the edge of her bureau, which she mistook for one of the children's toys and stooped to pick up.

"Oh, Aunt Helen!" exclaimed Manuel, "look at this procession of drink-water ants (*Bebeaguas*)! It looks as if bits of leaf were running along on the ground, but they are all on the backs of ants that live in long galleries under ground, which they fill with these bits of coffee leaf. Sometimes, papa says, they will strip a whole coffee-square in a night, when the leaves first grow. These ants are carrying them clear through this portrero to the other side, where papa had a great pit dug, as large as our house, on purpose to cut into their galleries."

A look from his mother stopped Manuel's description, for she did not wish the little girls to hear that the people cut down young trees and, cutting off their branches, thrust them into their galleries and set fire to them.

The children stooped down and saw the little ants, each with a bit of leaf about as large as the little finger-nail; and close by this procession was a row of ants going the other way, empty-backed.

"And here is another kind of ant that makes this great mound that is as tall as I am," and Manuel pounded the structure till he broke a hole in it and showed covered galleries which the ants had made to run all over it, and up and down which ants were travelling, laden with their bits of earth. These mounds stood on the ground, but Manuel pointed to others on the highest branches of the trees, which were reached by similar galleries wrought upon the trunks of the trees. He had names for all the different species, which Carlo had told him when he took his morning rides upon his head.

They saw too the little red guinea-peas with black spots, which grow on shrubs in the woods, and which the little girls had often played with, though they never before saw them growing in their pods. The cotton ball plant was also in flower and in seed — the flower a beautiful yellow, the seed a ball of cotton just bursting from its envelope. Helen recognized these from the portfolio of Juanita, who had painted them all, as well as many beautiful flowering vines that hung from the trees.

"Such wealth of nature!" she mentally ejaculated. "Why does it not speak more to the heart of man? Is it that the heart of man can only read this word of God when love — unselfish, divine love — guides it? That is the Father's face which the child beholds, and the sight of which he never must be allowed to lose."

"Birds were not made for cages," Manuel said one day, trying to console himself for the loss of the doves.

"It must be dreadful," replied Miss Wentworth, "to have wings and not be able to exercise them. Little birds are apt to beat themselves to death when taken from the free air. They must, at least, be born in cages to be able to bear it."

"But they know how to use their wings, do they not, even if they are born in cages, and they will fly out if the door is left open."

"Just think of a little boy in a cage — how he would long to run!" said Miss Wentworth.

"I'll never have a bird in a cage," said little Pepita

"Nor I," said Luisa.

"Then my little darlings have learnt something from the turtle doves," said their mother. "They have learned to be kind to little creatures that cannot speak and tell what they wish."

Bird-life was henceforth a fruitful topic, and Miss Wentworth told the story of Audubon's life and observation of birds in their own homes in the trees, which all agreed was far better than to shut them up in cages; and papa promised to send for the beautiful pictures Audubon painted of them, each bird resting on the plants or shrubs or trees they frequented in their real lives.

"Oh, how many stories you know, Aunt Helen!" said Luisa. "You know stories about everything! I like stories better than anything!" And to this all agreed.

The birds Juanita and Ludovico had painted on the walls were now seen with new eyes and new interest by the children, and when they went to the woods they hunted for birds as well as flowers. Birds in the tropics do not sing as melodiously as those in the temperate zones, but their plumage is more brilliant. The paroquets, which are very gorgeous in color, were taught new sayings, and were often let out of their cages, but they had become so much at home in them, they would come back without being called at night, and cats were banished the premises whenever seen.

"I love kitties, too," said little Pepita one day. "I can't have my kitty now — I wish they did not kill birds. Why does the Heavenly Father let them do it, mama?"

"When pussy catches a mouse," said mama, "she makes it so sleepy it cannot feel being bitten, and I think it must be so when they catch birds, for I am sure God makes everything right. There are birds enough to feed all the pussies, and if it does not hurt them to be eaten, it is no matter."

"But God lets people hurt other people," said Manuel. "Why does he do that, mama?"

"People are different from animals, my boy, and know what is right and what is wrong; they are different from the animals, who do not know anything about right and wrong. God gives them a conscience to guide themselves."

"Mama, my dog knows when he has done wrong," insisted Manuel. "He puts his tail between his legs and looks ashamed."

"He knows you are displeased with him, but he does not know, as you do, why things are wrong. He is afraid you will punish him if he displeases you, but he knows nothing about displeasing God."

"Did the first man that ever was born know about displeasing God?" asked Manuel.

"I have no doubt he did," said his mother, "for that is just the difference between men and beasts."

"I wish I did not know," pursued Manuel.

"My little boy, do you wish to be like the beasts?"

"But I feel so unhappy, mama, when I have done wrong. Carlo says we shall burn forever and ever in everlasting fire if we do wrong."

"Carlo is a poor ignorant man, my dear boy —

do not believe what he says, but always ask me or papa, for he may teach you many untrue things, not because he wishes to tell you anything that is not true, but because he is ignorant."

"Don Andres tells the people how to do right when he talks to them at night. He tells them that if white people steal, nobody likes them, and they have to be punished. I heard him tell them so when I was over there. Why can't somebody talk to them and read to them on Sunday as you do to us — it is better than dancing and making that dreadful noise on the drum."

"They do not know enough to be talked to much, my dear boy — and, besides, their dancing is like the dancing that is told about in the bible — it is religious dancing; — we don't know what it means, because we do not understand their language; but people tell us so who have been to Africa and have travelled amongst them. Even savage people know about some kind of God that they look up to, but the more people know about other things the better kind of God they worship, for all we can know about God is what we can think about him. I think the time will come, my darling, when these poor colored people will be free, and will have a chance to be as wise as any one else — but people have to learn to take care of each other. That is God's way, and we must all do the best we know. It is hard to wait, but the world is growing better slowly."

"Why can't papa talk to the people? They like him, and would listen to him."

"They understand very little of our language, my dear; only just enough to do the work they are told to do. They are not Spaniards, you know. Don Andres or papa can tell them a few things, but not many."

"In one country where they have made the slaves free," said Helen, "they taught the people a great deal to prepare them for being free, and when they were told of it, they fell upon their knees and thanked their Heavenly Father for their freedom. I know colored people in my country who remember all about that time, and who are good people and do not steal or tell falsehoods as you hear them do here. The world is growing better, dear. Even these ignorant people have their virtues. Many of them are kind to each other — they love good masters and mistresses and good children. Even poor old Camilla would work herself almost to death for you children, or for mama — and yet she gives mama much trouble because she is ignorant and does not know how to govern her own temper. Such good people as dear mama make every one better that lives with them. That is the best way of doing good to people — to be good one's self."

"Dear mama," said loving little Pepita, climbing into her mother's lap, "I want to hug you and kiss you, and I love you a hundred and a hundred and a hundred times."

"And I won't cry about my horses, mama," said Luisa. "I'm sorry I was so cross to Francisco when he broke Rosillo's neck — he may break them as much as he pleases." (These were the Guinea-grasses that served for steeds.)

"My darlings, how happy you make me," said their mother — "that is the only way to be good — to make ourselves do right. God has given us consciences, and if we listen to the voice of conscience, we shall always do right. — No one can do it for us but ourselves. I can help you think about it, but I cannot do right for you."

And yet, comforted as she was by the love and good consciences of her children, the heart of the mother sank within her when she thought of all the evil they might learn from the poor ignorant slaves.

"Conchita told me about that dreadful fire," said Carlito.

"Do not believe anything about your Heavenly Father that is not good, darling," said Helen. "He is all love and goodness."

"But he makes wicked people, like Don Ermite and Don Alfonso," said Manuel.

"He does not make them wicked, my boy," said his mother, "he makes people so that they can be good if they wish to, which is better than being only as good as the birds and fishes and other animals; don't you think so?"

"I don't know, mama."

"Don't you wish to be growing better and wiser all the time, since you are to live forever and ever? the animals know all they can know when they are born."

"Must I live forever and ever and ever?" said Carlito. "I don't want to live so long. I want to die and never wake up again when I hear of anything cruel, cruel, cruel, — " and he began to cry.

Luisa, who had been listening, burst into a violent fit of weeping, and little Pepita swelled and sobbed in sympathy.

"My darling children," said their mother, whose heart was sore almost to bursting, "let us not think of the wrong things people can do, but of the good the dear Heavenly Father wishes them to do and has made them able to do, and of this beautiful world that he has put us into to help us be good and kind and loving. We will all go to drive now, and see how many beautiful things there are to make us happy. Mrs. Warwick will get you ready while Aunt Helen and I go to find our shawls."

And the little party broke up for the moment.

"I believe my heart will break, Helen — these dear children are too young for such sad scenes as their eyes are now opened to. There is no such thing as shielding them from such knowledge here — I wish my husband had been with us just now."

Helen's heart was too full for speech — she

could only embrace her friend, for whose pain she saw no remedy — but around whom darkness seemed to be closing — moral darkness, the silver lining of whose cloud was not yet visible.

This precocity of experience in such a state of society is appalling, and, if fully realized in its effects upon characters, might well make the hearts of mother's break — but God's resources are unfathomable. The fair universe is his answer to the crying soul, if that soul can only be taught to read it aright. Its ministrations do meet the demand, if the moral evil can be kept out of sight till the heart is strengthened by its teachings. Youth is the time for happiness — but if love does not prevail where can the happiness be found? The child must be made to feel that God is love, or he loses his way in this otherwise dark valley. Isabella saw as she had never seen before what is the mission of the mother. She is the near Providence who must represent the Heavenly Father's love and wisdom.

A few mornings after this, as Helen was about to rise, she saw her door gently opened and heard a low knock upon it. She said "Come in," and little Pepita bounded to the bedside.

"Aunt Helen! won't you come into the nursery a moment after you are dressed? I want to show you something, oh, so beautiful!"

"I will, darling — give me a good kiss."

Pepita gave the kiss and disappeared.

When Helen entered the nursery, she saw upon the wall opposite the door an exquisite painting of the turtle dove and the young bird sitting upon a tea-rose bush such as grow in the piazza garden.

"How beautiful! did Juanita paint it?" said Helen.

"Yes, Juanita is always painting something pretty — there is a whole portfolio of her paintings."

"I must look at them if they are as beautiful as this."

"Oh, they are, they are — she can paint the whole world," said Manuel.

Carolina and Ludovico now came in to see the painted doves.

"They look real, not as if they were painted," said Ludovico — "and they look to me as if they were human doves — such beautiful expression in the eyes, as if they understood us all and our love for them," he continued, quite carried beyond himself — "Look, Carolina! did you ever see such painting as that?"

"Who taught Juanita to paint like that?" replied Carolina, but without a word of sympathy or admiration.

"I gave her her first lessons," said the Marchioness, "but she far transcends me now. I cannot paint the human soul looking through a dove's eyes. When you have time to look round, you will see her paintings in all the halls. Among others you will see a view of the beach at La Modestia."

"Are all these wall-paintings hers? She must go and paint the walls in La Modestia, for me."

Juanita was standing in the next room, whose door was ajar, and heard this; but no one responded to it. Juanita was happy at that moment because Ludovico had spoken warmly of her, but she did not appear.

As they passed to the breakfast-table on the gallery, Helen entered the studio and found Juanita leaning against a window, her eyes full of tears. Helen could not speak, but she put her arms around her and kissed her, which turned the fountain into a river. And, for the first time, Helen's eye caught the view of a splendid Madonna, that hung upon the walls.

"Is that yours, too?" she whispered.

Juanita gave a mute assent, and they parted.

When Helen sat down to breakfast she said: "I have for the first time seen that Madonna in the studio. Why did I not see it before?"

"It was covered, to protect it from one of Camilla's sweepings," said the Marchioness.

"Do give me its history!"

"The picture came into the hands of a friend of ours in Havana, in a cargo of old metal, that was brought to copper a vessel. We happened to be there and thought it might be something valuable, as the frame was very massive, but it was so obscured by time and soiling that we could not decipher it, till I sent for some nut oil and washed it all over, which brought out all its beauty. I was so desirous of copying it that my friend sent it to me, shortly after, for that purpose; but it came in the season of the sewing, and when that was passed, and I was preparing to paint it, I found it copied by Juanita, who had asked me to let her paint, that season, instead of helping about the sewing. She had always been so helpful to me that I thought it a strange request, but, as it was the first indulgence she ever asked for, I granted it. She had consulted Ludovico about it, and wished to do it then, for fear she might lose the opportunity if she waited. I have never thought it worth while to paint it myself, as I could not compete with her. It is called a perfect copy, and, to my eye, there is a beauty in it that Murillo did not put into his, — for it proves to be a masterpiece of that artist."

"Where did you get that wonderful creature?" asked Carolina, somewhat irreverently.

"Her mother and grandmother were slaves of my grandfather, and he gave them to me when I was married. They were all Mussulmans; there are many Mussulmans in Cuba, but these are the most gifted ones we have ever known of. They have kept their own faith through everything, and shown themselves capable of cultivation in every direction."

"Can she read?" inquired Carolina.

A latent smile appeared even on the face of the Marquis.

"Look behind her door in her sleeping apartment, and you will see a rare art library on her book-shelves," he replied. "Your aunt keeps her supplied with books, as well as artist's materials."

"Why! what a Phœnix!" exclaimed Carolina. "I presume she looks down upon us all. I thought I could draw and paint pretty well, but I cannot hold a candle to her. Did she ever go to America? for I saw on Miss Wentworth's walls what seemed to me to be American scenery."

"No," said the Marchioness; "that painting is mine — the only one that adorns these walls; for I have spent my artistic faculties in teaching the children to draw and paint, and have left them to adorn the walls. These flowers and birds that you see are Ludovico's work. We live such a retired life that we must make the most of such resources. When the holidays are over, I am afraid you will find it a little dull here, unless you can use your faculties well."

"Oh, I am no artist, — I care for society."

"A woman cannot do a finer work than to bear her part nobly in society, especially here," said the Marquis; and Isabella felt that he was thinking of her. Carolina felt, too, as if this was a personal remark, and that the conversation was getting too serious for her taste, and so she proposed to Ludovico to take a ride on their ponies, and the breakfast party dispersed. Helen went to the portfolios, for here was a new phase of life in the tropics. And in Juanita's portfolios she found abundant food for reflection. There was the history of a soul, as it were. The difference between Juanita's sketches, whether of a rare flower or tree or landscape, or of a head — of which there were innumerable specimens, — and the drawings of Ludovico, was the difference between talent and genius. Juanita's were not transcripts of anything, though portraits, but were expressive of the highest thought suggested by the image.

"That all this should be done in a corner!" was Helen's mental ejaculation. "But they will live after her," was the next thought.

In the portfolios of her friend, she found ample testimony to her love of New England, which was dear to Helen's heart. In the summers she had always taken Isabella in her visits among her friends, and here she found sketches of the lovely elm-tree valleys of Massachusetts and Connecticut, the azalea-covered hills of Vermont, the mountain-laurel reaches of New Hampshire, the hemlocks and pines of Maine, — for these jaunts were always enlivened by sketching; and the autumnal coloring, which, in the language of one of her native poets, gives the impression that the jewels imprisoned in the earth had struck their gorgeous dyes through the foliage, had not been forgotten by the little lover of beauty.

Helen possessed herself of many of these gems, sure she should obtain her friend's permission to hang them where she could always see them. Ludovico's work had been to find the rare tropical plants — the night-blooming cereus, the campanula, and other native products, trees and fruits which would vie in beauty with those of any land. Luxury so enjoyed bore its appropriate fruit, and harmed no soul; and it was balm to Helen's wounded spirits, to see what a noble life could be, no matter where passed.

Could this be made living and fruitful to Carolina, who seemed to have entered this domestic paradise like an evil spirit? — for what else are selfishness and vanity?

CHAPTER XXI.

PARTED FAMILIES.

"An invitation from the Countess Lopez! oh, how delightful!" exclaimed Carolina, dancing one morning into the salon, where sat the Marchioness and Helen. Ludovico followed, and looked rather inquiringly at his mother.

Encouraged by this recognition of her possible wishes, Isabella said, "It is many years since I visited that lady — I hardly feel willing to resume the acquaintance. Do you think, my son, that you had better number her among your future friends?"

Ludovico knew that the Countess of Lopez was not considered respectable among Spaniards even, although the whole neighborhood attended her fiestas, and he would not have accepted the invitation against even a suggestion from his mother to the contrary, had not Carolina vehemently, and even petulantly, insisted.

"What matter is it if she is not good, dear auntie? She cannot hurt us, and I have longed to see that splendid plantation, and herself too, for I hear she is the most beautiful woman in Cuba. Oh, you must let us go! I am not afraid to go alone, but I suppose that, according to your foolish Spanish customs, it will be proper for you to go too. Oh, do go, dear aunt, and perhaps Miss Wentworth will go. I am sure she is grave enough to balance all my flightiness — and I will be so good and discreet. I had rather go there than anywhere in Cuba, for every one says her parties are the pleasantest. Every one goes, and she always has splendid music from Havana. Pepe says it is the greatest fun in the world to catch her in one of her summer-houses, where she has decoyed some one in with her cards, and is fleecing him of all he has in the world. Oh, we must go there!" — and she looked to Ludovico for aid.

"Just this once, mother. You know every one goes. It will only look strange if we refuse and go everywhere else."

"But I cannot meet her as one lady should meet another, my son, — do you wish me to do it? I should see that murdered husband standing between us."

"Murdered husband!" exclaimed Carolina. "What! did she murder her husband? Why? Do tell me about it."

"She wished to get rid of him, probably, for he was a decent man."

"But, mama," said Ludovico, "was it ever proved?"

"No attempt was made to prove it, but does any one doubt it?"

"Perhaps not," said he; "and yet every one visits her just the same."

"Too many do that, I know, but I cannot make up my mind to do it. I never meant that you should be caught in her summer-houses, my son, where I know she is famous for gambling away people's birthrights, and I hope Carolina will give this up to please her aunt, and still more her uncle, who would object, I am sure."

The Marquis entered at the moment, and his objection was so decided that not another word could be said; but Helen heard Caroline mutter, as she sauntered out upon the piazza, "When I am my own mistress, I will do as I please." Nor did the self-willed beauty recover her good temper during the day, but evidently resented the authority of her guardians.

Helen hoped Ludovico's eyes would be unsealed by this and similar demonstrations of character, but Ludovico's sympathies were, for the time being, enlisted on Carolina's side. It would have been dangerous to his prospects if it had been otherwise, and this consciousness, not recognized by himself, often blinded him to the truth. The Marchioness knew that the society at La Mariposa, the splendid heritage of the Lopez, would be far from select, and hoped this check to Carolina's fancies would be followed up by Ludovico, when the power came into his hands. The Countess' entertainments were fabulously enchanting, and the whole world of the neighborhood would be there, but she had hitherto kept Ludovico from the snare, and could still less trust Carolina in it. Even in that community, the Marchioness of Rodriquez could do as she pleased, for she was respected even by those who did not dare to imitate her independence.

"When I meet the Countess of Lopez," she said to Helen, as the young people perambulated the gallery, "I speak to her as if she were the respectable woman she ought to be. Nor would my doing otherwise even be accredited to the true cause. I should be thought impolite not to do so, but many mothers who do the same would not take their daughters to her home. So, you see, we can hold up a little testimony of our principles, when it comes to treating a murderess cordially. Her other crimes, of quite as deep a dye, would be considered no disqualification for society, if this suspicion did not fill people's minds with horror."

"I hope she has no children," said Helen.

"Yes, she has several, and they are married well, as the world says, and they are very decent people in comparison. Their standing is in no wise affected by their mother's character. In fact, my dear Helen, gossip is not the fashion here, except among our slaves. The "people," as they are called, spread information about character and events. It is through them that we know what passes on the various plantations, and their testimony is rarely doubted. They are, indeed, the only persons who have the means of knowing the events of every-day life, for it is not considered etiquette to report of our neighbors' doings. In this case, it is not because people are above scandal, but because every man lives in a glass house. I should not dare to say why I refuse the Countess of Lopez' invitation, for society would only laugh at me, and think me a dishonorable neighbor for mentioning my reasons. Another mother, careful of her children's characters, might surmise my reason, but we should not be likely to speak of it together. Still less do we ever criticise each other in our relations of slave-holders."

At this moment, mumma Camilla came up the steps of the gallery, crying and wringing her hands.

"Ay de mi! my lady! Ave, sanctissima! poor mothers! poor little ones! much people down there! thank God, he has all my children!"

"What is the matter! what can it be? Perhaps it is nothing, after all. What is it, Camilla," said her mistress, with an appearance of calmness, for Helen's terror had startled her into the apprehension that something unusual might have occurred.

"There they are! there they go!" said Camilla, as a party of gentlemen passed the piazza in company with the Marquis. "Poor mothers! poor little ones!"

It was not the intention of the Marquis that the errand of his visitors should transpire to the family, at least till they had gone, for he was disturbed at the thought of his wife's distress on knowing it. But an event upon a plantation may be likened to a spark falling upon dead leaves. It spreads like wildfire. And Camilla was not the woman to keep a secret that would spread dismay. In this case, her own feelings were enlisted, for she had a heart, perverted though its emotions were.

The visitors were a party of whom the Marquis had purchased a plantation contiguous to his own, many years before, with a proviso that the slaves sold with it should be returned to their owner, if he claimed them, at the end of twelve years, but, in case he should do so, any children born in the interval should remain with the Marquis.

Isabella had not known of the transaction. It was one of frequent occurrence in slave communities, and even the Marquis had not hesitated to consummate the bargain, but, now the day of restitution had come, he would willingly have foregone the advantages of it, to have escaped the consequences. No intimation of the resumption of the slaves had been given, the circumstances had almost escaped his memory, when the other party to the bargain appeared to claim his right. The Marquis had met the carriage at some distance from the house, and had given orders that parents and children should be sent to another part of the plantation, but the servants who led the mules for exchange, upon the road, not having been charged with secrecy, had given the alarm, and it was soon known in every direction. Parents hurried in from the field, were called from the house and from the portreros; children were summoned from the chicken house for the parting, for the mothers were frantic, and all were frightened. A general feeling of consternation was diffused, for family relations had been formed, now to be torn asunder. Pazienza, the wife of Jacobo, the negro-driver, a dignified and respectable negress, was godmother to nearly all the younger children. She hastened to the scene of the rendevous to renew her promises to take care of the children, who were crying in their mother's arms. Some of the best and most useful negroes on the plantation were of the number called for. Stout men wept to leave their young wives and little ones — for though no marriage relation existed in form on the plantation, it was all the same to their simple hearts.

The Marquis had walked away from the scene, after those who were to be taken were assembled, but Isabella and Helen hurried to the spot. A few hours only were given, and they were to part without hope of reunion, for they were to be conveyed to a distant part of the island, and were nearly all field hands. The coachman and personal servants of the family are the only individuals on a plantation who travel or who have a chance of again meeting lost members of their family.

To Helen it seemed as if the foundations of things had given away. She stood aghast at the spectacle, and still more so at the fact that Isabella only wept, and did not remonstrate. Carolina's frivolity was hushed for the moment, but when Ludovico swore that he would leave the island and never be party to such a transaction, she drew him away from the place on the plea of its being too painful a scene to witness, but evidently, as Helen felt, willing to bear her part in it for the sake of being a wealthy planter's wife. Manuel hid his face in his mother's dress, while she vainly tried to bind up broken hearts by her kind words and promises of care for the children. It was a dark day at La Consolacion, and not even the presence of the guests at dinner, among whom were the gentlemen who brought all this dismay and terror, could rally the spirits of the family. The Marchioness was obliged to appear, but Helen persisted in remaining secluded, pondering upon the "the sum of all villanies." Could slavery show a deeper woe than this? It seemed to her that it could not. Yet it was passing before her eyes unchallenged, and, though tears and sobs and bitter wailings accompanied it, not even the victims remonstrated. What could be a greater proof of the tyranny that held them in bonds? No outward show of kindness could avail to blind her to the conviction that the Marquis ruled with an iron hand, and she felt that she could never look upon him again but with horror.

The sad procession passed the house toward evening, followed by the poor children and a motley assembly of negroes, who were allowed to go as far as the gate, and returned with the little ones in their arms. They were of all shades, from the deep black to the golden yellow, those in arms all unconscious of their coming fate, but some of the older ones knowing too well what their destiny was to be.

No one spoke to Pazienza on that day. She saw the last of the parents and led some of the little ones by the hand as she returned from the gate, and Helen thought she had never seen a face more expressive of grief and sympathy, and the dignity of sorrow, than that of this stately negress. She passed the house without turning her head or making the usual salutation.

"I must find Carlito," Helen said to herself, starting up. She found him lying on his little tent-bed, weeping bitterly. She led him away to her own room. The poor little boy knew too well what it all meant, and Helen really feared that his health would be impaired by his prolonged sorrows.

"When I brought you into the country with

me, darling," she said, as he rested in her arms, with his own round her neck, " I thought you would have some chance to forget what had pained you much at home, but when our eyes are once opened to what slavery means, there is always something to know that it is terrible to bear; but, Carlito, dear, this is God's world, and these poor people will live forever and ever in a better world than this, and be happy, and this part of their lives will then seem to have been very short."

"Will they live forever — and forever — and forever?" said the child, his voice sinking to a reverent whisper, as he repeated the words. "Am I going to live so long, too?"

"Yes, darling, all of us, and we must try to be good and remember that everybody belongs to God's family, no matter what is the color of his skin."

"And, then, are they all my brothers and sisters?"

"Yes, and we must treat them as kindly as we do the brothers and sisters that live in the house with us — they are all God's children."

Carlito sat up straight, and his beautiful face was lighted up with something like a happy look.

"These poor people," Helen went on, "are very ignorant, because nothing is taught them; but I have known very nice colored people, and once I had a little class of colored children come to my house every Sunday, after church, and I used to tell them stories about good children, and show them flowers and shells and every pretty thing I could find, and some of them became very good scholars at the school they went to, and grew up into lovely characters. One of those little girls lived in my mother's family when she grew up, and we all loved her dearly for her goodness and her kind care of my grandmother, who was very old and ill, — a great many such people lived in the town where I did. Their grandmothers had been slaves, but they were so no longer, and I think the time will come when the colored people in Cuba will be free, and then no one can punish them or sell them."

"When I grow up, I shall have none," said Carlito, "and Manuel says when he has been to college he shall come back and make all his free; — he has a whole plantation full that his aunt gave him — they are all his own, own, own," — this was a favorite mode of expression with Carlito when he wished to be forcible, — "and if any one gives me any, I will come too and make mine free."

"Then you and Manuel can do a great deal of good, and perhaps others will do the same when they see you do it."

"Manuel says Don Andres is very kind, and his dogs never hurt any one — they only bark, and that frightens the people enough to stop them from doing wrong; and then they love Don

Andres, too — Mrs. Warwick says they do — and mumma Camilla says so too."

"Yes, I know they do. When so many of them had the cholera last year, he came and took care of them — and put up huts on the driers so that they should not sleep on the ground."

"Oh, do they sleep on the ground?"

"They have a board, but that is laid on the ground, and sometimes the ground is wet. They have a warm blanket, too," Helen added, regretting that she had unwittingly told a fact Carlito seemed not to have heard — but she supposed Fanchon's revelations were known to Carlito as well as to others. She resolved not to forget again how much time he passed in Mrs. Warwick's nursery, where little transpired of a painful nature. She now proposed to go there, for she wished to divert his mind as much as possible from the horrors around him, and she passed the rest of the day with the children, the only happy, unconscious souls on the plantation. How short a period of their lives would be thus shielded, it was sad to think.

When she retired for the night, she sat long at her window, with the feeling that she needed the presence of the stars to reassure her that God reigned over this sad world — till Isabella came to bid her good-night.

Helen told her friend that she must return home, for her knowledge of slavery was getting to be unbearable, but Isabella begged her to remain through the trial of her son's wedding, and Helen was made aware that sorrow had wrought great ravages upon the mother, and promised to do so, whatever she might suffer — for was not Isabella's portion harder to bear than her own?

Isabella's hope that Ludovico would never return to Cuba to live after a residence in France was in danger of being cut off by this unfortunate alliance with his cousin. The force of circumstances might be too much for his resolution; it might even prevent his forming it, and probably would do so. Carolina would rush into every dissipation, which would rob travel of half its advantages, and, as for study, there would be no hope of that.

Isabella had a true mother's heart, and could better bear the thought of separation from her children, than any deterioration of character, such as she was apprehensive must ensue from living in such a society as that of Cuba. That Ludovico was to be absent from her had not given her the pain that his probable future now gave her. Her confidence in her husband's affection and fidelity had kept her happy, but it was that alone which reconciled her to exposing her children, even in their early years, to the contamination of Cuban life. Her disappointment in regard to Ludovico was her first domestic sorrow. She had thought herself afflicted when her kind father died — (she did not remember her mother) — but that was a natural sorrow. This was an unnatural one, and Helen began to feel alarmed for her. Isabella's usual quiet habits of life were entirely changed by the necessity of accompanying her niece to all the fiestas of the winter, where her presence was indispensable as protectress. Helen usually accompanied her, but remained at home when wearied in mind or body, and was always glad to be with Carlito and Manuel, whom she could comfort when the little girls were asleep.

Isabella had no choice, as Carolina had no thought but of self. Such had been the whirl of events that the friends had of late had but few opportunities to enjoy hours of quiet talk, and Helen became aware, for the first time, this evening, of the change that had taken place in Isabella. Serious injury had been done to her health by these dissipations and painful excitements, and she promised not to leave her while her sympathy could be any relief to her.

"I could have borne the terrible scene of to-day better," said Isabella, "if I could have felt that it would strengthen Ludovico in his growing dislike to Cuban life; but the strong influence that is upon him now overpowers every other consideration, and I fear he will steel himself against it. I have not seen my husband yet, but I cannot conceal from him that this new experience goes far to disgust me with life here. I wish we might all be released from it, and accompany Ludovico abroad. I do not know but what my life will depend upon it. I knew that these things were done, but it was never brought home to me before. How little we realize the woes of others by imagining them! I have just left Manuel, who has been frantic with grief till he fell asleep exhausted. Mrs. Warwick was so fortunate as to keep the little girls from much knowledge of this sad affair, but I do not know whether it can be kept wholly from them."

"You need rest now, dearest; lie down with me, will you not?"

"Oh, no, dear Helen; I must go to my husband. I know he dreads to meet me, — but I will bid you good-night now, and we will hope that this will do somebody good. It may soften a hard heart."

Helen shared the hope, but had no confidence that Carolina would be softened. Selfish frivolity is the most hopeless form of the demon that lies *perdu* in the human heart.

Her fears proved but too well founded. The neighborhood rang for many days with the praises of the Countess of Lopez' fiesta, and Carolina was duly pitied for not having assisted in it. The disappointment was so bitter a one that from that time her defiance of authority was almost open. Nothing restrained her but the fear of losing that opportunity of independence which her marriage would give her. Ludovico was the only one who did not feel the revolt keenly, and anticipate the consequences when she should be released from the thraldom of maidenhood.

The men who had carried away so many slaves had brought with them four stalwart young men, — bound hand to hand and foot to foot with iron chains — whom they had met on the way, in a coffle of slaves just brought from the city into the country for sale. By offering an advance price, the Marquis purchased these men, to take the place of some of those about to leave the plantation. They had been but a year in the island, and were evidently of a tribe superior to many who are brought from the African coast. There were too many opportunities of knowledge of escape in the city, and a trader had brought them into the rural districts, with more of their kind, to be disposed of upon the plantations. These were the last of the gang, the rest having been taken on the way. They were silent witnesses of the heart-rending scene of the day. They were left all night chained together on the piazza of the hospital, because no one was at leisure to attend to them. Some negroes visited them, carried them oranges, took them by the hand, and spoke the words of their native dialects, lest perchance they should have come from their distant homes. The Marchioness saw them as she returned from her visit to the afflicted group, and ordered them nourishing food, and inquired if any one had recognized them as countrymen, but apparently no one had done so. She did not know till the next day that neither the food she had ordered, nor the shelter of a cabin, was afforded them during the night; but Manuel brought in the information, from his morning ride, that they were still on the piazza, chained together, and must have been very uncomfortable. The Marquis ordered their release, and they were immediately sent into the field; for the important point in their case was to "break their spirits." When night came round again, they were assigned to their sleeping-places, and, after the evening roll was called, were locked into their cabins like their fellows. At midnight, the family was disturbed by the noise of horses' feet, which alarmed Helen, as it was an unusual sound. She refrained from asking an explanation in the morning, for Isabella's sake, and she remembered to have heard the duties of the night-guard explained as watchers of the horses, which are tethered to the lawn in that hot climate, instead of being shut up in close stables. But mumma Camilla never let any one suffer from ignorance, and when Helen took her early walk on the piazza, she found her sauntering there, with her arms folded and a handkerchief over her head, the very picture of disconsolate woe. Her theatrical airs were well understood by this time by her new victim, but yet Helen knew that the part was played — not to hide, but to reveal, some tragedy that might elicit an exclamation of pity from her.

"Toothache, mumma Camilla?" she said, kindly.

"No, lady — no — poor boy — poor boy — new hand — just out of the woods — don't know how to be a slave — caught, lady, caught — in the hospital — all over — poor boy — poor boy."

"It is a shame to worry you, Miss Helen," said Mrs. Warwick, opening her door; "that old thing can never keep anything to herself."

"What is it?" said Helen, faintly, fearing to hear.

"One of those new hands got away last night — nobody knows how — perhaps his mate answered for him in the cabin when Urbano went round and called out their names. They did not know it till just before bed-time, but they found him before morning — he was several miles away."

"And what was done?"

"Oh, there is no punishment like the one for that. I should have tried to beg him off — he was so new and so young — and perhaps I could have done it, if the old overseer had been there, — and when they do whip here, they always do it thoroughly; they say it only makes them worse to hurt them a little."

"Do not tell me any more, now," said Helen, gasping for breath; and she retreated to her own room.

"Papa," exclaimed Manuel at the breakfast-table, "I think it was too bad to whip that bozal for running away. I would if I —

"My son, do not speak of what you do not understand — the people must not run away."

There was something in his father's manner that silenced Manuel; but he followed his mother to her room, and they wept together over the sad necessity.

God's sun shines upon the just and the unjust. Helen felt, when she looked abroad on the festal world of that fair clime, that only in such lands could this crying sin exist — that in her own wintry one, where man is condemned to pass many of his days shut up in houses, and where inclement seasons bring their own peculiar suffering, this one added to the rest would be more than poor human nature could bear, even among the spectators and perpetrators of the iniquity. But in that glorious earth, where the very air is music, and where the great mother pours out from her full bosom such wonders of vegetable and animal life, one can never for a moment forget that God lives and reigns, and that one day or other this great wrong will be righted, because he lives and reigns.

"Now you are here, dear Helen, and all these sad things come before us, and I see them through your eyes, I am aware how I have comforted myself with the degrees of more and less iniquity.

When I think of some of the neighboring plantations, where cruelty is the rule, — and I had almost said, there are no exceptions, — I think how fortunate I am — indeed, we have been blest with a steady discipline and many ameliorations till now. It is not only that I see it all with your eyes, but this cruel man has made everything different from what it used to be. If the former overseer had been here, he would have taken every precaution to soften the prospect of bondage to those poor fellows, who looked so wild and untamed yesterday that my heart foreboded evil for them. Don Andres who sometimes comes over to help, was not here — perhaps he stayed away on purpose. I suspected Tono yesterday of being able to make those boys understand him, for I saw some muttering went on between them. I did not ask Tono if he could understand them, and now he would doubtless deny it, even if he did — but I am afraid he put dismay into their hearts."

"And they saw those poor fathers and mothers taking leave of their children," said Helen.

"Ah, yes; Helen, that is as new a feature of slavery to me as to you — I mean that I never saw it done before, although I knew it was done — but I never supposed it would be done in my home. You can no longer have any respect for us."

"I love and respect you, my darling — I know you cannot help it."

"I have often thought," resumed Isabella, after a long silence, in which both she and Helen realized that the love and respect could extend no farther, "that this island would be a good place on which to begin a system of gradual emancipation — for the children of the plantations might be bound out to the farmers of the mountains, who are not slave-holders, and taught not only to work, but to live like civilized beings — and thus the slaves might be fitted to be hired out as free laborers. It could be done if the Spaniards could conceive of such a thing as innovation. I have an uncle who was not made for a slaveholder, and whose plantation is a perfect scene of confusion and waste, and whose wealth is wearing away, because he cannot fall in with the views of discipline and service generally adopted."

"Will you explain a little?" said Helen.

"He is very lax in discipline, because he is so tender-hearted — and, as no other motives are put before his people, they, of course, take advantage of his leniency, and are idle, and troublesome to all the country round. He would gladly co-operate with others, I doubt not, in turning his slaves into freemen, if others would do it also, but he would lose caste to do it alone, so he contents himself with giving freedom to favorites who become part of his household and live in perfect idleness. Do you remember those tall, bedizened women you saw walking about when we called the other day?

You remarked upon their appearance. Those women are the daughters of an old servant, who, with his family, received his freedom many years since. Old Tomás still waits upon his master, but never has an eye for any one else — one may in vain nod at him to take one's plate — he sees no plate but his master's. Each of his three daughters owns a pony, and rides about where she likes. They all, father and children, dress better than their master's family. The women embroider muslin beautifully, which they sell to the pedlers, and, as they have no cares, they are truly the greatest ladies in the land. Their children are all free, and I sometimes think they may inherit the whole estate. My uncle has no foresight; he is very wealthy now, but by and by his children will begin to mortgage the patrimony, and the family wealth must run out. Estates here become encumbered with debts, which run for many years, till at last some terrible crash comes, or, more probably, some alliance is formed which patches things up for another generation."

"Are not these lands very productive?" asked Helen.

"Wonderfully so, if well taken care of, but there is very little science in the cultivation. My husband applies a little to the renewing of his lands, and makes them twice as productive as most other planters do. The B——s from the United States are introducing steam-engines in their sugar-mills, and are growing fabulously wealthy, because their people are thus released to cultivate new and more extensive estates. They bring all their Yankee shrewdness to bear upon their fortunes. I wish I could say they were as peculiar for their humanity, but it is not the poor people that get the benefit of their improvements."

CHAPTER XXII.

DON ANDRES.

"Mama! mama!" said Ludovico one morning as he sprang from his horse and ran up the steps, "Don Andres has returned and has consented to come! Is not that joyful?"

"It is indeed," replied the Marchioness. "I did not expect it."

Helen looked inquiringly.

"Don Andres is a character you do not yet know, dear Helen, and you will know how to rejoice with us when I tell you his history. He has consented to be our overseer, and it is such a relief that —"

And Isabella burst into tears.

"It does me good to cry this time, so do not look troubled," she explained.

The Marquis, at that moment, rode up to the door, accompanied by another Spaniard, with a fine, open countenance, who alighted and paid his respects to the ladies with much courtesy, but with fewer flourishes than characterized some of the guests whom Helen had seen.

"Don Andres has consented to come," said the Marquis, cheerfully, "and I hope you will feel happier, Bellita."

"I do indeed," she replied.

The gentlemen passed on to the Marquis' apartments.

"Do tell us all about him, dear aunt," said Carolina. "I like his looks very much — I hope there is something romantic about him."

"His history may be truly called romantic in the best sense of that word, for he is poetical in his goodness."

"Mama! mama! Don Andres is here," vociferated Manuel, trotting through the salon on one of his reed horses. "I am going to tell Mrs. Warwick!" and he scampered across the gallery, and disappeared in the nursery.

"How strange it is that we have heard nothing about Don Andres before," said Carolina — "mumma Camilla will come next."

"Here she is," said Ludovico.

"Ah! my lady! Ave, sanctissima. Don Andres here! — come back! Muchas grazias! — Don Andres! my lady!"

"Yes, I know he is come," said Isabella, "and I am very glad. It is not likely she knows of his coming here, however."

Camilla took up her tray of sweetmeats, which she had deposited on a table for a moment, and went into her pantry.

"Now for Don Andres, auntie dear, before any one else comes."

"Don Andres came from the island of Majorca," said the Marchioness, "to make his fortune in Cuba. No one knows his private history. Some people think he is Basque, and I am inclined to be of that opinion, for the Basques are all educated men, especially in an artistic direction. It is said every Basque child is taught to draw, and Don Andres is a superior draughtsman, and has genius for architecture. But the Majorcans speak all the languages of the Mediterranean shores, and he is versed in these.

"On his way he was shipwrecked, and lost all his effects but the letters on his person, one of which was to our old blind neighbor who died a short time ago."

"The man who cried himself to death?" asked Carolina.

"Yes; he was the kindest old man in the world, and showed every attention to Don Andres — lent him money to commence his profession here, which is that of an architect, and gave him a home until he became independent in it. Don Andres built many of the beautiful gateways and porter's-lodges that you have admired so much, and many fine houses also, and was highly respected by every one for his character and good judgment and benevolence. Wherever there is misfortune, he is always there. Even when the cholera raged here among the negroes, he attached himself to a skilful physician of this district, and carried through sanitary regulations on many plantations, which saved much life and much suffering; so that he is idolized by 'the people' as well as by their masters. He is a man of education and taste, and his name is another word for honor."

"Heaven bless him!" ejaculated Helen.

"Take care that you are not jealous, Ludovico," said Carolina.

"The better you like him, the better I shall like you," Ludovico replied.

"Our poor old neighbor suddenly lost all his property, by putting his name on his brother's notes. The brother was a bad man, and ruined all his family as well as himself by his extravagance, and had to flee from his creditors. All the negroes of our poor neighbor were sold except fifteen, who belonged to his wife; all his coffee was taken from his packing-house; his wife died of grief; his two daughters were perfectly helpless in their poverty, and then Don Andres Torres showed what he was. He came to them, dismissed their overseer, took charge of the family, and has supported them ever since, by cultivating a little patch of coffee and vegetables for family use, with the help of the few negroes; by working at his profession a little, when he had time; and by being the conduit through which the charities of the neighborhood have passed into the good old man's family. They never ask where anything comes from. They do not know enough about affairs to know that he cannot obtain all they need from the plantation, and he makes it appear that he can do so. The poor old man cried himself blind. He was quite infirm when his misfortunes came upon him, and has passed his time for several years in alternate weeping and praying, while Don Andres has told him all things were going on nicely, and that he was happy to requite his former kindness by acting the part of a son to him.

"My husband knew that Don Andres' means were running low, and he purposes to pay him such a salary that he can hire some one to take care of the small corner of the plantation by which the daily wants of the family are supplied, and lay up something for himself also. I was afraid he would not think it possible to leave his old friend, but it is easier to do so now the old man is gone, and, as he will still be in the neighborhood, he will constantly visit the ladies and superintend their affairs. He has probably found a substitute for the labors he performed already. We are indeed fortunate. Don Andres has been an honored guest everywhere."

"Which shows," said Ludovico, "that, even among us, virtue is honored, if it is real virtue. I hope Don Andres will make you think rather better of us, Miss Wentworth. Mama, we will go out when the roll is called this evening, and see how glad the people will look. It has made me melancholy to look at them since that wretch was here."

The ladies from the plantation of Don Tomás, as the old blind planter had been familiarly called, were sent for to dinner, and Helen realized for the first time what is the life of a country lady of moderate means on the plantations of Cuba. These ladies were somewhat advanced in life, and for many years had not been able to afford visits to the city. They were wholly uncultivated and very uninteresting, and the only variety in their monotonous lives was to stand at the gate of their avenue and look at the passers-by. If they had been younger, they would not have dared to do it, for a lady seen in a forbidden place at once loses character in Cuba; but the misfortunes of their good old father had created quite a sympathy in the neighborhood, as the circumstances under which they occurred were well known, and the high character and popularity of Don Andres Torres had thrown a sort of consecrated charm even over their mediocrity.

Helen listened to their prattle about the equipages they had seen and counted during the holidays, the fiestas they had heard described by friends who had been so fortunate as to attend them, while they were watching by the dying-bed of their good father; of his virtues and sufferings, and the kind things that every one had said of him since his death; of Don Andres' brotherly goodness and kind management of their few remaining negroes, and their sorrow even at a nominal parting with him, but their joy that he was to be so near. And it all had a certain musical flow to Helen's ear, which had listened so long to tales of woe that a story of poetic goodness bore healing on its wings, especially in that most musical of all languages. Nor was her subsequent acquaintance with Don Andres any disappointment.

At the evening roll-call the family went over to the gallery of the overseer's house, before which "the people" were ranged, and every one answered to his or her name with a cheerful voice and beaming face, for the Marquis had announced that Don Andres had come to rule over them. Encouragement and protection were in the very tones of his loud yet musical voice, and the people well remembered his kind ministrations when the fearful epidemic of the year before had prostrated them by hundreds.

From the overseer's house it was but a step to the hospital, and there Helen — who accompanied Don Andres and her friend to see poor Pedro — was convinced at the first glance that her conjecture had been a true one. Don Andres laid his hand kindly upon the head of the poor negro, who was lying on a blanket spread over a board, but enjoying the almost unheard-of luxury of a soft pillow, which Isabella had insisted upon at her first visit. It was a decided innovation, to which her husband had at first objected (for billets of wood are the only pillows usually allowed), because it will not answer to make the hospital too desirable an abode. Its friendly rest and nicer food were already too great an attraction; but it did not occur to Helen that there was any great luxury in being there when she saw the emaciated form of poor Pedro, and imagined the discomfort of his bare bones, without even a pallet of straw under them! She inquired the use of one structure that stood in a corner, and was told it was the *stocks*. It looked to her like a gallows, and she saw that the victim must lie on his back upon the floor, while his feet were fastened into the opening made for them, and without the possibility of turning over. She stood a moment transfixed before it, and when she again met Isabella's eye, everything swam before her vision. She did not know what was passing around her again till she found herself supported by the arm of Don Andres in the open air.

"You must hold your eyes in this country, lady," said the good man, in a low voice.

Isabella had seen the look in Helen's face and understood it, and it was reflected in her own heart; but she lingered a moment to speak another kind word to Pedro, in hopes that she should not be obliged to recognize it.

Dolores was not forgotten, and the two ladies accompanied Don Andres to her cabin. He at once advised her removal to the hospital, where he could oversee her more easily; and Helen saw her spring from her hard board bed when Urbano — whom they had taken as interpreter — made her understand the order.

Dolores knew very well that Pedro was still in the hospital, and Helen understood the alacrity with which she rose to go. Her haggard looks were sad to see. Helen hoped something might be done to prevent a final separation from Pedro, and resolved to make Don Andres a party to her knowledge of their circumstances, when a good opportunity offered. But she knew that Pedro was left to the tender mercies of Don Ermite, for the result of his brothers' conference with Don Alfonso was the requisition of a fine, which sent them all to their mountain home penniless, if they persisted in rescuing their brother from the grip of the cruel planter, which they concluded to do even at that price. Don Alfonso had failed to draw the Marquis into the plot, and, seeing the family feeling of Don Ermite's brothers, had used it to their destruction and his own gain.

No one knew when Pedro would be sent for, and he did not yet know what his fate was to be.

It was not long before Helen found the opportunity she desired. Don Andres was always a welcome guest in the family, which was quite an anomaly in that society, for the position of an overseer is uniformly a subordinate one. Don Andres' character was the sole cause of the exception. He was a man of varied information and experience, and much knowledge of the world, and made himself agreeable to young and old.

One evening, when pacing the gallery, and engaged in conversation with him, Helen took an opportunity to tell him the history of Dolores and Pedro, as far as she knew it, and he was deeply interested. She also told him that Pope Urban was a countryman of theirs, and Don Andres promised to draw from him some particulars of their history, and, if possible, interpose to prevent their separation. But he gave her little hope of success. The Marquis would not choose to buy him for the same reasons that he had avoided giving him aid when wounded. From time to time, Don Andres spoke with her upon the subject, and her respect for him increased as she saw proofs of his humanity.

One day Isabella startled her by saying in a playful way :—

"My dear Helen, you must not indulge Don Andres in walking apart with him, even on the piazza. I heard Camilla say to Urbano that Don Andres was going to marry the Americana. We have to be very circumspect before our critics, who judge us very severely, though they have another code of right for themselves. Seriously, too, I fear the good man will make himself unhappy about you. You show your regard for him very plainly."

"And I feel it," said Helen, "but I will take your warning both as a matter of propriety before these sable critics, who, you say, are the scandal-mongers of your society, and still more if there is any danger of Don Andres misunderstanding my regard for him. But I do not think there is, dear Isabella."

"I hope there may not be, but you do not know how interesting you are, and, much as you might esteem Don Andres, and much as we all esteem him, the influence of caste is such that he could not marry into our circle without scandal to us."

"I would not be influenced by that motive in my own case, I assure you, for Don Andres is not bound to this soil by any ties of preference, or by any affinity of taste with your institutions. I know that from himself, for our conversation has been chiefly upon that subject, when you have seen us talking apart. I promise you not to trifle with his heart — you know I would not do it."

"Yes, I do know it, darling, and therefore I speak frankly. I really believe he is attracted to you, but he is a man of too much honor to ask you to share his fortunes, and so I must take care of him," she added, laughing. "Do not look so grave, dear Helen. You are not hurt with me?"

"Oh, no, Isabella — not in the least; I am only thinking how sad it is that such a man should be in such a position. He is very noble, and I will be as careful of him as you wish. If I were younger and more susceptible, I do not know but my enthusiasm for Don Andres might endanger me, and my views of caste are so very independent that I probably should not be influenced by any such considerations as those you refer to. With us, you know, any man may take any position in society, if he fits himself for it by education and character. I have often thought we Americans do not live up to the theory of our society as we ought, but since I have looked back to my own country from this, I appreciate, as I never could before, its advanced position."

"You are right, dear. Such a state of society as yours is worthy of envy. I only wish my children could grow up in it."

"Will you not lend me one of your little girls when I leave you, dear Isabella?"

"Ah, can I do it, Helen? I will try to be as good a mother as that. But my heart is too sore, just now, to dwell upon it."

Helen was aware of this, and said no more.

CHAPTER XXIII.

TULITA.

"Whose splendid livery and carriage is that?" exclaimed Carolina, one afternoon, as the family were sitting on the piazza.

"It is the Countess of Lopez'," said Ludovico, "but I do not know the young lady she has brought."

"It is Tulita Abrides," said Helen.

The next moment the superb equipage, with its outriders, dashed up to the steps; Ludovico descended to meet the ladies.

The shameless woman, with unblushing face, greeted the Marchioness as if on terms of courteous friendship.

"I know this is not etiquette, la Marquesa, for you did not come to my fiesta, and have not been to see me since. But our little friend, here, was so eager to come to you that I waived all ceremony. — And these are your American friends, whom I so much wished to see —" and the Countess welcomed the ladies to Cuba with all the grace in the world.

The Marchioness was coolly civil to her, but affectionate to Tulita, whom she begged the

Countess to leave with her for a few days, promising to send her safely back. After a little parley, this was agreed to, and, with the usual Spanish blessings and courtesies, the visit passed, and the imposing lady was whirled away again.

"She is gloriously beautiful!" exclaimed Carolina.

"And so kind to me!" said Tulita. "I wish you had come to the fiesta; it was magnificent. Dear Miss Wentworth, how pleasant it is to see you again, and my darling Carlito."

"How long have you been in the country, Tulita?" inquired the Marchioness.

"Several weeks. Papa brought me up to the fiesta, and left me for a visit. I shall soon return, but I could not go home without seeing you, and I teased the Countess till she brought me here."

Isabella's heart ached to see the child of an old friend in such society, and she wondered at it as much as she grieved. But Helen observed that Tulita was not as blooming as when she had seen her last.

"Why did you not come to me, my dear," said the Marchioness, "if you needed country air. I begged your mother to send you at any time."

"Oh! mama said you were expecting guests from the States, and you know the Countess is an old friend of papa's."

Isabella knew it too well, but she did not know Don Miguel's reasons for sending Tulita away from home.

I was about to say it is difficult for an American to realize the desire for a title, in a land of titles. I can only say, however, that I wish it was difficult for an American to realize it, but there are too many proofs that even in our democratic land there is too much worship of privileged castes, and too much low aspiration for emulating them. In England, this tendency shows itself in servility to the aristocratic class. In Cuba it is a raging passion. In Cuba, the "sugar nobility," as it is called, is very numerous. This nickname takes its rise in the fact that it is easy for any man who is sufficiently wealthy to buy a title, and as the sugar estates cannot be taken for debt, the sugar-planters soon acquire great possessions, which are carefully hoarded till they can buy a Marquisate. Such usurpers of rank are looked down upon by the hereditary nobility, who are called, *par excellence*, Castilians, but it is necessary to inquire into pedigree to know who people are. This consuming passion also leads many young ladies to marry worthless men, while at the same time poor young nobles will marry untitled women if they are wealthy, to replenish exhausted coffers and keep up the patrimonies they must otherwise cease to enjoy, for coffee estates can be seized for debt, and, when these are secured by civil processes of law, the coffee can be seized at the very door.

Don Miguel Arbrides had married a lovely orphan girl, of a noble family, which he had aided, in the hour of need, for this price. The lady did not know his avocation of slaver when she consented to be his wife, for the knowledge of it had been carefully concealed from her by her heartless relatives, and his personal attractions were such that he won her heart as well as her hand. It was not an honored alliance in the eyes of the best portion of Cuban society, and the Marchioness, among others, had deplored the sacrifice, for Lucia Salvo was the daughter of her mother's friend. Yet such are the compromises of a corrupt society that, as long as Don Miguel was wealthy, he was admitted to titled houses, on the score of his wife's rank.

The prostitution of marriage must always be in the ratio of the estimation of character in a community. Holy and honored marriage ranks first among the ameliorations of society: its abuse is the first of calamities that can befall it.

Don Miguel's ambition now was to marry his daughter to a title, and he had therefore encouraged her acquaintance with the young Count of Carova, who was high-born, dissipated, and poor, but whom he despised.

The Countess of Lopez was one of the acquaintances of the young count, and her father had insisted that Tulita should accept the invitation the Countess had been petitioned by her youthful *protegé* to give. The Countess was a useful friend to the young nobleman because she afforded him an opportunity of gambling to advantage, and sometimes even lost at play herself, but perhaps the latter was one of her artifices to entrap the unwary.

Tulita's mother would fain have saved her daughter from the visit, but Don Miguel was imperative.

The visit had not been a happy one. Tulita was a good girl. She had been cherished by a careful mother, whose early life of dependence upon unwilling relatives had given her more knowledge of life bereft of its illusions than falls to the lot of most girls of her rank, and her present life was clouded by the fear that her only son would be made to follow a calling which she could not think humane or respectable.

The Countess of Lopez was not a proper guardian for a young girl, even on a visit of a few weeks, and the Count of Carova passed too many hours in card-playing, and paid attention to too many ladies of higher rank than Tulita, to allow her to feel satisfied that she possessed his affections. Her maiden delicacy had been alarmed at the thought that he had flattered her with attentions only because her father was wealthy, and that he might at any moment withdraw them if he could charm a titled and at the same time a rich wife. She had hoped the Marchioness of Rodriguez would keep her to while away the few days that would pass before her father should come or send for her.

Tulita and Carolina soon became as intimate as young and inexperienced girls can be in a few days. Carolina was thankful to learn more and more of the pleasures to be found in such a self-indulgent person as the Countess of Lopez, and secretly resolved, more and more, to share such pleasures when she should become her own mistress.

Tulita had never before heard the reports that had damaged the Countess' character, and indignantly defended her, with the impetuosity of generous youth.

"I will not believe it, either," said Carolina, "until it is proved. She is too beautiful and splendid to be so wicked."

"And every one loves her so dearly," insisted Tulita.

The Marchioness sighed, but did not think it best to excite Carolina's opposition farther. Ludovico walked away.

Carolina did not let him go unmolested. She skipped after him, and, seizing him by the hands, made him waltz down the piazza with her, exclaiming: —

"Come, Ludo, as I must not touch any gentleman but you, you must dance or sing whenever I wish you to."

And away they whirled, and reappeared at the opposite door of the salon a few moments after.

"Heigh-ho! I am all out of breath, and you are

more tired than I am, Ludo. What a dance I'll lead you when "—

The sentence was cut short by the appearance of the Marquis, whom Carolina was afraid to offend. . . .

"There is one thing we might do while Tulita is here," said Carolina, one day, "and that is to have some tableaux-vivants, for Tulita is a brunette and I am a blonde, and we could have some lovely pictures. I do not believe these Spaniards ever saw or heard of any, and they would not know who Rebecca the Jewess and the Lady Rowena are, but I have appeared more than once in that picture, and would not they open their eyes to see us? We might even get some ideas into their empty brains. Miss Wentworth, you have seen tableaux-vivants, have you not?"

"Oh, yes; it is a very pretty amusement, and I am sure there is enough artistic taste in this house to make very fine ones."

Carolina was quite wild with the idea, and the Marchioness giving her consent, for she was but too glad to have amusements at home, instead of seeking them in dangerous places, it was decided to have some now the regular holidays were past. Nothing must interfere with the balls or dances.

Helen found Ludovico had read Scott's novels, and there was no better quarry for tableaux-vivants. The Lady Rowena and the Jewess Rebecca would make a beautiful picture, and the Marchioness promised to hunt up the materials.

The games of society in Cuba are usually the most trivial, childish plays, involving forfeits and all the excitement of redeeming them. Tableaux-vivants are a great resource in the best society, and artists are needed to make them good.

The chief difficulty was how to light them up; candles are the only means of lighting houses here. It was decided to set Tom to work to make a frame in which several hundred candles could stand, and the picture frame was formed in one of the great folding doors that led from the salon to the studio. Black cloth filled up the space encircling the frame, and black lace stretched across the opening gave the softening effect to the figures. Helen had often assisted at this pretty amusement, and was glad to introduce something a little more intellectual than usual. The interview between Rowena and Rebecca the Jewess made a fine show of the two beautiful girls, and many a Spaniard resolved on the spot to study English, in order to read the beautiful story whose outline the Marchioness indicated in a few words. The lovely children were utilized also, and children are so dramatic in their own plays that they readily fell into Helen's plans in this pretty play, quite unconscious what an unwonted display they were making of themselves.

There were strangers present at some of these tableaux, who had seen them arranged in the States and in Europe, with the most costly appliances, and who said they had never seen a more artistic display, and with so few materials. A few rules observed in the construction gave all the effects of good paintings. The three prime colors must enter into every picture. Helen did not forget this, and Juanita's native genius for coloring knew where to apply the rule. A scarf of pure color thrown across a table or couch, Helen's maroon riding-habit, and an ancient blue satin skirt did much duty on these occasions, and every one was enchanted. Carolina usurped all the glory, for it was her suggestion, but the skill of true artists produced the effects which she could not have done.

"The proper tableaux for Spanish people should be taken from Don Quixote's adventures and experiences," Ludovico remarked to Helen. "It is the only literature people here know. Can't you make some tableaux from the pictures that illustrate the work? I think they would set the Spaniards quite wild."

"If you and Don Pepe will be the subjects of my pictures, I will try my best," said Miss Wentworth.

The audience was at home in Don Quixote, and so much were they excited when Pepe personated the knight of La Mancha doing penance on the Sierra Morena, that they could scarcely preserve that peculiar decorum which pervades a crowd in Spanish society on public occasions. Pepe's tall, lank figure, clad in appropriate garments, or perhaps some might say want of garments, excited inexhaustible merriment. Pepe little realized how he appropriated to himself the sobriquet of Don Quixote for the forever of this world; and the repetition was called for on every occasion of tableaux. Even the Spanish women understood these tableaux.

"If you have ever observed Spanish conversation much," said the Marchioness, one day, "you will recognize the proverbs from Don Quixote in their every-day talk, for the style is to illustrate all they say with a proverb from Don Quixote."

"I am not sufficiently conversant with the work," said Helen, "to have understood the source of those sententious remarks. I have credited them as original with their utterers."

Carolina's curiosity was much stimulated by this suggestion, and, as Don Quixote lies on every one's table in Cuba, she soon made herself acquainted with many of its witty sayings, and Pepe was very happy to help her find them.

Pepe was doubly assiduous in his visits since the arrival of Tulita, and fertile in excuses for his frequent calls. He came very earnestly one day to say: —

"I want to get up a carnival ride, and, if you will go with me in my ox-cart, I will be the negro driver, and we will go to see my aunt, who lives on a beautiful estate, and whom we can puzzle completely, for she only knows la Marquesa — all the rest of you ladies are strangers to her."

"Oh, delightful!" said Carolina. "We can go, can we not, dear aunt?"

"If you will be very discreet, and if Don Fernando will go, so as to keep Pepe in order," said the Marchioness.

"Oh, yes; never fear! I have plenty of masks, and can disguise you all. It will not be the first time my grave brother has chaperoned me on a carnival frolic. I have some beautiful oxen, and Fernando's Alejo will dress up the cart. I shall be here by nine o'clock in the morning day after to-morrow, and to-morrow I will send the masks. Manuel must go as a deaf and dumb boy, else he would be sure to betray us all."

"I can keep a secret as well as any one," declared Manuel.

"I would not trust you," persisted Pepe.

"You must take Don Pepe's terms, my dear," said his mother. "You would not like to spoil his sport." So it was agreed that Manuel should be the deaf and dumb boy.

The Marchioness assured Helen it was very innocent fun, as enacted at that time. Formerly a good many accidents had occurred by the wanton use of the privilege, and a law now existed that no one should appear in a carnival party in the public roads, but only within the limits of the plantations.

The next day came the masks, which were Pepe's work, and worthy of his talent.

The Marchioness and Helen personated New England witches (this was Helen's suggestion) and were dressed in old plaid woollen cloaks, with hoods that had figured on the voyage to Cuba. The hoods were trimmed with black and white horse-hair, and each sported a stick, and took on the character of fortune-teller. Carolina and Tulita were the belles of the party, dressed like Greeks, their garments and scarfs trimmed with Greek borders, that Helen drew for them; and Ludovico, a Turk, who had them in charge. Fernando, an old portly Spanish lady, covered with jewelry, whose shape was determined by a huge pillow worn under her flowing garments, her neck and arms bare, and adorned with bracelets. It is true she was rather of the gigantic order in height as well as girth, but the disguise was complete. The two little girls were fairies floating in gossamer.

The cart was elaborately decorated with branches of cocoa and palm, and Pepe was disguised by a black silk handkerchief drawn over his head, with a broad negro face painted upon it, grinning with merriment, his eyes gleaming from the slits made for them, his costume that of a dashing calesero with a steeple-crowned hat, and floating red ribbons. The masks had long noses, of various shapes, asses' ears, and black **veils.**

The little girls did not like the masks, and were only reconciled to them by knowing the wearers intimately.

As they threaded their way through a neighboring plantation of a French gentleman, somewhat advanced in life, who had a wife and sister of corresponding age, and a daughter with two charming children, the negroes whom they passed, and looked out upon from behind their masks, fled in every direction, terrified by the long noses and asses' ears. — The negroes always run towards the mansion when alarmed, but Pepe drove his oxen as rapidly as he could make them go with the goad which guides oxen in that country, the two heads bound to one yoke; and the whole party alighted upon the low piazza, and took the family by surprise. The elder members understood the frolic, but the children screamed so fearfully that the Marchioness insisted at once upon the masks being taken off, which resolved the company into a party of friends, well known to the neighbors, and soon they resumed their jaunt to the coffee estate of la Señora Doña Maraquita, the aunt of Don Pepe. A lofty flight of steps were to be ascended, and when the party, preceded by flying and frightened negroes, appeared on the great gallery, the Aunt Maraquita came forward to meet them. The great sport of the occasion was the impenetrable disguise, and it was truly baffling until the aunt spied upon the finger of Pepe, who had strangely forgotten to disguise his hands, a ring which she had herself presented to him.

"Pepe! Pepe!" she exclaimed, delighted to find a clew to the unexpected party.

"The ring! the ring! that has betrayed you — Now you must all unmask and come to lunch, for you must be tired and hungry."

"First let the American witches tell your fortune," insisted Pepe.

"Ah, there are your American friends. Now I begin to see the light."

The Marchioness threw off her mask, but Helen did not wish to follow her example. She could not help herself, however, and, after rapping with her stick in mock anger, she too unmasked, and was cordially greeted by the lady.

The beauty of the young ladies was its own apology for being, and the dear children added their charm to the scene.

Manuel was the only one who persisted in wearing his mask. When addressed, he only made signs, but not a murmer escaped his lips. Helen had taken the pains to teach him the finger alphabet, the day before, and he did his part well.

When they all sat down to the delicious lunch provided, they rested from their labors, and Pepe was rewarded for all his exertions by the success of his fun.

When they arrived at home by the glorious moonlight, they found themselves perfectly exhausted by the much laughing all their droll adventures had elicited. Even Helen had been beguiled into merriment, and the Marquis, who had not accompanied them, felt much relieved to see them safely back again, though their three cavaliers were as safe guides as they could have had. He knew they had to cross from one avenue to another, and was not sure but that Pepe had made some unlucky venture. . . .

Don Pepe ran up the steps unexpectedly one day. His approach had not been observed.

"What now?" thought Helen. "Don Pepe looks quite excited."

"Good-morning, ladies; La Marquesa, to-morrow is your annual snow-storm. Young ladies, to-morrow you must dress yourselves in white, pure white, and make part of the snow-storm; no colors are to be worn on that day. I shall be happy to come and make part of your escort."

"Snowstorm?" said Helen, with an inquiring look at Isabella.

"That is my word for the first coffee-blooming, and Don Pepe has never forgotten it. If he had only seen a New England snow-storm he would appreciate it still better. Yes, we will all be ready. It is a spectacle never to be neglected. I hope it will be a happy day. We have three blossomings of the coffee-tree in the spring, but the first is the fullest."

"I don't know which is the most beautiful spectacle on that day," said Pepe, "the ladies or the coffee-flowers."

"We can have the ladies every day," suggested Ludovico.

"But not all together like a flock of angels," insisted Pepe.

"Shall we wear our fairy dresses, dear mama?" inquired Luisa.

"Yes, my darling."

"And mama, you shall be Queen of the Fairies," said Pepita.

"You should ask Aunt Helen to be Queen of the Fairies," said mama, "in gratitude for reading you the beautiful play about Titania."

"But we won't have any ugly men such as were in the play, mama," said Manuel.

"No; to-morrow is a lady's-day, and you gentlemen must be very modest and humble."

And when Miss Wentworth took her walk on the piazza, next morning, every coffee-square was like a snow-bank, indeed. The orange-like flowers bloom the whole length of every coffee-twig, and fill the air with their rich perfume, and, contrary to the usual custom, which is to keep housed during the heat of the sun, the gay quitrins, in their most beautiful liveries, threaded the walks of the plantations, laden with beautiful ladies and children dressed in pure white, and escorted by the young men in white pantaloons and gay-colored parasols; and long white ribbons floated from the steeple-crowned hats of the caleseros, who were dressed for the occasion.

By night the blossoms had withered, and the next morning fell blackened from the coffee-trees. It was a day not to be forgotten, but put away in the memory as the only one of its kind in one's experience.

"Don't you like snow-storm day, Aunt Helen?" inquired Manuel, at breakfast-time next day.

"I do, indeed; it was a day without a blot."

"Even the people looked happy," said Manuel, rousing himself, as if he had mused upon the fact.

"I wish mama had been here," said dear little Carlito, who loved to think of his mama, but did not wish to return to Havana, where there were no little girls or Guinea-grass steeds, and Miss Wentworth could comfort him, when unhappy, even better than his mother could, for she, too, was made unhappy by slavery. She was doomed to pass her life in it, while Miss Wentworth lived in a country that seemed more like God's world to poor little Carlito's tender heart.

Juanita amused herself all day painting coffee-trees in bloom.

"As to painting, Helen," said Isabella, "I am entirely outdone by Juanita. I have always made drawing and painting the chief occupations and amusements of the children. They all inherit my taste for it, and I may truly say it has been the solace of my life. I painted the sketch you so much admire, soon after I came here, when my soul hungered and thirsted for my New England home. I did not love palm-trees nor their kind at first — I pined for elms, and oaks, and beeches. If you should turn over my portfolios, you would find many sketches that you would recognize — not the sketches, but the places sketched. But after the children grew older, they painted — not I. Ludovico painted still-life. But Juanita is the genius of painting. She copied my New England sketches over and over again. She taught herself the art with them, and you will find her portfolios full of them. She once made a visit with us in the Mountains of San Salvador, which you can see from here some clear days, and there we commanded beautiful sea-views. Juanita steeped her soul in them, and after our return she painted some views that you will see in another room, which I call my studio, because it has always been my painting-room. You will find the Berkshire Hills quite pale before two views there, upon which she wrought many months. I had quite as lief look at them as at the views themselves. She seemed to add something to nature. She has never talked much, for hers has been a sad and strange history, but we all understand her. Ludovico has always taken great pleasure in teaching her what he knew.

"Indeed, as she hung over the table where he was studying his lessons, her quick perceptions caught everything he did, and it was this readiness to learn which had at first interested him in teaching her. Her brilliancy, her piquant grace, her devotion to his every wish and whim, and his want of other playmates, united them more than was best, perhaps. You have made me question it more than I ever did before.

"I had sometimes questioned the expediency of such an intimate intercourse, but the beauty and loveliness of the child were very great, her position isolated, being the last of her race, always subject to the envy and consequent hatred of the other slaves, and my desire to shield her from contact with them has made me disregard too much, I sometimes think, the fact that she is still a slave. I think they are a little superstitious about her power of taking likenesses, which is very great. They seem to be a little frightened by it, as if it gave her some power over the individuals. She once drew the likeness of Don Fernando and his brother Pepe, at the request of Ludovico, and I have been amused to see them sit and gaze at these drawings as if for the first time they had seen themselves."

"I wonder she had the courage to do it," said Helen.

"She would not have had, if it had been necessary for them to sit to her. I must show you the group of my children which she took several years ago. Our purpose is to give her her freedom; but the taint of African blood would still remain, and if she were free to dispose of herself, all the chances are that she would be led into temptation by the wicked. These pretty, lady-like girls that are brought up with the children are in a terrible position. There is hardly a chance of their keeping their virtue. They do not hesitate to give themselves to a white man if he is kind and attentive. I keep her out of the way of our guests as much as possible. Thus far she is entirely able to take care of herself. She never comes into their company unless I bid her, and I do not believe a stranger ever caught her eye."

"Her reserve is wonderful to behold," replied Helen.

"Yes — her attachment to me and to Ludovico is the absorbing sentiment of her being. Separation from us would be a death-blow to her. The only circumstances that would make her freedom desirable are those of possible removal from the island, and this is but a shadowy possibility, contingent upon Ludovico's future.

"Again, planters are very circumspect about bestowing freedom upon their slaves, because freedom given to one makes others discontented. The race from which Juanita had sprung had been haughty and overbearing, for they knew they were *emancipados*, and a strong hand had always been required to keep them in subjection. The mother and grandmother of Juanita had demanded their freedom as a right, a demand which had been sternly resisted, for its admission might have necessitated its application to many other individuals entitled to it on the same ground, all unwitting as they might be of the fact."

Neither the Marchioness nor Helen knew the secret fire that burned in Juanita's heart. She had carefully guarded the knowledge her mother had imparted. As she grew older and shared in Ludovico's knowledge, and knew what freedom meant, she had lost her vivacity and fallen into a deep melancholy. The Marchioness accounted for it easily on the common principles of human nature, and had often felt that to her ignorance would indeed have been bliss. She now allowed her to occupy herself very much as she pleased. Her tastes were decidedly artistic, and she soon surpassed Ludovico in both execution and conception. She could not only imitate flowers with her brush, but with her needle, and the exquisite decorations of curtains, towelling, table-linen, etc., that made the palace of the Marquis celebrated, were the work and inspiration of her hands, to say nothing of the walls that constantly brought strangers there. It is a national custom to paint the walls both inside and outside of houses, and it is generally the work of the tutors who are hired to teach the children, and these are often cultivated men, but their position in the family is little above that of an upper servant. Juanita's decorations were not so exceptional therefore, except in quality, but that made them sufficiently famous to attract much attention.

While busied in the creation of beauty around her, the smouldering fires of Juanita's inward being were restrained from bursting into flame. Every day the family board was arranged like a work of art. Every flowering vine and tree appeared in its season upon the tables. All was performed in the spirit of a service of love. When not with her mistress, her home was the nursery, where she assisted Mrs. Warwick in the care of the younger children, whose taste she formed unconsciously by the exercise of her own, while the good Mrs. Warwick serenely presided over all, the Marchioness herself included, — for Mrs. Warwick was one of those substantial New England matrons who command every one's respect, and are mothers and nurses by nature, as well as by craft, to all around them.

Helen listened to this strange history with ever increased amazement that her friend should have dared to let the two children risk each other's happiness to such a degree as she felt it to be; for are not all hearts made alike, no matter what the outside semblance or circumstance may be?

"I know what you must think of all this, Helen; but I have never had any serious fears. Ludovico is noble and pure, and so is Juanita. They both know how completely their positions in society forbid anything like marriage between them."

"I cannot share your confidence, dear Isabella; I only hope you are in the right. You sleep on a volcano. May it never burst forth into flame! I rejoice that your splendid gifts bring such resources to yourself and your children."

One afternoon the Marquis invited the family to accompany him to the scene of the "sleeve of wind" that had passed across the island in the last storm, on the memorable night of Pedro's capture. The devastation it had wrought in its path was quite curious to see, and had been much talked of.

It was arranged that the elder ladies should take the volante, with Manuel between them, and the rest of the party go on horseback. The Marquis, after viewing the pathway of the storm, was to leave them to Ludovico's escort, which would be all-sufficient.

Traces of the ravages of the hurricane were visible all the way, in broken limbs of trees and heaps of whirled leaves, but, at the distance of six miles from La Consolacion, it had taken a definite shape, a quarter of a mile in width, and everything had perished in its grasp. The line of hedges looked as if the lightning had scathed them; every leaf was shrivelled and red with the mahogany-colored dust, that seemed to have been the heated instrument of the lightning. Trees seventy feet in height were uprooted, and stood upon their heads. Sugar-cane and coffee-shrubs were laid low. Every vestige of the plantation mansion was swept away. These structures are light, the lignum-vitæ posts being only lathed with cocoa-leaves, and covered with plaster. Not one post was to be seen within fifty yards of the spot. The roof had been lifted first, the inmates raised into the air, as if by suction, and then dropped. The negro quarters were entirely demolished, and fifteen of "the people" had been killed. Outside the path of devastation, everything grew and bloomed as if no besom of heaven had passed that way. Farther on, a royal forest had been traversed by the wind-spout, — if so it might be termed, — and everything it touched had the appearance of being twisted by giant hands. Yet, outside this path, the vines still hung upon the trees, which had been broken on one side and left unscathed on the other.

It was a wondrous spectacle. And its contrasts seemed to Helen analogous to those she had seen in the moral world, in that fairest of climes, — the heart-wringings and despair of one class, the fiestas and gayeties that rang their fairy-bells within hearing by the other. Forever associated in her mind would be the howlings of the pitiless storm and the raging passions and terrors of that night of horrors. The young people prattled of the tempest, but Helen and the Marchioness had no words for the external sign; and, when they rode away from the scene, "the poor man in the hospital," as little José called him, — for he was Pedro only to Helen, — was the topic of their conversation, and not the storm.

As they passed a stately gateway that stood open, a loose horse rushed by them, and Tulita's pony, excited and startled, dashed up the avenue with headlong speed. The Marquis had parted from them half an hour before, and Ludovico was the only gentleman in attendance. He followed Tulita, as did Carolina and the rest, and found her lying on the ground, close to a house that stood at the extremity of the avenue, and the pony gone, no one knew where.

Tulita's ankle was sprained, and she was carefully lifted from the ground by Ludovico and the fine, Jewess-looking lady Helen had seen at the village balls, and laid upon a couch on the piazza.

The Marchioness was faint with alarm when she stepped out of her volante; but Tulita was apparently not much hurt, and every attention was paid to the party by the lady and her beautiful daughter. A physician was immediately summoned from a neighboring village, but the hostess had bathed and soothed the sprained ankle with so much skill that when he came he pronounced it all the treatment that was needed.

An urgent invitation was given to the party to stay all night, but the Marchioness, when she declined, said her young friend was a guest of the Countess of Lopez, who resided on the very next plantation, and she would restore Tulita to her care rather than remove her so far as her own residence.

Ludovico said he would notify the Countess at once, and sprang upon his horse to do the errand. Before the Marchioness was aware, Carolina had done the same and sped after him. It was too good an opportunity to be lost, and she had now gained her point, which was to see the far-famed estate of *La Maripoosa*.

They soon returned with the Countess and a light hammock, on which Tulita was carefully placed and carried to *la Maripoosa* by four athletic men, who kept step so skilfully that she was scarcely jarred. Helen remarked the care, and when Tulita was asked if she was pained, she replied, "Not much," and, in a moment, added, "These are some of the bozals that I nursed with my own hand before they were sold. They have been so good to me since I have been here! Good-bye! good-bye!" and Tulita kissed her hands to her friends with tearful eyes.

Helen inquired of Isabella before they retired who those fine-looking ladies were whom they had by constraint visited that day.

"Are they Jewesses?"

"No, my dear Helen; they are the freed slaves of a wealthy man who died when his daughter was still a child, and left her and her mother all his riches. You saw them at the village balls. Strange to say, they always go there, evidently hoping to be noticed; but they are never spoken to. The young cavaliers who spend the holidays in the country visit them in their beautiful home, but never speak to them or recognize them elsewhere. That is the way with Spaniards. They often visit in the country families they do not recognize in the city, and even this one is not exempt from their meanness. Some men are too gentlemanly to do it, but the Countess of Lopez' visitors are of a class that will do anything to amuse themselves. I have seen that young girl grow more and more melancholy as she came to the balls year after year. She is exceptionally well educated (but what do Spaniards care for that?), and all the diamonds of the House of Almonte will not purchase her an honorable alliance; and it is said her mother's ambition runs high."

"I hope they will both die of broken hearts before they will accept anything lower," said Helen.

"I hope so too, but I fear they will not. A suspicion of negro blood in women who are apparently equal in manners and education to any of us, will prevent marriage. This mother was one of those beautiful girls brought up in the house to wait upon the children, and, ever after the death of the old Marquis of Almonte, she presided at the son's table, and was in every way treated as his wife, except that he did not marry her. He never was married at all, but was very much attached to her, and left all his riches to her and her daughter. But the young girl can have no respectable pride, or she would not expose herself to this public neglect from those whom she is weak enough to receive as guests at home."

"What a strange state of things!" said Helen.

"Yes," said her friend, "society here cannot be easily understood."

CHAPTER XXIV.

THE FLIGHT.

Dolores was better as soon as she became an inmate of the hospital. Her strange condition had ceased to command attention, her "fits" recurring often, and also the subsequent prostration inevitably following them.

A little fellow, eight years old, belonging to Don Ermite, had been left to take care of Pedro, and through him she let Pedro know that she was near him. Don Andres winked at the messages and magic words that were borne back and forth by José, and at the oranges and bits of bread he often saw transferred from one apartment to the other, for in the hospital the men and women had separate rooms. Bread is an article unknown to the slave on the plantations, unless a kind mistress sends it to the hospital, and it ranks in his estimation very much as plum-cake does with our little boys and girls, not to say with some older children.

José had always been silent and moping in the presence of his master. He filled the office of personal attendant to him, and endeavored by devotion to his duty to avoid punishment, but Don

Ermite's bad temper was often wreaked upon him. When his master was absent in the field, José would fill the air with his melody, and the character of his songs was so peculiar that he was very attractive to the family. He sang songs of the most sentimental character, Spanish and Italian, and, when asked where he learned them, always replied "the niñas sang so." Who "the niñas" were no one could ever discover. After Pedro was left in his care, he refused to come and sit on the steps of the piazza to sing, always giving as excuse "sing to poor man in the hospital"; and when not in attendance upon the poor sufferer, he would sit outside, under his window, and sing his sweet songs. No doubt, they soothed the wretched man, for José's voice was sweetly wild and pathetic to the most refined ears. He varied the Spanish and Italian songs with hummings of his own, that were like the warblings of birds, and it seemed as if he broke out into words when his own wild notes happened to touch some key that brought them to mind. Manuel never let him want for good things for himself or his patient, and José had been a happy little boy since his master had finally left the plantation.

But the summons came at last. One day a cart was sent for Pedro and José. One of the brothers of Don Ermite, who had been sent back penniless to the mountains by Don Alfonso, came with it, and gruffly demanded the property of his brother.

Pedro was laid upon some straw in the bottom of the cart, and José, weeping aloud in evident terror, was placed at his feet, and they were driven away. There was not a heart unmoved upon the plantation.

Ludovico entreated his father to buy the man, and the Marquis would have been glad to do it, to gratify him, but for his troublesome neighbor, who might have made it an excuse for farther persecution. Dolores again rent the air with her cries, and Pope Urban held her as she raged and foamed at the mouth.

The next morning, two of the swiftest horses, and Urbano and Dolores had disappeared. The country was scoured in pursuit. The horses were found loose in the road at twenty miles distance, but no trace of the fugitives. No bozal could have done it, but Urbano knew the way, and it was not difficult to hide in the tangled woods that were frequent in the king's public ways, the districts being in the form of circles, in which the plantations are located, and the gores of land, as they are called, belonging to the crown, filled with timber of the rankest growth.

Don Andres was obliged to conduct the pursuit, but he assured Helen afterwards that he let slip no blood-hounds in the chase. His dogs never hurt any one. Dolores and Urbano were never seen again, and Helen hoped the Pope found means to rescue or buy his young chief. He had doubtless laid by money enough, and there was no danger that the peasantry would betray him, for they were incensed with the Marquis, for his supposed neglect of one of their class, who had suffered in his service.

The negroes conceal it by burying it in the ground, and the floor of Urbano's cabin showed evident signs of having been well dug over, as if it had contained hidden treasures.

Helen longed to tell Isabella the story of these poor lovers, but she feared to do so, lest the Marquis might think her to blame for not imparting the knowledge before, however unjust it might be for him to do so. As she had taken no part in their flight, her conscience was wholly at rest, and by her silence she would certainly avoid the possibility of implicating Don Andres, who was as innocent as herself. She therefore allowed the vain conjectures of others as to the connection between Pedro and the two who had fled, to exhaust themselves, as they were sure to do in time.

CHAPTER XXV.

SEWING.

THE time had now arrived when the scanty but extensive wardrobe of the 150 slaves must be attended to, and Mrs. Warwick and Helen insisted that Isabella should not incur the fatigue in her present state of health. Helen therefore assumed the care of the work, assisted by Mrs. Warwick, and it gave her much opportunity for observation of "the people." The field women assembled every morning for several hours to sew upon the piazza, and the new hands were to be trained to the use of the needle. Some of them took hold of it readily, and as if not unskilled in a more delicate use of the fingers than the handling of the weeding knife, while others found it very difficult. Don Andres presided over the whole with admirable tact, not ostensibly, but with a sort of omnipresence that checked any insubordination or idleness, and this made Helen's task more easy. It had always been an occasion when the Marchioness gained much moral power on the plantation, simply by not exacting more than was reasonable from these uncultured creatures. All were cleanly washed, and those who owned any garment but the inevitable duck chemise drawn over the breast with a string arrayed themselves in it for the sewing hours. The decoration might be only a colored handkerchief for the head, a scarf round the neck, or ear-rings bought from the pedlers, who are encouraged to come upon the plantations to keep down the possible funds the slaves may accumulate for the purchase of their freedom; of which there are instances of success in the better class of household slaves. These are dressed in more respectable garments than the field hands, and the privilege is made the most of, creating quite a difference of caste.

The Marchioness assumed the care of the children, in the nursery, with Juanita's help. She was obliged to recline upon the sofa, and the daily studies were partially remitted. Juanita had long been engaged in embroidering the wedding-dress for Carolina, who had chosen the design, and well knew the superiority of Juanita's handiwork. Patiently and sadly she wrought day after day, weaving her poor heart into the hated garment. Isabella, who watched her with painful interest, and felt self-reproached that her kindness to the girl had taken the form that it had, willingly interrupted her often for the amusement of the children, and Carlito and Manuel seemed to divine Isabella's condition. One morning Juanita was needed to assist a young field hand to hold her needle, and unwittingly took her embroidery in her hand when she was called out. It was the waist of the dress, a delicate fabric of gossamer linen, a marvel of beautiful workmanship, nearly completed.

Mumma Camilla was the chronic torment of the sewing-women at these seasons. Their presence operated like an elixir upon her every day. She often moved them about to sweep around them when she thought too much litter of scraps and thread ends had accumulated to look picturesque, and if they dropped a needle or a thimble, she would run to the spot to help seek it, and it would be sure never to reappear. The defiant looks of the women who were sometimes suspected of thus securing to themselves a few moments of leisure, only stimulated her troublesome activity.

When Juanita turned to the chair on which she had laid her work for a few moments, it was gone. She was betrayed into an expression of dismay that attracted Helen's attention. An immediate bustle ensued. Mumma Camilla was the busiest of the hunters. Every woman was turned and shaken. Every chair was moved. Some of the women cried for fear of being suspected; others looked angry, but dared not speak if they knew what had become of it. Camilla whirled round the poor bozal who had been the object of Juanita's sympathy, till she was perfectly dizzy, Camilla the while filling the air with her vociferations.

"Dress of the niña gone! wedding-dress of the

niña! Much work — many days work — poor Juanita! thieving bozals — sell such work to the pedlers! enough money to buy liberty —" and she laughed her bitter laugh.

"Yes, my lady," she went on, "let me search her — who else could have taken it? — perhaps she passed it — much cunning — bozals play ball with the mud — pass them along — much cunning — I must search them all —" and, passing rapidly about, she twitched away their work, thrust her hands into their bosoms, and the more dismay the better she liked it."

Don Andres, who stood upon the piazza, at the moment, seeing an unusual commotion, in his clear and commanding voice silenced the tumult at once, and soon they were again seated, Camilla, however, voluble as ever, describing to him the accident and its probable effect on poor Juanita, who had resigned the search at once when Mumma Camilla assumed it.

It was too good an opportunity for Camilla to lose in convincing the large public before whom she performed that Juanita was one of them.

"Poor Juanita!" she suddenly exclaimed, as if a new thought struck her. "So much work! so tiresome! eyes ache! back ache! fine stitches, many stitches — poor Juanita — Ave, sanctissima — do not punish her — much tired — too many stitches — pardon for Juanita — young people foolish — young people do not think; work towels, work curtains, work forever — too many stitches, poor Juanita."

"Madama," said Don Andres, to Helen, in answer to this tirade, "has this old woman been searched?"

"I searched! I'm the seeker! I searched!" screamed Camilla. "Who'll search me? Poor Juanita. I searched all — moved the chairs — shook the women. I searched," and she laughed defiantly.

"It is not on mumma Camilla," said Juanita, deprecatingly, for she knew the old thing too well to suppose it would be found upon her person, and she feared the consequences of the accusation to herself.

"On mumma Camilla? no, indeed! on me, indeed! Poor Juanita! don't punish her."

"Solidad!" said Don Andres, in a loud, clear voice, "come and search this old woman."

"Ay de mi! La Señora! — ave, sanctissima! — do not let her touch me."

"It is but fair, Camilla," said Helen.

"Go on, Solidad," said Don Andres.

Camilla looked defiant, and Solidad looked timid, but Don Andres approached a few steps nearer, and fixed his eye upon the former, motioning with his head to Solidad to proceed. The search, which Camilla saw it was not best to resist, was fruitless. Camilla was too cunning for that. When it was over, she laughed, more like a hyena than like a human being, and darted into her pantry to conceal her rage, carrying her displaced head-handkerchief in her hand.

"There, Miss Wentworth," said Carolina, in English, "you see she had not got it. I have no doubt she was in the right, and that Juanita has hidden it, because she was tired of it."

Both Helen and Mrs. Warwick protested against this, and endeavored to signify to her that Juanita might hear her; but Carolina, much excited, went on : —

"That girl is more cunning than you think. She takes you all in. I do not care if she does hear me."

Juanita had heard, and walked away, disdaining to reply.

As soon as the women had gone to their cabins and other work, Camilla called her washers, and for a second time that day the gallery was flooded with water, a running soliloquy of the old woman varying the scene.

"Ave, sanctissima! much women, much bad air! poor Juanita! — too many stitches! — Ay de mi! searching me! who else to look for things? Poor Juanita! tired, no wonder — much sewing, much tired. Ah! la Marquesa! not yet — not dry yet! lazy people! wipe the floor! more dry cloths! Canailla! no head! la Marquesa wants air — dry here, mi alma!" Whirls a long settee across the gallery.

"I will walk on the other side a few moments," said the Marchioness.

"Too much sun, lady! headache!"—runs round with a chair.

"I do not wish for a chair, Camilla; keep at your work."

"Yes, yes, lady! soon dry—dry now." Whirls the settee back again.

"Camilla, let the settees alone; you will break them all to pieces."

When the Marchioness sat down, Carolina came to relate her grievances, and to accuse Juanita.

"You do not know that wicked old woman, Carolina. She has often done such things before. No juggler has more sleight-of-hand, and we shall probably never see it again, at least until the occasion for which it was worked has passed, and then it may reappear. The reappearance of things is often as mysterious as their disappearance. Juanita is wholly incapable of any such act."

Camilla, who had retired a moment to her pantry, to readjust her turban and put on dry shoes, hearing voices, peeped out, and soon emerged with her duster.

The Marchioness, who was very willing that she should know her opinion of her, went on.

"One day she broke a guardabrisa while dusting the buffet. It was a very valuable one, of cut-glass, and could not be replaced here. I expressed a great deal of regret and vexation at her carelessness. I was not wise, for a few days afterward the mate to it disappeared. I accused her of having broken it; but she denied it vehemently, invoking all the saints. I let it pass as I could not help myself. If I had let her be punished, it would not have restored the vase. I only begged her to hunt for it, which she often assured me that she had done, but that it must have been hidden away and sold secretly to some pedler. Camilla, you have dusted everything now — do not make any more noise. I am wearied, and wish to rest — go now!"

Camilla disappeared down the steps. After a little while she came upon the gallery again from outside the house, half covered with a shawl, and evidently carrying something. Suddenly she stood before the Marchioness, and held out the guardabrisa, safe and sound.

"There it is, my lady — hidden away — hidden away; but I have found it! Much cunning — but I'm too much for them." She laughed sardonically.

"I am very glad to see it again," said the Marchioness, quietly. "I have no doubt you hid it yourself two years ago; put it on the buffet."

"Ave, sanctissima! hid it myself! no, indeed! hunted everywhere — but I have found it!"

"Where did you find it?"

"Ay de mi! I would not tell — much punishment, poor thing."

"Go now," said the Marchioness, "and do not come back till dinner time."

Camilla slowly retired, somewhat crestfallen.

"You see, my dear, that she understands English. Her wits do sometimes betray her. It was not a lucky moment in which to bring it back." She did not go on to say that she presumed Camilla was trying to involve Juanita. She thought it probable she would hardly have dared to play the trick she had played upon Juanita that morning, if she had been present, and this last she did say.

"I am afraid you must forego the beautiful waist; there will not be time to work another, but the rest of the dress is finished, and a pretty bertha of lace will cover a plainer waist."

"Can she not work another, if not quite so much?" said Carolina, pettishly. Her pity was all for herself, not for Juanita.

"Even Camilla thought there were too many stitches," said Helen, playfully, hoping to disarm Carolina's selfishness.

"I have no doubt the old thing was in the right about one thing," persisted Carolina.

The Marchioness rose from her reclining posture, and said she would lie down alone until dinner, and, pale and exhausted, she left the gallery.

"You will look quite as well to me without the worked dress as with it," said Ludovico, who now appeared and heard the whole story from Carolina.

He keenly felt her selfishness, and was almost indignant in Juanita's behalf; but he contented himself with expressing his dissent.

"Let us have a little music, now," he said, wishing to change the subject.

"No, I do not feel like it," said Carolina, and she walked into the house and closed the door of her apartment with a clap that thrilled upon Ludovico's nerves.

"I wonder where the old woman could have put the work?" said Ludovico; "where was Juanita?"

"She stood near that door," said Helen, "and laid her work upon that chair. It is astonishing how suddenly it disappeared."

Ludovico turned the chair over. It had a leather seat. There was a slit in the leather at the back of the seat.

"I wonder if she could have tucked it in there," he said. He took a penknife from his pocket, and thrust it in, and drew out the identical bit of fine linen.

"Mumma Camilla!" said Ludovico to that functionary, who just then appeared at the door of her pantry; "I have found the place where you hid Juanita's work,— are you not ashamed of yourself?"

"Ah, pupil of my eye! I hid it!"—laughs. "Ave, sanctissima, not I!—it was very easy to hide it—poor Juanita! many stitches—do not punish her — young people foolish! Ave, sanctissima!"

"Nothing was easier than for you to tuck it in there. Miss Wentworth says that was the chair Juanita laid the work upon. It is you who ought to be punished! It must have been you that hid it — we all know you very well. It is not the first time."

Camilla let her long ape-like arms fall at her side, then covered her face with her shawl, and fell into a fit of violent weeping, as she moved slowly away, and the more willingly as she heard the Marquis ascending the steps.

"I wish that hateful thing was not in the house," said Ludovico.

"I wish so, too; but your mother could not do without her, in her present state of health," said Helen, who was very willing to call Ludovico's attention to his mother's condition.

"Where is mama?" inquired Ludovico, as if struck with a sudden thought.

"She went to lie down by herself till dinner-time, she was so pained by Camilla's behavior."

Ludovico, however, softly opened his mother's door, which led from the hall, and Helen hoped the interview would be a soothing one. If he had known how much she had been pained by Carolina, perhaps he would not have ventured upon one; but they spoke only of Juanita and Camilla, and the mother had a few moments of happiness in her son's affectionate caress. He restored the work to Juanita in the nursery, and she, too, was made momentarily happy by his kind manner.

At the Marchioness' request, nothing was said upon the subject at dinner, which Camilla served with swollen and downcast eyes, and a look of injured innocence. The jet black of her complexion prevented her from looking pale, as she would undoubtedly have liked to do, but it was amazing to see what a look of injured innocence she could put on. Indeed, there was no character which her genius could not assume.

When the women had gone from the piazza, the little naked plantation children came skipping across it where they had been sitting, just as a swarm of ants gathered upon a fruit skin that might have been left upon the floor.

"These children," said Mrs. Warwick, "are sure to pick up every stray knot of thread or dropped needle or end of tape, after the sewing is over."

"Why should not they be taught to sew?" said Helen, to whom this remark was addressed. "I should like to teach them myself."

"Ah, miss, it would be of no use to try," said Mrs. Warwick. "I tried it thoroughly, when I first came here, though the Marchioness told me I should not succeed, — that they would like it very much at first, but they would soon get tired of it, and begin to lose their needles. I was so bent upon it, however, that she let me try, and the French overseer, who was a kind-hearted man, let me collect them together on the piazza of his pavilion. I went to the village and bought fifty thimbles, and fairly went to work; but it was just as the Marchioness said, — they did not like to be confined long enough to do anything, and, as I could not talk to them, the overseer said there was no way but to whip them into it. That was enough for me, so I gave it up in despair."

"But I can talk to them," said Miss Wentworth, "and I never yet saw the children that I could not manage by telling them stories. I had a class in the African Sunday-school in S——, when I was only twelve years old, and I found the children very bright and teachable even then, and still more when I was older and could talk to them better."

"But the children here don't know enough to hitch anything to," said Mrs. Warwick.

"I would like to try, nevertheless," persisted Helen.

"I suppose you can, if you wish to, and it would be a good thing, and some of the children are very docile, but they are all as wild as little animals. I tried my best to make them wear some garment, and the Marchioness tried that, too, finding how disagreeable it was to me to see them running about naked; but it would not be an hour before the clothes would be tucked under a bush, or hidden somewhere else. They found it much more comfortable to be naked in this hot climate, and you could not get the first idea into their heads of any reason why they should wear them. If any of them are going to the village to be baptized, they are willing enough to dress up in all the finery their mothers can find for them; and it is a pretty sight to see them then."

"What idea have they about the baptism, do you think?"

"Oh, none whatever, except that if they die they can then be buried in holy ground, and that is everything to a Catholic."

"But they cannot be called Catholics."

"Oh, no, not with any meaning, but it is something the white people do."

Helen used to carry flowers into her Sunday-school at home, and show pictures to the children, and she could imagine many ways in which she might interest these; but the Marchioness was too ill to be consulted about it, and her conferences with Don Andres had been necessarily checked.

"Honi soit qui mal y pense."

CHAPTER XXVI.

DECEPTION.

THE next day, Carolina proposed a ride on horseback with Ludovico. The Marchioness had feared she would propose calling upon Tulita, and had sent to inquire for her health in the morning, that there might be no excuse for doing so. Tulita was doing well, and begged to see them; but Isabella did not think it necessary to repeat the invitation in the family circle.

It was late before the riders returned. They had visited many beautiful plantations, the gates of which are always opened to riders, even when they are strangers. They did not speak of seeing any one in their ride.

But Ludovico was not happy this evening. At nine o'clock the family assembled round a little tea-table, in honor of American customs, for tea-drinking is unknown to the Spaniards, who do not eat in the evening, the Spanish dining hour being late in the day; and when guests were present, they were much amused with this evening meal, which was always light. It had been instituted since Helen's arrival, wholly in her honor. Ludovico would fain have declined to sit down with the rest of the party, but Carolina insisted. Helen had little doubt that they had been on forbidden ground, because of their unusual silence, and a little excitement in Carolina's manner confirmed her suspicions. She rattled away more recklessly even than usual at the evening meal.

Helen was right. Carolina had insisted upon accepting the Countess' urgent invitation, given the morning before, while she sat upon her horse at her door, and on her way home she had rallied Ludovico for his gravity, and defied him to tell his mother. It was the first time any one had come between him and his beloved parent, or turned him aside from his life-long allegiance to her. But the serpent had fascinated him, and more than once the baleful influence overcame him.

He had turned his face from his mother and from truth. His descent was rapid. His mother felt it deeply, and her heart sank within her. But she did not suspect the whole truth; she had no suspicion that he would so far forget what was due to Carolina's position. If Ludovico had been a girl, he would have known the impropriety of the step; but, as it was, and as he had seen no sisters trained, and had had no young relatives to be restrained, it must be said in his favor that he did not know the full extent of the indiscretion. If he had persisted in being frank about the first visit, as he wished to be, the indiscretion could easily have been forgiven, and his mother would have had an opportunity of giving him such instructions as might have been a safeguard in future.

"It is the first step that costs." And the saddest misfortune to youth is, not to be found out in these first downward steps.

But "murder will out."

One morning, among other guests who frequented the attractive circle at La Consolacion, arrived Tulita with her father, accompanied by the young Count of Carova.

If the earth had opened under Ludovico's feet, he could not have been more dismayed than when Carova greeted Carolina familiarly, evidently not a stranger.

The Marchioness was sufficiently chagrined to see Don Miguel, who did not often profane her threshold. Her blood always chilled at the sight of him, and she was in the habit of going to see the daughter of her mother's friend only during his absence on the slave-coast, purposely to avoid him. But when she saw the evidence that Ludovico and Carolina had frequented the Countess of Lopez' mansion, — for Carolina's confusion, as well as the young man's manner, were as plainly to be read as words, — her cheeks blanched, and it was only by a superhuman effort that she commanded herself.

The mother's solicitude for her child's reputation acted quick as thought, and, in her endeavor to recover herself, she welcomed Don Miguel more cordially than she would otherwise have done. This put him quite at ease, and the light jest went round, the Spanish suavity of the company dissolved all private sentiments in a mellifluous flow of nothings; and it was not till the last sonorous farewell was sounded from the volantes, and responded to from the steps of the piazza, that Isabella fell heavily upon the marble floor.

"Mama, I have killed you!" burst from Ludovico, in a wild cry that curdled every one's blood.

He lifted her from the floor and bore her in his arms into her own apartment. All was terror and astonishment among the servants. The others knew well enough what it all meant. When Isabella, under the care of Helen and Mrs. Warwick, opened her eyes again, Ludovico bowed his head upon her hand, and, with bitter weeping, begged her forgiveness.

"Come, Carolina," he said to the partner of his deception, "come and beg mama's pardon too."

Carolina, who stood a little apart, pale and trembling, approached, and, bursting into tears, sank down by Ludovico's side. She was thoroughly frightened. Yet she could see no reason for such serious apprehensions. She was too ignorant to know of the worldly consequences that might possibly ensue from what she had tempted Ludovico to do, and it never occurred to her that her aunt suffered from the loss of her son's confidence, or from his defection from truth; for she had not had the sentiment or the principle cultivated. She had had no home, no mother to watch over her young life. A fashionable boarding-school is no nursery of the virtues. Truth of character especially, which must be so carefully guarded and often so carefully instilled into the young, is frequently destroyed by that fearful ordeal. Carolina had been through all stages of experience in her boarding-school life, from the time when she was made the instrument of the older girls to obtain hidden pleasures, and to take cake and sweetmeats, up to that when she was old enough to carry notes, and to take them from the post-office under false names. She was always favored by teachers, for she was wealthy and pretty and piquant, quick to learn her appointed lessons, and ambitious of distinction even in the school. This was the first time an act of her own had frightened her. Fainting, or any semblance of death, always alarmed her, and she was ready to promise anything now.

Ludovico believed all her protestations, and accepted all her excuses. He had not opposed her with sufficient earnestness to make any moral impression, and he took all the blame of the impropriety of the step upon himself. His mother was satisfied with his repentance, but she felt the shallowness of Carolina's, and grieved that his fate was to be clouded by such a companionship. Indeed she could not be consoled.

The Marquis did not share her apprehensions. His displeasure was expressed in no measured terms that Ludovico should so far violate the customs of society as to take an unmarried lady to make a call at any house, but he did not feel the moral separation from his son which had paled the cheek and made heavy the heart of Isabella. Indeed he had feared that Ludovico would be estranged from Cuban life too much. The alliance was too valuable a one to be lightly given up, and Isabella felt that she must henceforth sorrow alone. Helen alone estimated the significance of the wasting form and failing step. In that climate all processes of nature are rapid — that of decay as well as that of growth.

Meantime, the preparations for the wedding were rapidly progressing. Carolina was wholly absorbed in the thought of her trousseau, and of the gay life she was to lead in the city during the summer rains, which would be so dismal in the country. The plan was to take possession of her own house for a few weeks, receive the attentions of her neighbors, and then make the desired visit. The seasons are so imperative in that climate that delay would derange all their plans, and Isabella would not suggest any modification of them on her own account, except that she was unable to make of the occasion a fiesta such as is usual on marriage days with the pleasure-loving Spaniards, who make a holiday of every saint's day in the calendar, and intensify the feast whenever there is an apology for so doing.

She was also unable to continue the dissipated life she had led during the winter, and, as Carolina could not go out alone, she was obliged to be contented with the ordinary amusements of home. La Consolacion was still the resort of all the families that remained in the neighborhood, and domestic dances, tableaux, drives, and arrivals of goods from the city for the bride's trousseau, occupied the time of the young people.

CHAPTER XXVII.

CONSEQUENCES.

The wedding shall pass undescribed. It was a private one, owing to the Marchioness' state of health, and the young people went to their splendid abode.

Carolina was a married woman now, and no longer needed, she thought, protection in the eye of the world. The Marchioness saw that she needed it more than ever, and so did Ludovico.

Why should not the Countess of Lopez make early calls upon the new married couple? She must have known that the visits Carolina and Ludovico had made upon Tulita were unsanctioned visits. She had not been invited to repeat hers to the Marchioness, and even the visit of her young friend had brought no interchange of courtesies. It was a feather in the Countess' cap to have a call from Ludovico, for the Rodriguez were people of character, and the Countess knew that she had no claim to that distinction. There was no doubt that she would make the best of her opportunity to get back so far into the society from which she knew suspicion had partially banished her. In spite of the horror of this suspicion, the Marchioness shrunk from her less as a murderer than as a corrupter of the morals of the young. But Carolina was exceedingly tenacious of her own prerogative, and to every gentle remonstrance or word of warning tossed her pretty head, and replied, "I am a married woman now."

For ten days, Carolina was overwhelmed with visitors and invitations. Fiestas occupied every evening. The Marchioness attended a few of these, but every day she became more feeble, and at the end of the second week she failed so rapidly that every one was alarmed. Ludovico rode over every morning to inquire for her, but Carolina's nights were turned into days, and therefore her days were turned into nights.

The Marquis wilfully shut his eyes to his wife's condition. He would not, could not see it. He too was anxious for his son, and for the reputation of his son's wife, as he saw them mingle in society that he had never cultivated. If they had remained in the family mansion, he might have controlled their movements in a degree, but Carolina had resisted his urgent invitation to do so. He did not mean to die about it, however, and he would not think that Isabella would do so.

Helen meant to have returned home soon after the wedding, for it was important to go sufficiently early in the season to avoid the yellow fever, which infests vessels after the month of May. But she would not leave her friend so ill, for any selfish reasons.

One evening, as Isabella reclined upon her couch on the piazza, for in that climate invalids are not condemned to the close and darkened chamber, she suddenly exclaimed to Helen: —

"Will you take my little girls home with you? Manuel must stay with his father."

"Isabella, my darling!"

"I am sorry I am so weak, but I cannot bear it. She has killed me, dear. Where is Hernando? I I cannot see you, Helen!"

Helen's heart stopped beating. Isabella's weakness had increased rapidly within a few days, but she had not anticipated this sudden summons.

Juanita sat at the window of the inner apartment. Helen pronounced her name, and pointed to the door of the Marquis' apartment.

Juanita had heard Isabella's remark, and flew to open it, for she understood the look, but she could not speak.

"What is the matter?" said the Marquis, rushing by her, for Juanita's agony was in her face.

"Hernando, dearest," said Isabella, opening her eyes as he knelt by her couch, and she made a last effort and threw both arms around his neck.

The next moment they fell, and all was over. The poor Marquis remained upon his knees, his gaze riveted on Isabella's face. Not a sound escaped him. Juanita fled with a piercing cry into the nursery, from which Mrs. Warwick and the children burst with frantic weeping. All was confusion and terror, but the Marquis still gazed, and as he gazed, the wan, faded look on the once beautiful face passed away and a celestial smile took its place. Still he gazed, and gradually all were affected by the spell of his silence; the children nestled close to him, and he threw his arms around them, but still gazed upon the wonderful spectacle before him. They were all hushed at last by this statue-like gaze, for she seemed only sleeping. At last he suddenly swayed over and laid prostrate on the floor. The terrified children were gathered into the arms of Helen and Mrs. Warwick, the stricken man was lifted up and carried to his own apartment, to which Manuel followed him with piercing screams.

"See how beautiful mama is now she is an angel!" said Helen to little Pepita, who had buried her face in her bosom, for she felt that this moment was the one in which to take away the fearful impression of death.

"May I kiss mama, nurse?" sobbed Luisa.

"Yes, darling; you know how she loved you," said Helen, for Mrs. Warwick was speechless.

"And I too," said dear little Pepita, bending over; "she loved me too. Oh, what shall I do without mama? mama! mama!" shrieked the poor child.

"Mama will take care of you still — she will be

always with you, darling, though you cannot see her. She is an angel now and cannot open her earthly eyes any more, but see how she smiles upon us. She is very happy with God. One of these days you will go to her."

"Oh, I want to go now! mama! mama! I must go now," said Luisa. "I am afraid to stay here without mama!"

"What! and leave dear papa?"

"Oh, where is papa?" said Pepita. "I must go to papa!" and she struggled out of Helen's arms and ran to his room. "But first I must kiss mama again!" and she ran back.

Helen followed her into the Marquis' apartment, the door of which stood open, and lifted her upon the bed. Manuel was nestled close to his father, with his face hidden, his little form in a convulsion of sorrow. Little Pepita, the Marquis' favorite, was drawn to the other side, and Helen left them together and returned to Luisa, for she felt sure there could be no ministration as sweet as theirs.

Gradually she soothed Luisa, whose passionate nature made sorrow dangerous, and whose vivid imagination needed to be led into pleasant pastures and by living waters.

Ludovico came. His pale, haggard face startled Helen.

"It is I — I killed her. Mother! mother!" and he knelt down and laid his head on the bosom that had so loved him.

Luisa burst into a fresh paroxysm of grief, and Helen forcibly drew her away, that the poor boy might have no witness to his anguish. And she kept others away yet a little while from both apartments, for she judged even herself, near and dear as they were to her, an intruder upon the sacredness of that sorrow. Luisa wandered in to her father, who, when all were gone but his own, rose to look again upon the celestial countenance of his beloved wife. Its radiant, heavenly calm, soothed them all at last. Was it not the conscious spirit that illuminated the form at will? The heart answers the question in the affirmative, surely.

Helen found Juanita prostrate upon her own little bed, and with a despairing look on her beautiful features, that went to her very heart. She had lost her friend and protectress. Helen in vain tried to rouse her. The wailings of the other servants, whose grief was sincere perhaps, but superficial, were less piteous than the silent despair of this poor child of the sun. Her devotion to the Marchioness had been wholly self-forgetting. She had never left her at night since her strength had begun to fail, but, whoever else might watch, she had insisted upon sleeping on the floor, and was always awake to serve her. Helen was sure that she had shared her apprehensions of the final result, but presumed she was as much shocked as herself at the suddenness of the death.

She wound her arms round the poor girl and whispered : —

"If I take — the — little — girls with me, perhaps you can go with me too."

Juanita started and returned her caress gently, then fell back with a low cry, and tears burst from her closed eyelids. Helen was glad to see them flow, and, laying her head by Juanita's, she gave way at last to her own sorrow.

But that low cry which was wrung from Juanita's heart, haunted her long after, for it meant much that only Helen suspected. She looked upon the slave as a being endowed with affections like her own, and she had suffered enough in her own right to carry the touchstone of the hidden woes of others.

Helen found ample occupation in her care of the bereaved children, who became very dependent upon her cheerfulness for power to bear this great sorrow.

CHAPTER XXVIII.

REPENTANCE.

"Dear Miss Wentworth, will you go to Carolina, and stay with her till I come to-morrow?" pleaded Ludovico, when the motherless children were all soothed to sleep. "Mrs. Warwick will take care of the children, and I wish to stay here to-night — I cannot leave papa. Will you go?"

"Certainly I will. Shall I go now?"

"The volante is ready, and I prefer that Carolina should not come over here to-night. Papa could not see her. He can scarcely bear to see me."

Helen lost no time in preventing the possibility of Carolina's arrival.

She found her in the midst of gay company, who were only awaiting the arrival of her husband to take their leave, as it was hardly courteous to leave her alone, and he had apologized for absenting himself in order to inquire for his mother. Carolina was always terrified by the word death. She had never set her own house in order, in reference to that event. Her half-Catholic, half-Protestant education — for the former mode of faith had been kept up by request during her school life — had resulted in a confused mingling of ideas upon the subject, both of this life and the future one.

She was therefore glad to see Helen, and to be released from joining her husband, though Helen was no special favorite of hers. Helen told her all she needed to know, but she thought it best to leave Ludovico to give his own account of his mother's rapid decline.

Juanita had begged permission to pass the night in the apartment of her beloved mistress. It was late when she was left to her watch, and Ludovico did not know of the arrangement. After bidding his father good-night at his own bedside, he stole back to weep once more in solitude over that beloved form.

In the bitterness of the experience through which he had passed, Ludovico had learned to feel a new sympathy for his mother. Before his love and marriage, his life had passed in a happy unconsciousness of any want of harmony in her domestic relations; but, when he looked at the ashes of his own hopes and dreams, he became sensitive to the relations of others. The fearful features of slavery that had transpired to Miss Wentworth had made him feel that there was no one to whom his mother could fully unbosom herself; and he often had longed to tell her of all his disappointments and regrets, and to assure her that she could confide in him without fear of hurting his feelings, as she might be doing to those of her husband. But the occasion had been neglected, and he could only say to himself, "Too late! too late!"

When a son ceases to be in the attitude of a child who must be reproved, if need be, his intercourse with his mother gradually becomes signally like that of a lover, with only this difference, that the confidence is more unwavering — that, whatever may be the mood of the moment, or the apparent neglect growing out of the very assurance of love, no suspicion of love's alteration occurs; whereas, between lovers, even after marriage, there is always a sensitiveness in each party lest the other, just in proportion as his or her ideal becomes more fair, may see a discrepancy or want. Conjugal love needs to be fed continually by sweet assurance of appreciation, but the parental and filial sentiments are based upon a life-long knowledge, and identity of fibre which precludes all fear. Ludovico had left his mother's side to cleave to that of his wife, and in that natural act there was no implication of want of affection; but, in this instance, all sympathy with the wife had long ceased, and he often had left his mother's side with regret. In this terrible moment, he felt that she might not have understood his reticence, which was purely for her sake, and that she might have supposed his heart was in the gay and reckless career which his wife led him. He could only ejaculate to himself: "She knows me now! she knows me now! She must see me, know me, but would to God I were sure of it!" He was unaware that there was any other person present when he threw himself into the boutacle which his mother always occupied in that room.

When his first paroxysm of bitter weeping had subsided, he heard a suppressed breathing that made him start from the chair. For one second he thought it was his mother, but the next he saw Juanita sitting on a footstool with her head on the bed beside her.

A few *curculios* in a gourd gave a fitful light as they beat their wings against their prison walls.

She looked up as he sprang to his feet.

"Juanita! I did not know you were here! how you startled me!"

"Where else should I be?" was her sad reply.

"Juanita! dear Juanita! how can I ever repay you for your care of my dear, dear mother? Ah! God, forgive me! how I neglected her, and you who are not her child, how you have watched over her, nursed her, wearied yourself out with her, when I seemed to be amusing myself with what my heart hated! Why did you not tell me she was dying, Juanita? Did you know it? Do you think I should have gone on dancing and singing if I had known it? Do you think she thought me neglectful? Won't you speak to me,

Juanita? you used to love me, dear Juanita — speak, or I shall go mad."

"She never said so," sobbed Juanita.

"No, but that means that she thought so, and it was true. Don't you think so? you must talk to me, Juanita!"

And with these words he seized her round the waist and drew her forcibly up to him.

She flung him from her.

"What if I should tell you yes? would it make you feel any better?" she said, in a hollow voice. Ludovico uttered a cry of agony, and staggered to a seat.

Juanita sprang towards him, and seized his hands.

"Cruel! cruel!" was all he could say.

"Why did you ask me? She never said so, but you did neglect her wishes, Ludovico. She saw that you had no thought but for one; and she did not love her; you know she did not."

"I know! I know! Oh God! my mother! my mother!" And again he started to his feet, and paced the room wildly; then stopped short before the trembling girl.

"Juanita! you loved me once! can you ever love me again? I am not worth your loving, or any one's loving. Oh, my mother! my mother! Juanita, what are you going to do? Come and live with me! — I will take care of you! Do you want your freedom? What shall I do for you? You were my mother's child, and I was not. Juanita, what do you wish?"

"My freedom! what good would that do me now? Where could I go with my freedom? Oh, I want to die. That is the only freedom I can have. I have nothing to live for now; I am worse off than a slave, for I am more wretched than any."

"You are a slave, Juanita, it is true enough; but there is no justice in heaven if you must always be one. Come and live with me — I will take care of you."

"Your wife will never wish me to do that," said Juanita, bitterly. "She hates me now. In the sight of God I am as free as you are, even according to your own wicked laws. My ancestors were not slaves. They were free in their own land, and here they were *emancipados*, and so are many others who are called slaves, though they do not know it. My soul has always been free. The money that bought my grandmother was perjured money, for she was free when she touched this island, by your own laws. She planted the seeds of freedom in the heart of my mother, and my mother planted them in mine. She thought the day might come when justice would be done. But it will never be done. Give me my form of freedom if you can, and I will take care of myself. Perhaps I can find my poor brother — he vowed he would get his freedom or die. Take me away from here — I will take care of myself."

"You would not forsake me, Juanita!"

"Forsake you! you have friends enough — a wife to love you."

"Hush, for God's sake, hush!"

He approached her and whispered, "She does not love me, Juanita. She does not know how to love any one but herself. She is incapable of devotion to me or to any one."

Juanita placed her finger on his lips.

"Yes, I must not say it, I know; but I will say it to you, for you are capable of devotion, you can love me. You are my best friend. I have neglected you. She has ill-treated you. She never shall have a chance to do it again. If I had known you wanted to be free, I would have gone down on my knees to get your freedom. I hate this life; I hate slavery more every day. If you had not been a slave, you would have been my wife perhaps — how I wish you were!"

Juanita sank at his feet, and clasped his knees.

"Take me with you — I will serve you always! even if I am free, but let me be free so that I may not do it as a slave, and then she cannot treat me ill."

"You shall go home with Miss Wentworth if you wish to," said Ludovico, for he saw at a glance the desolate position of the poor girl — "and you shall go a free woman —"

When she found herself alone, Juanita threw open the broad shutter to cool her burning brow.

The rich moonlight poured into the room, and who can interpret the thoughts that poured through that distracted brain, as she gazed long and intently at the broad disc of the beautiful moon, in which so many hearts have been sown!

Morning dawned as she stood there, and at the sound of a footstep she started, and returned to her watch.

The angelic light had faded from the countenance, now rigid and cold in death; Juanita shuddered.

Ludovico returned in the morning for Helen and Carolina, and a long train of mourners attended the Marchioness to her temporary resting-place in the village graveyard, to be removed at a future time to the proud tomb of the Rodriguez in the cemetery of Havana.

It was not a common occasion in the neighborhood, for, though vice was winked at, virtue is honored everywhere, even there.

Wearily to all, the season of mourning passed away. To Carolina it was only a privation that tried her temper, and brought out more strikingly her innate selfishness. Ludovico did not reproach her, but neither did he express an affection he had ceased to feel. He was wholly disenchanted, and could with difficulty summon resolution to meet the frivolous companions of Carolina's summer hours.

The Countess of Lopez was her frequent guest.

Ludovico did not attempt to oppose Carolina upon this point. He was resolved to live no longer in Cuba if he could persuade his father to go abroad, and that matter would take care of itself. The Countess was too much a woman of the world not to read a character of Ludovico's simplicity, and took care not to intrude herself into his presence, but she came at the hours he devoted to his father. The Marquis gave himself up exclusively to his children, and their innocent prattle gradually won him from the depths of his first sorrow. To his children alone did he ever speak of their dear mother. He grieved, when it was too late, that he had so rashly committed the happiness of Ludovico to one so unworthy to fill her place. The father and son drew nearer together than even in the days of their unbroken happiness, for the deeper suffering of disappointed affection made Ludovico more truly wretched than even the bereaved husband could be, whose record of love was pure.

CHAPTER XXIX.

HOMEWARD BOUND.

IN this hour of crushing bereavement, Helen was sustained by the only friend she had yet made in the island, excepting Isabella. Don Andres Torres had proved not only the humane and efficient overseer, under whose rule no punishments were necessary, for he ruled wisely and kindly, and knew how to hold even those poor souls up to some sense of duty, which helped also to make him their idol; but he was the honored friend of the family, and both the Marquis and Ludovico, as well as Helen, had leaned upon his strong arm. He had beguiled many an hour of languid suffering to the invalid, by his graphic descriptions of countries visited, and by his sensible criticisms of men and things, and in his own profession he was an amateur, and had the rare power of making his hearers see with him the beauty of the architectural masterpieces of the world, which he had carefully studied not only in their principles but the structures themselves. The Basque tribe of the Pyrenees, of which he was one, have a national education, among other peculiarities of their institutions, which raise them immeasurably above all other Spanish nationalities. A love of freedom characterizes them also, which would only throw them by accident, as in this instance, into the rank of overseers in a slave-holding community, but Don Andres felt bound by his own inward monitions to devote himself to the family of his benefactor, and this was the only way in which he could combine that duty with the bettering of his fortunes, which had now become necessary for their sakes. He filled the office in a manner which showed that a good man can make himself useful to his fellow-creatures even in such a position. If he could inspire others of his class to labor on the same principles, the wretched population of the plantations might by degrees be fitted for the care of themselves. This subject had often been discussed with him in the family of the Marquis of Rodriguez, but there were difficulties in Cuba, where the slave-trade was in such active operation, that might not be found in the United States. The constant succession of fresh slaves, who are purchased from many different tribes, speaking different dialects and inheriting different traditions, makes it impossible to prepare Cuban slaves for freedom, except by training them in the families of the mountain peasantry. Another difficulty is that of making innovations among a people so nationally ignorant as the inhabitants of the Spanish Colonies. No hope of such a change existed, except in the possibility of annexation to the United States.

But there were two aspects to this annexation. One was that the progress of society would eventually destroy slavery in a land whose government was based on freedom, the other, and this was widely entertained, that slavery would be the more firmly secured, but that its condition would admit of ameliorations sooner than in Cuba, because of the general superiority of the masses in the States, growing out of the idea of popular education. Upon the whole, it was rather a vague notion of benefit, and there was therefore a want of vitality in it. The United States government desired the annexation for commercial and political interests, but these advantages would be accompanied by many evils, and thus it has remained for the colonists to realize the weight of Spanish greed before anything like a revolution transpired.

Since this narrative was written, slavery in the United States has been abolished, at least in name, and the movement, has been initiated in Cuba. Such institutions as slavery leave their traces long and deeply scored on the public mind. That no human being can legally be enslaved again in our land must satisfy us for the present. The generation that has been in slavery must pass away before its traditions can make it possible for anything like equality to exist, but may we not justly hope that in a land where all men have a right to education and to the enjoyments of their own earnings, the day may come when, as in England, whose soil has never been polluted by slavery, the mere color of the skin will be no bar to social equality. Practically, it is no bar to the affections. The basis of mutual respect will alone elevate the inferior race. I use the word *inferior* in a popular sense, not in a radical one, for the natural characteristics of the colored race have more affinity with what we call the Christian graces than those of the one whose powerful grasp has so long held it in bondage. We laugh unreflectingly at the boast we sometimes hear from the colored race, that it *is a better one than the white race.* If to give the other cheek to the aggressor is a Christian grace, which race deserves the preponderance in that Christian forbearance? Surely not the one that has all the power.

Helen had the pleasure of often hearing the Spaniards express kindly and sympathetic feelings for the slaves, but it rested there, proving only how difficult it is for even the worst institutions to ruin the souls, created in the image of God, by which is meant endowed with his attributes of love and mercy.

No word of Don Andres' private history had ever transpired to his present friend. There was in him a certain barrier of dignified reserve that guarded him from all inquiry. But Helen often felt that it would melt at the touch of a friendship near enough to be an assurance of confidence, and, with the true sensibility and delicacy of a noble woman, she avoided lifting a veil which might admit her into a sanctuary that she had no right to invade, and which it would therefore be cruel to penetrate.

The Marquis had become very dependent upon him, and Helen rejoiced to leave Ludovico with so wise and sympathizing a friend, and one who entered with so much humanity into his plans for ameliorating the condition of his sugar-plantation. If he could not educate his slaves, he could lighten their labors by the introduction of the mills worked by the steam-engine which some American planters had, with Yankee energy, brought into use there. The standstill Spaniards were gradually opening their eyes to the advantages of these wonderful innovations, at the same time that they swore at the innovators over the lime hedges. And they had already borrowed them in many instances.

When the Marquis spoke with Helen of the children, he could only say that he could not yet part with them, but by and by he would himself take them to Helen and place them under her care while he prosecuted with Ludovico the long projected tour. He wished him to shut up his house, or still leave it under the care of Larimon; but Carolina objected to this arrangement. She knew too well what would be the penalties under the firm rule of her uncle.

Carolina's ennuyed neighbors were only too glad

for a place of resort, and came to her in ox-carts when the mud was too deep for other vehicles and more slender-legged animals than the sturdy oxen. Carolina was not unwilling that Ludovico should absent himself on such occasions, for his deep melancholy was neither understood nor sympathized with by her shallow companions.

Ludovico turned his attention now to the condition of his "people," and succeeded in interesting his father upon the subject. He could not set them free nor forsake a slave-holder's life without the concurrence of Carolina, but he could make less sugar rather than waste the lives of his slaves, or kill off their children by unnatural labors.

It was necessary now to facilitate Helen's departure before the roads became impassable by the summer rains, or the yellow fever infested the vessels. The Marquis accompanied her to the city. Don Andres had hoped this escort might devolve upon himself, for to him Helen's departure was as the withdrawal of the sun from the heavens. But the Marquis could not so far forget what was due to his wife's friend as to allow such a departure from established customs, and, placing Helen in one volante, with Mrs. Warwick to matronize her, he took another himself, leaving Ludovico to preside over the nursery, and at daybreak they left the plantation.

Don Andres was in waiting at the great gate, which he opened for the travellers. Helen held out her hand to him, which he reverently kissed. "God be thanked that I have known you!" were his parting words. "I ask nothing more of him!" he added, after a moment's pause.

Helen could not answer them, but her tearful eyes assured him that she valued his regard and respected his reserve, which she had never given him an opportunity to break.

"That man is out of place here," said Mrs. Warwick, after they had left the plantation entirely behind them.

"A good man is always in place," said Helen, "and I think the poor slaves would hardly agree with you."

"Indeed, they would not; it is a happy day for them. I could not stay there alone, if he were not to be there."

It was the Marquis' purpose to send his little daughter, and probably Manuel, with Mrs. Warwick, to Helen's care, in the fall, and then to accompany his son to France. Helen had petitioned that Juanita might be sent with them, and this request was readily acceded to. Helen was happy to be able to inform Juanita of this arrangement before she left her. She also spoke of it to Ludovico, who gladly assented, and expressed himself so well pleased, indeed, that Helen was sure he would promote it when the hour of fulfilment came. She commended Juanita most earnestly to the care of Mrs. Warwick, who promised to shield her from harm to the best of her power.

It was a sad day for the little girls when they parted with their kind friend, but the promised visit filled their imaginations with delight. Helen was confident they would be tenderly watched over by their father, and of Mrs. Warwick's devotion there could not be a suspicion. She rejoiced that Carolina was to remain in her own house, for her influence could be only baleful.

When they arrived in Havana, the Marquis remained but an hour in the house of the friend who received them, and with fresh horses immediately left the city, for fear of heavy rains that might detain him from his family, to which Mrs. Warwick was also too important to remain absent more than a single day.

A hurried visit to Doña Lucia and Tulita revealed the fact to Helen that Tulita had been secretly married to the young Count of Carova since her visit to the country. The word "secretly" is not perhaps the appropriate one here, for the ceremony had taken place in the Governor's mansion, and under his own eye and sanction. The young man knew that his father would not consent to his marriage with the daughter of the slaver while there was a chance left that his title might make him acceptable to a more respectable match; but the son had tried his fortunes, too often with other offers to be willing to relinquish this prospect of wealth, and the Governor-General has power to sanction stolen marriages when he thinks fit. The Count's father had sorely offended him once, and when the young man represented the wealth he should enjoy by the alliance — and no one knows what more substantial interests of his own might be added, for why is not the bribe of a Castilian noble as respectable as the blood-money of a slave? — his petition was granted. The irreproachable character of the lady could not be gainsaid, and the opportunity of revenge on the part of the Governor-General was not to be lost.

But neither Doña Lucia nor Tulita was happy. They had been unwilling parties to the marriage, strange as it may appear. Tulita's confidence in the young Count's affection had been destroyed during her visit to the country, which her father had favored for the sake of securing the match for his daughter; but Doña Lucia was too good a mother to wish for such a connection. Nor was the object yet attained of forcing Tulita into the aristocratic circles of the city, for as yet the old Marquis had refused to receive her. It was not probable, till the young Count should inherit his title, that Tulita would attain the position for which her father had sacrificed her happiness.

Helen was glad to bid adieu to the unhappy mother and daughter and the dissipated husband, who evidently felt himself made of a superior stratum of the clay which covers this mundane sphere. But the money of the slaver was as good as the money of nobles, to pay for wines, horses, operas, and the debts incurred at the gambling-table. In such states of society as exist in the Spanish colonies, the heart is the last thing to be consulted in marriage. Even the titled leper, a form of humanity not rare in Cuba, can command a beautiful and a wealthy wife, for *raisons de convenance*, as the French phrase expresses *marrying* for an establishment or a title.

But the pure ocean would soon roll between her and this corruption, and she was still under the delusion that her own country was free from it. She knew, however, that the giant form of Caste had not been exorcised from the most advanced state of human brotherhood that yet existed; but her heart bounded at the thought of returning to a society founded upon the theory of equality in human rights, and in which a more equal culture had already begun to establish an equality in social privileges. Our ideals go before us, ever beckoning on; and, in spite of her late experience, her faith was still unshaken that the influence of that theory would filter through the lowest depths of evil, even to slavery itself, the "sum of all villanies." A little leaven leaveneth the whole lump.

CHAPTER XXX.

DISSIPATION.

WHEN the season of mourning had passed away, which custom in Cuban life fixes at six months, Carolina threw off her sable dress, and launched again into the dissipations of plantation life. Ludovico found it necessary to follow her into these gay scenes, but it was with such an altered mien that every one remarked the change. It seemed as if all whom he met sympathized in his sorrow, except his thoughtless wife, who, disappointed of her city visit, determined to compensate herself by making the most of country pleasures. Even the Countess of Lopez had deserted her in the heavy rains, and left her to the society of a few families who could not afford to solace the tedious months of bad weather in the city. But that lady now returned to her plantation with a retinue of visitors, and music and dancing were the order of the day, as well as of the evening. The Marquis did not come out of his solitude except to accompany Ludovico in the superintendence of his plantation, and so highly had the Marchioness been respected that no one intruded at present upon his retirement.

Juanita devoted herself to the children, whom Ludovico often visited, and to whom he endeavored partially to fill the place of that tender mother whom they so fondly loved and remembered. He was glad to have them remain at home for a time, that this memory might not be obliterated by new scenes, as well as for his own solace.

Carolina had never shown the least interest in them, and was now too much occupied with her independent pleasures to give them either her time or her thoughts. She could hardly find leisure to dwell upon her own expectations of becoming a mother, and when she did think of it, it was only with a vague terror, and this dread made her rush more recklessly than ever into dissipation. Mrs. Warwick once ventured to give her a friendly warning, and even suggested that she should make *La Consolacion* her home for the winter, that she might take care of her, but Carolina preferred to take her chance with old Celia rather than submit to the comparative solitude to which a winter at *La Consolacion* would condemn her.

Carolina could not resist the temptation of attending the first village ball of the holidays, and on her way home was suddenly taken ill and brought to *La Consolacion*, which was on the way to her own residence. Before morning she was the mother of a daughter, and the young wife and mother lay all unconscious of her new relation and responsibilities, ready to pay the dearest price for the reckless imprudence she had indulged in, — even that of her own life.

In the confusion and terror consequent upon this scene, the new-born babe was wrapped in a blanket and laid upon a couch, while Mrs. Warwick and old Camilla were engaged in endeavoring to restore Carolina.

Ludovico had heard the cry of his child with a feeling wholly unknown to his breast before, and he left his watch by Carolina's side for a few moments to take it in his arms. His impulse was to carry it to Juanita, whom he now perceived was not present. He darted from the room with it to seek her apartment, which was at some distance. The door was closed, and he knocked, but received no answer. He opened it. It was just at dawn, and by the faint light he saw that Juanita was lying in the bed, with her head partially covered.

"Are you ill, Juanita?" he said, stepping in.

Juanita started on hearing his voice, and saw him with his infant, whom he placed by her side.

"Will you take care of it for me, Juanita? I fear its mother is dying."

She held out her arms for it.

"God bless you, Juanita, and I will take care of you both."

He stooped and kissed her forehead, and rushed from the room, to find that Carolina had breathed her last.

Ludovico was thrown back into his old home by the death of Carolina, and devoted himself to his father and to watching over the motherless little ones that surrounded him. He said little to Juanita, but looked upon the miracle of her love for his child with reverence and awe. He truly felt that he had had no wife, — that he was the victim of an empty delusion. There was something in the atmosphere of Juanita's presence that forbade his approaching her on terms of former ease, but it purified and ennobled him to witness her devotion to her charge. She allowed no one to share the care. No vigils wearied her, but her figure rounded into the proportions of perfect health and symmetrical beauty, and as the time approached when they were to go to Helen, even melodious song, such as had been the natural language of her childish days, was heard to issue from her lips when she was conscious of no presence but that of the child. As Mrs. Warwick expressed it, she had "turned into a mother!"

When spring came and made it possible to visit northern shores with impunity, both father and son, leaving their estates in the care of the good and wise Don Andres, accompanied the children to Massachusetts, where Helen had already secured a house in a rural village for their reception. Her life now had an object worthy to engross all her thoughts. She adopted the children of her friend in the true spirit of a mother, and felt that all the experiences of her life had but fitted her for the duty. The Marquis and Ludovico passed a few weeks with them, and then went upon their long-anticipated tour, which had become a needed change for the Marquis.

When Ludovico visited them again, Isabella was three years old, and as lovely a child as the eye could see. She bore no resemblance to her mother, but a very close one to Ludovico. He did not come unexpectedly, but the occasion was one of feverish anxiety to Juanita. The Marquis had returned to Cuba, and wished Ludovico to join him there. Juanita feared he might wish to take the child, and how could she part with it? She had been made free by the act of the Marquis, at Helen's earnest entreaty; but what position could she fill in her former home? Her beauty, refinement, and cultivated mind suggested no thought of the bondwoman, and Helen had put her into the position of a relative of the family who had taken charge of the orphaned babe.

Ludovico's letters had at first been frequent and full of fatherly feeling, but Helen had begun to wonder at his prolonged absence, and was much relieved at last to learn from him that the travellers had visited the mother-country, at the suggestion of Don Andres, where his father thought it possible the home government, with which he had some relations, might be influenced, by one who had no selfish aims, to check the increasing encroachments on Cuban liberties, that had inspired much discontent in the inhabitants who were disposed to be loyal, but would not bear oppression, and already showed strong inclination to be annexed to the United States. He represented the capacities of the island as immeasurable, and that in fact but a small part of its resources had been developed. But the home government continued to pile the imposts upon every industry and interest, until prosperity was impossible in any direction. When the exorbitant prices of the island merchants were complained of, the answer was that even the slightest privileges of trade were so heavily taxed that prices could not be reasonable. Hatred of the mother-country was increasing rapidly. The increase of commercial relations which was marked at that period brought no fruits to Cuba, and it was desirable that the truth should be told by patriotic Cubans. The Marquis returned disappointed and full of forebodings. His efforts proved to be in vain.

When the South American colonies had thrown off the Spanish yoke in 1810, and asserted their independence, Cuba did not follow the lead, and was then designated by the home government as "our ever faithful isle of Cuba." But the Cuban people were descendants of the very Spaniards who tyrannized over them, and gradually learned to hate the mother-country, which showed such rapacious greed, and so little sympathy for their true interests.

Neither Ludovico nor his father had been aware of the changes that had taken place in the island during their absence. Tacon was deposed in 1838 — which was due partly to the despotism he showed, and partly because he threatened to overhaul the slave-trade. Thousands of free negroes were found in the city of Havana. A syndic there enabled them to purchase their freedom if they could hoard the means to do it, which syndic did not operate in the rural districts. Some of these free negroes are artisans, many are musicians. The public coachmen, or caleseros, form a strong body, and, in truth, life in the island city is one long nightmare of terror. It is impossible to give any history here of the effects of bad legislation, of the cupidity of many of the governors of the island, of the iniquitous practices that are constantly put in use to conceal the landing and selling of slaves, which have been illegal since 1820. Large buildings may be seen, by those who know how to seek for them, in which bozals who have been well fed, — fattened, one may say, — and cured of the terrible diseases consequent upon the middle passage, are held for sale, sometimes openly, sometimes covertly According to the best known statistics upon the subject, the policy being to work the slaves to the top of their strength and import new ones when they are exhausted, the average life of a Cuban slave is from seven to eight years only. The importations consist, of course, of various tribes, some of which are more easily subdued than others. Those who care to look over the details of the slave-trade, gleaned often from the narrations of the slaves themselves, and often from the reports of the missionaries, must be aware that many slaves are brought from localities where much domestic happiness and even worldly prosperity are found. Little opportunity is afforded for any play of natural character in the life of a slave, especially in a country where they are worked as no man works an ox or a horse. But when they emerge from bondage, if any health and strength are left in them, native characteristics reappear, and great sagacity and thrift are often seen in their modes of life and self-maintenance, for they do learn something from their painful experiences.

The confusion created by a succession of rulers each following the policy his own self-interest suggests, gives rise to many evils that are not found in United States slavery. Within a few years, great suspicions had arisen in regard to the free negroes. It was supposed they were forming a wide conspiracy, and unusual cruelties had been exercised to extort confessions. By the laws of the island, any slave could purchase his freedom for five hundred dollars. On the plantations every means was resorted to to prevent the accumulation of so much money, and when it was fairly in possession it would often disappear mysteriously, sometimes by the connivance of the masters themselves. But in cities, where slaves were hired out, it was not so difficult for them to obtain and successfully conceal money.

CHAPTER XXXI.

THE RETURN.

LUDOVICO came upon Helen one evening unexpectedly. The children were playing upon the piazza, after a warm day: Luisa knew him at once, and her joyful exclamation brought Helen to the door. Isabella was already in her father's arms, but a little frightened, and stretched out hers to Helen, who took her from him.

"What a lovely little being!" he exclaimed. She bore no resemblance to her mother, but a marked one to himself. "And is this tall boy Manuel? And my little Pepita grown up too! It seems as if I were at home again, indeed. And dear Mrs. Warwick! And where is Juanita?" he added, with some difficulty.

"I will find her," said Luisa, springing into the house; and she called, "Juanita! Juanita! Ludovico has come!" and dragged Juanita forth, who had lingered within to compose herself for the dreaded interview.

"Are you going to Cuba, Ludo?" said Luisa. "Oh, do stay here with Aunt Helen."

"I am not going back to Cuba," said Manuel. "I shall stay here and go to college."

"Why did not papa come?" inquired Pepita. "Is not papa coming?" and her lip quivered.

"Papa has gone to Cuba," said Ludovico, "and wants his daughters to come and live with him and Aunt Maria."

"I do not know Aunt Maria," said Luisa; "papa must come here. Can't papa live with us here, Aunt Helen?"

"If he would like to, we should be very glad," said Helen, "but Cuba is papa's home. I hoped your father would remain in France, at least, where we could have joined him," she added, addressing Ludovico.

"I hoped it, but business called him back, and I fear I shall not win him from there again."

"Will Bella and Juanita go?" said Pepita. "I want to see papa, but I wish he would come here. If I write him a letter, will he come? Do you want to go, Juanita? I don't like to see those black people; do you?"

"I like this better, dear," replied Juanita.

"I shall let my little daughter stay with Aunt Helen for the present," said Ludovico. "We will not go yet; perhaps papa will go back to France, if I urge him very much, and then we will all go there."

"And Aunt Helen and Mrs. Warwick?"

"Yes, indeed; we cannot live without them; can we?"

"Will you go, Aunt Helen?" inquired Pepita.

"Perhaps so," said Helen, smiling.

"Oh, joyful, joyful! Will you write to papa and tell him so, Ludo?"

"Yes, I will, my little Pepita. I do not know what we should all have done but for Aunt Helen. Miss Wentworth, you must let me call you Aunt Helen too. I have not had a home feeling since I left you till now. I wish papa was with us, indeed."

And, saying this, he started up, and walked down the path that led to the garden.

Helen withdrew the children, whose hour for retiring had come, and left Juanita still sitting upon the piazza. When Ludovico returned from his walk, he found her still there.

"Juanita, you are free now. Does it make you happy?"

"Happy? Yes — no — I do not know. Oh, my God! if I could only die!"

"No, you shall not die! Live for me — be my wife! I wish it, and the world is big enough. No one need to interfere," and he drew her head upon his breast, where she gradually sobbed herself into calmness.

"Go, now," he said at last, caressing her fondly, "and I will tell Miss Wentworth." He took the sleeping child in his arms, and carried it to her door.

"Oh, my mother, my mother! Perhaps she will forgive me now!"

Ludovico excused himself for the night, for he did not feel equal to the task of imparting to Helen the fruits of his long banishment.

Long and deeply did Juanita commune with herself as she tossed sleepless that night.

"Can I do this thing?" she asked herself. "It will ruin his earthly life. His father will never consent to it or forgive him. It is enough for me that he wishes it. If I marry him, I shall be a dark cloud upon his life."

With this resolve she at last slept; and, when she rose in the morning, her first care was to find Ludovico, and tell him her decision. He remonstrated, but she was firm.

There was something in her mien that awed him into silence. She told him she would devote herself to his child, and that should be her happiness.

"You have made me as happy as I ever can be by wishing me to be your wife, but do not tell your father even of your wish. There would be no happiness for either of us in marrying. Nor would your mother sanction our marriage, I am very sure. I should feel as if I betrayed her confidence in me, if I should comply with your request. But I am not afraid to return to Cuba under your protection, though it must be as Isabella's nurse."

She did not appear at the breakfast table that morning, for she did not know what might have been said to Miss Wentworth; but when the latter at last sought her in her room, she found her languid and silent, but tranquil, and was convinced that the interview on the piazza the evening before had soothed the feverish agitation with which she had awaited Ludovico's coming.

Juanita's habitual life-long reserve did not yield, and it was easier for her to keep the secret of her happiness than would have been possible to one who had not always veiled her soul from human eyes. Indeed, she did not know what to do with happiness. The hopeless suffering of her life had almost destroyed the capacity for enjoyment. The nearest approach to it had been in the care of Isabella. She had felt that here she could in some measure requite her beloved protectress for her care and culture — for she had imbibed her principle of disinterested love, and felt power to impart it again, — and was it not Ludovico's child, too? She bore no malice to its mother, for malice was not an ingredient of her nature.

No movement could be made in regard to the children till letters should come from the Marquis. They came in due time. Ludovico communicated the intelligence that his father was safe at home, and the next time he saw Helen alone he said to her: —

"You will be surprised at what I have to tell you, dear Miss Wentworth, but I hope it will be a pleasant surprise. My father begs me to return at once with all the family, for he feels that his own health is failing, and he wishes to gather them about him again. I shall never return to Cuba to live, and I regret the necessity of this visit, but how can I refuse it to a dying father?"

He paused a moment before he added: —

"Miss Wentworth, I wish to marry Juanita."

Helen's heart gave a bound.

"Thank God, if you can do it! Have you told her so?"

"I have, and she received it as a pure woman should. She has long known of my love for her; she knew it even before she ought to have done so. She knew I ought not to have told her, but she had the moral strength to make me feel it, and I found her unapproachable. I am sure my mother would approve our marriage, but she does not think so, and is sure that my father would probably discard me. I do not suppose he would ever forgive me. I could not marry her there, for it is against the laws of the country; but even my father's disapproval would not deter me from doing it elsewhere, if Juanita would consent to it. But she refuses it decidedly, and is impervious to all remonstrances. She says she will neither ruin my life, nor embitter the end of my father's. She is capable of the highest action, Miss Wentworth, and I realize my inferiority to her. Do not call my proposal to marry her a sacrifice on my part, for it is not so. This purpose is all that has kept me from going mad since I killed my mother. Ah, Miss Wentworth, you know it was I that killed her! Do you believe the departed watch over us?"

"I do, indeed," said Helen, speaking through her tears, but they were not tears of sorrow. "Your mother is happier in heaven for all this noble purpose in you, if I know what heaven is."

"Oh, make me believe it, and I can be happy again."

"Your own heart will assure you of it. These affections were not given us to perish with the body. Life is but a school in which we learn ourselves, our powers, and our duties, and sometimes we learn only through failures; but I have a happy faith that we shall grow into all that is noble and holy at last, and you are on the right path, Ludovico. Juanita is in every way worthy of you, and you are worthy of her. You have conquered a prejudice that holds half the world in thrall, — for the prejudice of caste is the most difficult one to overcome. I hope that even your father may see the nobleness of your act. You will go to France, I suppose?"

"Yes, as soon as I can bring the children back, and if he will join us. If he will come to me there, we can all be happy; but, if not, we shall all suffer to the end. He thinks he shall not live long; he cannot lay down the burden of grief, and I fear that it is wearing him away."

"But you must not expect Juanita ever to forget the horrors of bondage, or to be gay and light-hearted. Her happiness will be as solemn as her despair has been. I have watched over her with such intense interest that I think I know her well. She is a rare creature. Her devotion to your child proves it, and proves her love for you, which is not new to me, for I have always seen that it existed."

"I have often wondered," said Ludovico, "how the slaves can have any feeling but one of enmity towards us. They are certainly a forgiving race, and I do not think, as many do, that they are wanting in manliness because they do not strike for their freedom. Such measures are taken to subdue them that, in proportion to their intelligence, they give up the endeavor. They show much ability when they have any opportunity of acting freely, as the free negroes of the city prove; and, for my part, I do not like them any the less for being false to their masters, for it is the only way in which they can exercise their free will. Ah, it is a sad subject! I wish I could forget it!"

"It will never be done away with," said Helen, "till those who feel its wickedness dwell upon it long enough to find a remedy for it. I have faith, not founded in experience but in hope, that it will yet be abolished in my own country; not because I see any steps taken toward that end by our government, but because it must fade before the advancing light of truth."

"I wish I knew what to do for the cause of freedom for all men," said Ludovico, after a pause. "Wherever I travel, I see men free in proportion to their enlightenment, and so I wish to give those in my power the help of supporting themselves, which is the first step. Cuba is in a sad state of anarchy, as we see when we look at it from abroad, and I wish it could be annexed to the United States, as the first step in reform."

Little did the friends then know that the responsive wish for annexation, which the States had so clearly expressed, had far different objects in view in forming that wish. To extend the area of slavery was their aim at that day.

The conversation flowed back into a more personal character, and ended with Ludovico's saying that he wished to make his home in Switzerland, and that the time might come when he could overcome Juanita's scruples, but Helen could not encourage him in this hope. She felt satisfied that the love which had been Juanita's religion had purified her, that the divine life had flowed into her through that sentiment, untarnished by any alloy of selfishness, but that she loved Ludovico too well to marry him.

"What shall I do without my darling little family?" she said; "I could hardly love children of my own more."

"Do not speak of separating yourself from us, dear Miss Wentworth. I cannot ask you to go to Cuba with the little girls, but I shall hope to persuade my father to go to France, and then we can all be together. I do not think America would be congenial for him. He is as earnest as I am that you should have the care of the children's education. Does any one here know that Juanita was a slave?"

"No one has ever suspected it. I have always given her your family name, and left it to be inferred that she is a Spanish relative. I do not think the children ever thought of her as a slave, or as one of the 'black people' of whom they often speak. If Manuel regards her as such, he has never intimated it to me."

"The little girls wrote you that I had opened a small family school for their benefit, as there is no good school in this village, and companionship adds so much to the pleasure of study. Since that time I have taken Juanita as my assistant in drawing, and paid her a salary, which gives her a feeling of independence and a realizing sense of her freedom, which nothing else could give. She refused all compensation at first, but I was imperative upon that point.

"Such has been her success in the school that she has been importuned to take outside pupils. I have always adorned my home with her beautiful works, so that they have spoken for themselves.

"I told her that if anything happened to me now she could feel that she stood on her own feet, as I do myself. Next to being a slave it is humiliating to be a pauper.

"Dear Aunt Helen! I too inherit a degree of mathematical talent that will at any time give me an independent position if other resources fail." And Ludovico laughed with a feeling of pleasure that quite surprised himself. "I might be your mathematical professor, perhaps."

"When I was a child I was always amusing myself with inventing mathematical games, which dear mama would play with me, and I once taught her algebra, of which she proved quite an apt scholar. I suppose she too inherited the talent from my grandfather."

"I am so much of a New Englander," said Helen, "as to think it is better to inherit talents than fortunes. I wish Manuel was your mathematical pupil, for he finds it difficult to excel in that direction."

"No, Manuel is a dreamer, and will always be one," said Ludovico. "Let him follow his bent. That is the only way to excel in anything. I remember how you were Pallas-Minerva to him after you read them the Iliad, and you will always fill that place to him."

"He is very happy here among the boys," said Miss Wentworth, "and I never can rejoice enough that he is no longer in Cuba. The fact of slavery and its attendant horrors spoiled the universe to him. With that blot upon it, it was not God's world. I hope Cuba will in future be more of a dream than a reality to him."

To return to his desolate home under these circumstances, was no panacea for the Marquis' failing health. The next letters Ludovico received were from Don Andres, informing him that his father was failing rapidly, and begging him, in his name, to come home, and bring all the children. It would only be a visit, for the most skilful physicians had assured him that his father's days were numbered. He also wrote that old Camilla had died just before his father's return.

No time was to be lost, and preparations were hurried through to comply with the request. Ludovico left it optional with Juanita to accompany them or to remain with Helen till his return, but Juanita chose to go.

Nothing that proved Juanita's nobility of character could surprise Helen, as she freely told her; but when Juanita said that to marry her would be Ludovico's ruin with his father and his Cuban friends, she saw that it was so indeed.

Juanita chose to go back, with the clear understanding that in so doing she resumed the subordinate position of a servant for the time.

"She is as wise as she is good!" was Mrs. Warwick's comment when Helen told her of Juanita's decision.

CHAPTER XXXII.

CUBA.

LUDOVICO and his little family were hospitably entertained on their arrival at the house of a friend, as was the usual custom in Cuba at that time, hotels being unknown, unless certain boarding-houses where foreigners were received for a few days on their transit to the interior could be so called. Ludovico lost not an hour, but hastened home the very night of his arrival, hoping to have one more glimpse of his father, who was said to be dying. Mrs. Warwick, Juanita, and the children were to go on as soon as he could send a trusty escort, or return for them himself.

In the evening, Juanita was called down to the door. Some one wished to see her. For a moment she hesitated, for the sights and sounds of the city terrified her; but it might be Juan. Who else could it be?

The house in which they were staying was, like many genteel residences, a suite of apartments in the second story, the lower story being occupied as warehouses. Lofty flights of steps led up to the apartments above. Juanita descended, alone and cautiously, and when she reached the lower step she was seized in an eager embrace.

It was indeed Juan. He told her he was free, and that he had seen her land that morning. She told him she too was free, and had just returned from the United States, but only for a time, and was just about to urge him to leave Cuba also, when they were both seized, gagged, and borne away.

Juan had been dogged. He had long been watched for a suspicious character, being suspected of taking part in the supposed conspiracy. His remarkable figure, noble bearing, and dauntless air had long marked him for destruction, and he knew it. By day he had carefully disguised himself of late, but the temptation to see and speak to Juanita had overcome his prudence, and he had ventured out without that precaution, under the protection of the shades of evening.

They were conveyed to a remote quarter, and placed with a crowd of other suspected ones in a large building outside the walls.

When Juanita opened her eyes, — for she had fainted with pain and terror on the way, — "Pope Urban" was standing over her. He looked wan and wasted, and soon cut off all hopes of escape. The city was in a fearful tumult of rage and suspicion, and even the rural districts had been searched for victims. His endeavors to run off Pedro from the mountain sitio where Don Ermite had sent him had ended in the arrest of both. Dolores was still in the mountains, he knew not where.

It proved the night of a fearful outrage that rang widely over the island the next day. There is no trial in Cuba, any more than in the southern United States, for a suspected slave, nor even for a suspected colored freeman. The building was surrounded by an infuriated crowd, and fired, and Juanita, Juan, Urbano, and twelve hundred other negroes, free and enslaved, perished in the flames.

Are we told that the horrors of slavery are exaggerated? Those who know its history know that to be impossible. This holocaust is a matter of history, and included many individuals of a superior caste, for it was the more intelligent and able negroes who were most readily suspected. Besides the suspected freemen, many valuable slaves of well known and powerful families disappeared that night, and no one dared to inquire of their fate.

When Juanita failed to return, Mrs. Warwick became anxious, and inquiries were instituted. The first suspicion in the family was that she had fled; but Mrs. Warwick knew the fallacy of that suspicion. The store-keeper at the foot of the steps could only testify that the police had arrested and bound a man and woman who stood there. He had seen this through a crack in his shutter, but in Cuba no one gives an alarm when an outrage is perpetrated. Every one shuts his own door, and pleads ignorance. No one would have dared at that time to investigate the mysterious disappearance even of a white man, and the Catalonian, who had revealed these facts, must have been newly arrived, or he would not have ventured to tell so much. The inquiry was immediately hushed, both for his sake and that of the other residents. Mrs. Warwick passed the night in agony, but could not speak again of her distress till she should see Ludovico.

The conflagration outside the walls that night was nothing to the authorities within the gates but a confirmation of their suspicions, except to those who might have lost slaves, for whom they never dared even to inquire. Horror secretly filled every heart when rumor brought the intelligence the next day of the human sacrifice; but, again, they were negroes, and it was thought probable they had deserved it. It was not till long after, and till similar if not worse cruelties had been perpetrated on hundreds, nay, thousands of helpless beings, that a reaction of the public mind came; and then it was said that sufficient proof of the supposed conspiracy had never been afforded to warrant them!

But enough! Those who wish to know more can seek the information where it is to be found, duly accredited.

Ludovico, who arrived too late to find his father

living, remained on the plantation only long enough to bring the bodies of his parents to the family tomb in Havana. His first care, on hearing of the horrible tragedy of the conflagration, was to put Mrs. Warwick and the children on board a vessel for the United States, and send them away under safe escort. On his way home he had heard of the arrest of Urbano and Pedro in the mountains, and that they had been sent to Havana with other captured fugitives. When he was on his way back, he heard of the conflagration, and was convinced by Mrs. Warwick's story that it was Juan who had called down Juanita, and that he was the distinguished leader who had perished then. But he found it useless to make any investigations. Stunned and baffled, he mechanically followed the pageant of his parents' funeral, for the Marquis of Rodriguez was widely connected with the nobility of the island.

Ludovico returned to La Consolacion, where alone he could find any sympathetic care. His haggard appearance alarmed Don Andres, who knew how to sustain as well as sympathize, and that beneficent action was the best restorative for a broken life. Ludovico was young; he was generous; he had sisters and a brother and a child of his own, and these relations involved duties : and duty leads the soul into a higher world even than the natural affections, and into an immortal life, where the still wider relation with the human race lifts us above the sphere of this world's happiness. Gradually the truth dawned upon him that man's extremity is God's opportunity, and that all he had known and suffered from slavery fitted him to do his part to ameliorate, perhaps to help to abolish, it. Gladly would he have turned his back upon the island; but this he felt that he had no right to do. Don Andres had wrought beneficent changes in substituting his grand, melodious voice for the overseer's whip, and Ludovico could see in the faces of the people that something better and higher than fear and trickery had taken possession of them. Don Andres had promoted Pancho — the best coffee-planter in the gang — to superintend that work, while he gave some attention to the sugar estate, and had rewarded him by giving him a small interest in the crop. This had transformed him into a man, apparently, and Ludovico resolved to act upon Helen's idea of creating self-respect by independence, and gradually he threw himself into the work with his native ardor and energy. Don Andres assured him that the time was approaching when great changes would take place, and, inspired with the feeling that he could do something to elevate character among them, he turned away from personal sorrows, and gave himself up to the reforms he saw possible.

How difficult it was to do this, only those can estimate who realize the pang the thought gave him that he had disappointed his mother, and the consolation he hoped to feel from requiting by tardy happiness the years of suffering he had unwittingly caused Juanita, whose noble character had at last made itself manifest to him. But in Don Andres he had an adequate friend, who had read the whole by the touchstone of his own private sorrows and disappointments, and together they were a host. But the reforms they could effect were limited, because no one was free, and the espionage was such that even the wealthiest planters could not do as they pleased while the home government connived at iniquity. He could free a slave if he chose to keep him on his estate and maintain him, but he could not sell him without a license. If he gave him an interest in the estate, it must be solely at his own expense. This he was prepared to accept. He could make less sugar if he chose, but he must be the loser, for he would be taxed according to the number of his slaves and his acres. He found, however, that the amount and quality of work done by men who felt themselves men and not beasts was of a superior order, and balanced the loss.

Sugar could be made better or worse by care or carelessness, and the manuring of the coffee estate by the débris of the coffee-plant so far increased the value of that product that it was sought and sold at its own gates.

The children's voices were no longer heard

driving the oxen; the mills Ludovico introduced so far mitigated the labors of the sugar season, which must be nearly unremitting or the sugar would be spoiled, that it was unnecessary to perform night labor, as is usual on sugar estates, so that the people were not overworked, and, when the sugar season was over, lighter labor was given, and the rest of the year was even easier than on the coffee plantations. Good cane-feeding, added to other food, made fat instead of gaunt workmen, such as Larimon had exhibited, and cheerfulness and alacrity took the place of languor and idleness. It soon came to be understood that skilled labor was remunerative, for whoever proved himself capable was paid something. The improved manliness of the people was Ludovico's reward. He replaced the frail bamboo barracks, which a conflagration sometimes swept away in a night, by separate houses, furnished with comfortable bunks, and surrounded by small gardens, and promoted the institution of marriage, to which he gave the character of a festival, which revived the traditions of their native land, hitherto celebrated in their wild dances only. The wedding-cake made of tropical fruits, and not of butterflies, gave a sanction and dignity to the daily life which had hitherto been wanting. Ever so small a home is sacred ground.

Muerta-Viva had been promoted by Don Andres to take Camilla's place in the household, being always a cripple and unfit for hard labor, but having learned the arts of housekeeping by her frequent assistance of Camilla. She was now told that she would be paid a small stipend for her services and for her nice pastry work and the candying of fruits, in which she excelled; and Ludovico encouraged her to be thrifty of the money which might buy her freedom at a future time, for he now constituted himself his people's banker, and showed them the books in which he recorded their work. Solidad excelled in in sewing, and the prospect was held out to her that she should have the charge of the annual sewing, if she showed herself capable of managing the women, which she did very soon, under Don Andres' auspices. Don Andres was endowed with a grand voice, sweet as well as sonorous, and it was music to Ludovico's ears to hear him give his orders, which were not only promptly obeyed, but, when possible, anticipated — for he had gained the people's confidence. Old Panchita was gone, but Pazienza, the good god-mother, was installed over the children in a comfortable chicken-house, with a lignum-vitæ floor, which insects do not infest, and stalwart maidens assisted her in the care of the little ones. No overseer's lash had to be invoked, for Pazienza made them love her, and she trained them to weed the borders and take care of their mothers' gardens. The caleseros, who had been inhumanly punished for carelessness in their department, were made responsible for the horses. As fast as they proved themselves worthy, Ludovico offered his slaves their freedom, but they did not wish to leave his paternal care, even when the day came for insurrectionary movements. There were none such on Ludovico's estate, but he could carry his reforms no farther without subjecting himself to interference by the local government, which became more and more rapacious and oppressive, till every interest of the island was curtailed, and the imposts made so burdensome that discontent increased rapidly, and fresh forces were sent from the mother-country to meet increasing rebellion. The world knows the general features of the revolution that became the only means of redress. It is vain to try to describe it. Suffice it to say that in 1888 slavery will end in Cuba, according to the present arrangements; but what the actual condition of things will be, who will venture to say? Not more devotedly did Cespedes, Varona, and other patriots lay down their lives for their beloved island later in time than did Ludovico and Don Andres at that remote period give theirs to prepare the way for changes, which were not consummated till long after their day and generation. Ludovico at last joined his family, and took them to Switzerland to finish their education, leaving his estates for future disposal in the hands of Don Andres, with such improvements as they had been able to effect.

He had kept Helen informed of these improvements, and she had cheered him on till she felt that he was losing family life too long, and she then urged him to return to it, and give it the happiness so long withheld.

Carlito, who returned to his parents after the death of the Marchioness, was never forgotten by Helen or Ludovico, and the time came when Doña Lucia and Tulita, their respective husbands being dead, accompanied him to the States to finish his education, and finally followed to Switzerland. Carlito's only idea of happiness was associated with the Rodriguez family, and his childish love for Pepita ripened at last into an enduring affection.

It may be said that a tale of fiction should be a perfect artistic work, an epitome of all life that can be covered by its events, and that poetic justice should be done to all the characters who play their part in it, because God is just, and in the great whole of existence virtue brings happiness and vice misery. This may be true in depicting any state of society in which all the actors enjoy the inalienable right of ownership in themselves, but when that first essential condition of life and growth is ravished from man, the forces of nature cannot play freely, and the reward of virtue must be not only postponed to another state of existence, which must follow this as inevitably as thought follows thought, but the expectation that all things shall be adjusted in this life must give way to the sad earthly fact that justice is not always meted out here. Let us keep our faith unsullied, that God teaches man by his failures as well as by success and happiness, and that, with his due endeavors, he can effect that better adjustment of the spirit to the event which secures the best ends of existence here and hereafter.

EXPLANATORY NOTE,

By ELIZABETH P. PEABODY.

It was one of the last acts of Mrs. Mann's mortal life to put into the hands of the publisher the foregoing tale, and she intended to write a preface, indicating what was the "romance" and what was the "real life"; but the manuscript was temporarily mislaid, and her death prevented the preface from being written.

I think she intended to say that the bulk of the book was written without any conscious moral object in view, or for the public; but, as she used to say, *it wrote itself*, being a transcript of what was present to her observation, *as a relief* to her soul, in letters home, while she was living in Cuba, in a position not unlike that in which she has represented Helen.

Many friends who read the original letters at the time they were written, urged her, on her return to New England, to print them, for the subject of slavery was just then beginning to be agitated by Garrison. But while any member of the family in whose bosom she had received hospitality yet lived, she doubted the propriety of doing so.

Not one of that family is portrayed in the book, for the Marquis and Marchioness Rodriguez, Carolina, Ludovico, Doña Lucia, Tulita, and Carlito are creatures entirely of her imagination, and their story her Romance. Every other personage named, whether white or black, was real, and also every incident and scene described — even Juanita, though *her* story is idealized. And the action of Ludovico, at the end, which lights up the tragedy with a moral glory, is copied from actual life.

The death of the last member of the family of her host, a few years since, left her free to publish what she had seen and known of real life in Cuba, woven into a work of art of her own imagining. She thought it would be felt to be a timely publication, coming out so hard upon the time of the emancipation of the slaves of Cuba, in 1888.

THE SCHOOL OF HOME.

Let the school of home be a good one. Let reading be such as to quicken the mind for better reading still; for the school at home is progressive.

The baby is to be read to. What shall mother and sister and father and brother read to the baby?

BABYLAND. Babyland rhymes and jingles; great big letters and little thoughts and words out of BABYLAND. Pictures so easy to understand that baby quickly learns the meaning of light and shade, of distance, of tree, of cloud. The grass is green; the sky is blue; the flowers —are they red or yellow? That depends on mother's house-plants. Baby sees in the picture what she sees in the home and out of the window.

BABYLAND, mother's monthly picture-and-jingle primer for baby's diversion, and baby's mother-help; 50 cents a year.

What, when baby begins to read for herself? OUR LITTLE MEN AND WOMEN is made to go on with. BABYLAND forms the reading habit. Think of a baby with the reading habit! After a little she picks up the letters and wants to know what they mean. The jingles are jingles still; but the tales that lie under the jingles begin to ask questions.

What do Jack and Jill go up the hill after water for? Isn't water down hill? Baby is outgrowing BABYLAND.

No more nonsense. There is fun enough in sense. The world is full of interesting things; and, if they come to a growing child not in discouraging tangles but an easy one at a time, there is fun enough in getting hold of them. That is the way to grow. OUR LITTLE MEN AND WOMEN helps such growth as that. Beginnings of things made easy by words and pictures; not too easy. The reading habit has got to another stage.

A dollar for such a school as that for a year.

Then comes THE PANSY with stories of child-life, travel at home and abroad, adventure, history old and new, religion at home and over the seas, and roundabout tales on the International Sunday School Lesson.

Pansy the editor; THE PANSY the magazine. There are thousands and thousands of children and children of larger growth all over the country who know about Pansy the writer, and THE PANSY the magazine. There are thousands and thousands more who will be glad to know.

A dollar a year for THE PANSY.

The reading habit is now pretty well established; not only the reading habit, but liking for useful reading; and useful reading leads to learning.

Now comes WIDE AWAKE, vigorous, hearty, not to say heavy. No, it isn't heavy, though full as it can be of practical help along the road to sober manhood and womanhood. Full as it can be! There is need of play as well as of work; and WIDE AWAKE has its mixture of work and rest and play. The work is all toward self-improvement; so is the rest; and so is the play. $2.40 a year.

Specimen copies of all the Lothrop magazines for fifteen cents; any one for five — in postage stamps.

Address D. Lothrop Company, Boston.

You little know what help there is in books for the average housewife.

Take *Domestic Problems*, for instance, beginning with this hard question: "How may a woman enjoy the delights of culture and at the same time fulfil her duties to family and household?" The second chapter quotes from somebody else: "It can't be done. I've tried it: but, as things now are, it can't be done."

Mrs. Diaz looks below the surface. Want of preparation and culture, she says, is at the bottom of a woman's failure, just as it is of a man's.

The proper training of children, for instance, can't be done without some comprehension of children themselves, of what they ought to grow to, their stages, the means of their guidance, the laws of their health, and manners. But mothers get no hint of most of these things until they have to blunder through them. Why not? Isn't the training of children woman's mission? Yes, in print, but not in practice. What is her mission in practice? Cooking and sewing!

Woman's worst failure then is due to the stupid blunder of putting comparatively trivial things before the most important of all. The result is bad children and waste of a generation or two — all for putting cooking and sewing before the training of children.

Now will any one venture to say that any particular mother, you for instance, has got to put cooking and sewing before the training of children?

Any mother who really makes up her mind to put her children first can find out how to grow tolerable children at least.

And that is what Mrs. Diaz means by preparation — a little knowledge beforehand — the little that leads to more.

It *can* be done; and *you* can do it! Will you? It's a matter of choice; and you are the chooser.

<small>Domestic Problems. By Mrs. A. M. Diaz. $1. D. Lothrop Company, Boston.</small>

We have touched on only one subject. The author treats of many.

Dr. Buckley the brilliant and versatile editor of the *Christian Advocate* says in the preface of his book on northern Europe "I hope to impart to such as have never seen those countries as clear a view as can be obtained from reading" and "My chief reason for traveling in Russia was to study Nihilism and kindred subjects."

This affords the best clue to his book to those who know the writer's quickness, freshness, independence, force, and penetration.

<small>The Midnight Sun, the Tsar and the Nihilist. Adventures and Observations in Norway, Sweden and Russia. By J. M. Buckley, LL. D. 72 illustrations, 376 pages. $3. D. Lothrop Company, Boston.</small>

Just short of the luxurious in paper, pictures and print.

The writer best equipped for such a task has put into one illustrated book a brief account of every American voyage for polar exploration, including one to the south almost forgotten.

<small>American Explorations in the Ice Zones. By Professor J. E. Nourse, U. S. N. 10 maps, 120 illustrations, 624 pages. Cloth, $3, gilt edges $3.50, half-calf $6. D. Lothrop Company, Boston.</small>

Not written especially for boys; but they claim it.

The wife of a U. S. lighthouse inspector, Mary Bradford Crowninshield, writes the story of a tour of inspection along the coast of Maine with two boys on board — for other boys of course. A most instructive as well as delightful excursion.

The boys go up the towers and study the lamps and lanterns and all the devices by which a light in the night is made to tell the wary sailor the coast he is on; and so does the reader. Stories of wrecks and rescues beguile the waiting times. There are no waiting times in the story.

<small>All Among the Lighthouses, or Cruise of the Goldenrod. By Mary Bradford Crowninshield. 32 illustrations, 392 pages. $2.50. D. Lothrop Company, Boston.</small>

There's a vast amount of coast-lore besides.

Mr. Grant Allen, who knows almost as much as anybody, has been making a book of twenty-eight separate parts, and says of it: "These little essays are mostly endeavors to put some of the latest results of science in simple, clear and intelligible language."

Now that is exactly what nine hundred and ninety-nine in a thousand of us want, if it isn't dry. And it isn't dry. Few of those who have the wonderful knowledge of what is going on in the learned world have the gift of popular explanation — the gift of telling of it. Mr. Allen has that gift; the knowledge, the teaching grace, the popular faculty.

<small>Common Sense Science. By Grant Allen. 318 pages. $1.50. D. Lothrop Company, Boston.</small>

By no means a list of new-found facts; but the bearings of them on common subjects.

We don't go on talking as if the earth were the centre of things, as if Galileo never lived. Huxley and Spencer have got to be heard. Shall we wait two hundred and fifty years?

The book is simply an easy means of intelligence.

There is nothing more dreary than chemistry taught as it used to be taught to beginners. There is nothing brighter and fuller of keen delight than chemistry taught as it can be taught to little children even.

Real Fairy Folks. By Lucy Rider Meyer, A. M. 385 pages. $1.25. D. Lothrop Company, Boston.

"I'll be their teacher — give them private scientific lectures! Trust me to manage the school part!" The book is alive with the secrets of things.

It takes a learned man to write an easy book on almost any subject.

Arthur Gilman, of the College for Women, at Cambridge, known as the "Harvard Annex," has made a little book to help young people along in the use of the dictionary. One can devour it in an hour or two; but the reading multiplies knowledge and means of knowledge.

Short Stories from the Dictionary. By Arthur Gilman, M. A. 120 pages. 60 cents. D. Lothrop Company, Boston.

An unconscious beginning of what may grow to be philology, if one's faculty lies that way. Such bits of education are of vastly more importance than most of us know. They are the seeds of learning.

Elizabeth P. Peabody at the age of eighty-four years has made a book of a number of essays, written during fifty years of a most productive life, on subjects of lasting interest, published forgotten years ago in *Emerson's Magazine*, *The Dial*, Lowell's *Pioneer*, etc.

Last Evening with Allston and Other Papers, 350 pages. $1.50. D. Lothrop Company, Boston.

The wife of Frémont, the Pathfinder of forty years ago and almost President thirty years ago, has written a bookful of reminiscences.

Souvenirs of My Time. By Jessie Benton Frémont. 393 pages. $1.50. D. Lothrop Company, Boston.

Mrs. Frémont has long been known as a brilliant converser and story-teller. Her later years have been given to making books; and the books have the freshness and sparkle of youth.

The literary editor of the *Nation* gathers together nearly a hundred poems and parts of poems to read to children going to sleep.

Bedside Poetry, a Parents' Assistant in Moral Discipline. 143 pages. Two bindings, 75 cents and $1. D. Lothrop Company, Boston.

The poems have their various bearings on morals and graces; and there is an index called a key to the moralities. The mother can turn, with little search, to verses that put in a pleasant light the thoughts the little one needs to harbor. Hence the sub-title.

Readers of poetry are almost as scarce as poetry — Have you noticed how little there is in the world? how wide the desert, how few the little oases?

<small>Through the Year with the Poets. Edited by Oscar Fay Adams. 12 bijou books of the months, of about 130 pages each. 75 cents each. D. Lothrop Company, Boston.</small>

Is it possible? Is there enough sweet singing ringing lustrous verse between heaven and earth to make twelve such books? There is indeed; and heaven and earth are in it!

Ginx's Baby, a burlesque book of most serious purpose, made a stir in England some years ago; and, what is of more account, went far to accomplish the author's object.

<small>Evolution of Dodd. By William Hawley Smith. 153 pages. $1. D. Lothrop Company, Boston.</small>

Dodd is the terrible schoolboy. How he became so; who is responsible; what is the remedy — such is the gist of the book.

As bright as Ginx's Baby. A bookful of managing wisdom for parents as well as teachers.

Questions such as practical boys and girls are asking their mothers all the year round about things that come up. Not one in ten of the mothers can answer one in ten of the questions.

<small>Household Notes and Queries, A Family Reference-Book. By the Wise Blackbird. 115 pages. 60 cents.</small>

It is handy to have such a book on the shelf, and handier yet to have the knowledge that's in it in one's head.

www.ingramcontent.com/pod-product-compliance
Lightning Source LLC
Chambersburg PA
CBHW022147300426
44115CB00006B/389